CO-OPERATIVE SOCIETIES Law and Practice in Nigeria

Containing The Law & Regulation

Miakpo Emiaso
LL.M, BL, Dip. (Journalism)

All Correspondence To
The Author
Miakpo Emiaso
P.O.Box 425 Ughelli
Delta State
miakpo@yahoo.com

Published by
SOS Publications
sospublications@yahoo.com

CONTENTS

DEDICATION

To God the Almighty.
To His Son of divine birth - Jesus the Christ who is my Lord and Saviour.
To the Holy Spirit my comforter and advocate.

To my father 'Chief' Warri Durie Emiaso a.k.a Ogbodu – the edho no re aze who departed this sinful world in 1990 long before his lawyer-son blossomed into what it has pleased God the Almighty to make him.

To a woman who truly loved me – the late Mrs Elizabeth Efoda Ogomudia, my mother-in-law.

To all my students whom I had the rare privilege to teach in Emore Grammar School, Oleh; Peakmans Academy, Lagos; and the Times Journalism Institute, Lagos.

FOREWORD

Cooperatives evolved from the need to jointly pool resources for the socio-economic advancement of the members within the confines of the cooperative principles and the enabling laws. The cooperative movement has evolved rapidly from the peasantry level some decades ago to a highly sophisticated business concern following the wide acceptance of cooperative way of life by a spectrum of all classes of people.

The complexity of the modern cooperative enterprise with the high volume of business turn-over makes it imperative for cooperative managers, ordinary members and other stakeholders to be well vast with the cooperative laws and practices as most societies have gone underground due to the contravention of the laws and the underlying principles and practices of cooperatives.

Accordingly, the publishing of this textbook now is considered both timely and valuable as the author has based his writings substantially on the prevailing legal instruments regulating the conduct of the business of cooperative societies in Nigeria using the Delta State law and regulations which are substantially *impari materia* with all other cooperative statutes in Nigeria as particular guide.

One of the major problems hindering cooperative education in Nigeria is the paucity of textbooks especially in cooperative laws and regulations, perhaps, due to the fact that cooperatives appears not to be a common field of academic study by students coupled with the fact that disputes on cooperatives are currently not handled by civil courts – an issue the author has very vigorously attacked.

But the publication of this text, coupled with the full reproduction of the Cooperative Societies Law and the Cooperative Societies Regulations as appendices A and B respectively, will make the laws more accessible to a larger number of cooperators with the attendant positive benefits for the continuing contribution of the cooperative sector to the socio-economic development of the Nigerian economy.

Having carefully read through the textbook, I strongly believe that any member and officer of cooperative societies equipped with the body of knowledge contained in this well-researched book will not only avert corporate collapse or failure but also achieve corporate excellence thereby achieving the cooperative goal of wealth creation and maximization for their members. Accordingly, Miakpo Emiaso's book on cooperative law and practice in Nigeria will be of immense assistance to cooperators, students not only of cooperatives in tertiary institutions but also of business law generally, legal practitioners, and cooperative field officers/inspectors.

This work – Co-operative Societies Law and Practice in Nigeria – by Miakpo Emiaso is evidently a thorough research work in which the learned author has exhibited an in-depth knowledge of the workings and dynamism of the cooperative enterprise which I believe will contribute to the ever growing literature on cooperative matters. I therefore recommend this highly readable book written by an experienced and erudite writer like Mr. Emiaso to all stakeholders in the cooperative enterprise.

CHIEF A.E. ENEBELI (FNHR)
DIRECTOR OF COOPERATIVES
DELTA STATE
May 2011

PREFACE

It never ceased to amusingly baffle me the kind of reaction I got from professional colleagues each time I said I was doing a research on co-operatives laws with a view to writing a book on the subject.

'Why co-operatives of all things?'

'Because it is an area of the law which has undeservingly been neglected for too long', I would say.

Then I would proceed to draw attention to the fact that there is so much money circulating in Nigeria in the name of co-operative societies but sadly in an uncontrolled manner which has consequently created a fertile ground for monumental ignorance and fraud.

Recently, the Lagos State Commissioner in charge of co-operatives announced that the capital base of co-operative societies in Lagos alone had hit the five hundred billion Naira (N500 billion) mark with a co-operative asset base of over twenty billion Naira (20 billion). The commissioner however lamented that with over 15,000 registered societies involving over a million families in Lagos, his ministry was inundated with petitions alleging co-operatives related fraud.

Elsewhere in Niger State about the same period, the National President of the Co-operatives Federation of Nigeria was also lamenting the 'series of reports about ... activities of ... unscrupulous elements (using co-operatives) for dubious (ends) and who are fond of collecting money from people and vanishing' with over three hundred million Naira (N300 million) in depositors' funds.

I was myself shocked in the course of my research and gathering of materials for this book to realize how little I knew on the law of co-operatives, how many knew so little, and how so little literature was available on the subject in Nigeria. Not a single book could I find. Judicial authorities were, understandably, no exception.

Something had to be done to arrest the situation. At least, arrest the ignorance which abound about co-operatives. A book would just do it. A book on the law of co-operatives. Hence this effort as my humble contribution to learning and knowledge in relation to the specialized field of the law on co-operatives with a view to generally enhancing the quality of co-operative practice in Nigeria.

This self-imposed assignment turned to be a most arduous undertaking as I soon discovered in the course of the research that I had to contend with statutes on the subject enacted by different regions and states in Nigeria. Each of the former regions had a co-operative societies law which the states that sprang from them had adopted. Luckily, these statutory adoptions, safe for slight modifications in numbering of sections, are substantially *impari materia* so that a reference to one is as good as reference to all the others.

I therefore chose to adopt the Delta State statute, which is also directly applicable in Edo State, as standard reference in this work only because of my location and of the Lagos State for reasons of the co-operative vibrancy in that state. Ample references have also been made to the Eastern and Northern statutes where appropriate.

The present lull in judicial activity in the area of co-operative societies and their activities would not persist for long especially after the publication of this book. In a sense, therefore, this book carries with it the prophetic flavor with which most co-operative litigation in Nigeria would be resolved.

The effort in writing this book on the law of co-operative societies in Nigeria is indisputably a pioneering one. It comes therefore with some of the obvious inadequacies which all such pioneering activity is naturally associated with. I have made strenuous effort to avoid or reduce them and am almost sure I have succeeded in this respect but notwithstanding my effort, I take responsibility for any lapses and for which I apologise.

In my pioneering effort herein, I have struggled to throw some illumination on almost all areas of the law on co-operatives using language, not necessarily as lawyers do but as the proverbial 'man on the street' so that I can carry my non-lawyer readers, whom I presume will be in the majority, along. In the course of my struggles at illumination therefore, I have raised issues in connection with

(a) the legal place of co-operative societies *vis-a-vis* other business and social organizations;
(b) the corporate status of co-operative societies;
(c) why the Nigerian Co-operative Societies Act (Decree 90) is unconstitutional;
(d) why co-operative societies do not need to appoint trustees;
(e) the excessive and overbearing powers of the co-operative society registrars/directors;
(f) the unlawful ouster of jurisdiction of courts with respect to co-operative matters;
(g) the antiquated nature of all current co-operative statutes in Nigeria;
(h) the need to elevate the office of the co-operative registrar to a status equal or near-so to that of the Corporate Affairs Commission and thereby depersonalizing the office etc.

These illuminations, it is hoped, would not only make all persons associated with co-operatives a lot better informed but will give rise to very healthy debates on co-operative practices in relation to law and, especially, generate legislative action with a view to not only bringing our laws on co-operatives to reflect current social, economic, and legal realities of our times but also to bringing the various co-operative statutes in Nigeria in conformity with the Nigerian constitution.

In addition to the above, this book will assist the various co-operative colleges in Ibadan, Kaduna, and Enugu as well as all other tertiary institutions offering courses in co-operative studies to update and elevate their curricula as appropriate.

To all lawyers, particularly dynamic ones with vision, this book is a must not just on the shelf but also a must read.

From the date of publication of this book, no state department or directorate of co-operatives will feel safe and complete without copies of this book to guide their operations so as to keep always on the right side of the law.

MIAKPO EMIASO
President's Chambers
Area Customary Court, Effurun Warri
Delta State
May 2011

ACKNOWLEDGEMENT

I wish to thank and acknowledge all persons who encouraged me directly and indirectly to continue to write by patronizing my earlier work on the *Law, Practice and Procedure: Area Customary Courts in Nigeria.* Without such patronage, I would have had no courage to write the present book.

These persons are too numerous to mention here but I crave the indulgence of all else to specially mention the Hon. Justice S.O.N. Ogene (Mrs), the honourable President of the Delta State Customary Court of Appeal whose support, beyond patronage, deserves special mention in gratitude; and the Hon. Justice R.P.I Bozimo (Mrs), the immediate past Chief Judge, Delta State whose motherly love I feel even from a distance. Also worthy of mention here are all members of the Nigerian Bar Association especially of the Warri branch. Thanks my learned friends.

For writing the foreword to this work, I say a big 'thank you sir' to Chief A.E. Enebeli (FNHR), Director of Co-operatives Delta State. Also deserving of gratitude is the Assistant Director of Co-operatives Delta State, Mr. Frank Aghara who, after going through this book in manuscript, could not hide his excitement.

I thank in a very special way Mr. Muhammed S. Bello of the Lagos State Ministry of Agriculture and Co-operatives for not only providing me with a bundle of the initial literature with which this work took off but also found time to read the work in manuscript and made very useful suggestions and for linking me up with a great number of individuals in the co-operative movement from whom I learnt quite a lot for the purpose of this work.

One such individual whose link Muhammed Bello arranged who deserves special mention here is Mr. Ogunsanmi of the Institute of Advanced Legal Studies, Lagos who promptly rose to my assistance with a bundle of materials on co-operative societies. To him I am indebted and I say thank you sir.

Mrs. Helen E. O. Erhurun, author of *Co-operatives: Principles, Practice and Field Administration* obliged me with a copy of her work, from which this book has also benefitted, at a concessional price. Thanks madam.

To Mr. Idowu Adegbite, Dean Faculty of Law, Olabisi Onabanjo University, Ago-Iwoye, Ogun State; Mr. Folorunsho Omojola, Head of Department, Department of Social Sciences, Yaba College of Technology, Lagos – a multiple author one of whose works, *Omojola's General Principles of Business & Co-operative Law in Nigeria*, contains a chapter on co-operative societies law from which this work has benefitted; and Mr. M.O. Sofowora, Senior Lecturer, Faculty of Law, Lagos State University, Ojo Lagos – another multiple author whose works include *General Principles of Business and Co-operative Law* from which this book has immensely benefitted, I say thank you for finding time from your very busy schedules to go through this work in manuscript and for your immensely useful inputs.

I must also mention in gratitude Mrs. Ruth Aweto, Provost of the Federal Co-operatives College, Ibadan and Mr. Leonard Nwaosuagwu, Law Lecturer at the Federal Co-operatives College, Oji River, Enugu for their enthusiastic responses for inputs to this work.

Mr. Moses Ogbalor who is the president of one of the largest co-operative societies in Delta State deserves my special gratitude for inviting me to chair the bye-laws review committee of that society and thereby further exposing my co-operative horizon to a higher profundity.

To all members of the Lagos Cooperators Group on Facebook, I say *thanx 4 d* useful interactions.

MIAKPO EMIASO
President's Chambers
Area Customary Court, Effurun Warri
Delta State
May 2011

Table of Cases

Table of Statutes

Chapter One

Concepts and Origin of Co-operative Societies

'... the company of those who believed were of one heart and soul, ... and they had everything in common'.
- Acts 4:32 RSV

Co-operative societies are a very common feature of today's rural and semi-urban communities. However, what co-operative societies are, legally speaking, and what they mean seem to be taken for granted.

From the ordinary meaning of the word 'co-operative', the meaning of co-operative society should ordinarily be obvious. It must mean a 'society' where 'co-operation' is the guiding philosophy. A society where such ideas of collaboration, joint effort, team spirit, symbiosis, spirit *de corps,* combined operation etc form the basis of the coming together of a group.

In almost every part of Nigeria, it is not uncommon to find persons who come together to form a unity of purpose for the protection of their common interests and assuming an identity and calling themselves a name which includes the word 'co-operative' without appreciating the legal implications of doing so. The term 'co-operative society' is not a mere social terminology but a legal one with legal implications.

Origin of the Co-operative Movement

Available records seem to suggest that the first grouping in Nigeria with a conception and a semblance of a co-operative society was founded in 1907. It was known as the Agege Planters Union and was said to have been founded by one Chief A. Coker of Ifako. The object for which it was founded was to, among other purposes,

> curb the excesses of European merchants ... and to serve as a means of furthering political agitation ... on the agricultural cum economic front.[1]

Was this a co-operative society? What is a co-operative society? Although the meaning of 'co-operative society' appears rather obvious, its real intendments may be better appreciated from the following passage:

> **The Rochdale Society**
>
> The story of the Rochdale Co-operative Society, in 1844, which became the working model for thousands of others, is a most romantic one and in some of its aspects the history of its progress reads like a fairy tale. A hundred years ago wages were very low, and it was a terrible struggle for working people to secure a bare subsistence. They were compelled to buy the necessities of life from small retail shopkeepers, who usually supplied wretched provisions at extremely high prices.
>
> The price of bread alone was as great as it is now. In the midst of this poverty, twenty-eight poor but intelligent weavers of Rochdale determined to try to improve their lot. As this could not be done by increasing their earnings, they decided upon a plan whereby they could lessen their expenditure, purchase better provisions with their money, and at the same time keep in their own pockets the profits previously secured by the shopkeepers from whom they bought their provisions. They soon discovered that by buying in large quantities, and by paying in cash, they could buy at a cheaper rate and thus obtain greater

1. Muhammed S. Bello (1992) *Essentials of Co-operative Administration for Primary Societies in Nigeria* (CLERC Publications) at p.6.

> benefits. But this required ready money; which they did not possess.
>
> They determined however, though it cost each one a severe struggle, to give two pence a week to raise some capital. Afterwards, by great sacrifice, their weekly contribution was increased to three pence, until their combined savings amounted to twenty-eight pounds.
>
> A room was taken in Toad Lane as a store, and from this small beginning a society gradually developed which now numbers its members by thousands and its annual business by hundreds of thousands of pounds while in the place of the humble room is a huge central warehouse with numbers of branches.[2]

From the humble beginnings of these twenty-eight weavers in the tiny English city of Rochdale, the concept of co-operative societies developed into a universal movement and from the rather simple social grouping of individuals to a complex institution regulated by law not only at local levels but at national and even international levels.

When over 150 years ago, these 'poor but intelligent weavers' got together to achieve the objectives poverty had compelled them to seek, they probably saw themselves only as a neighbourhood social grouping confronted by a common problem which required their concerted efforts to solve. What they least considered must have been the place of the law. They are today universally credited with pioneering a co-operative movement that has come to be embraced worldwide.

The Rochdale Co-operative Society story brings to the fore that:

---

2. Culled unedited from L.Gartside: *English for Business Studies* (Macdonald and Evans, London 1969) at pp. 241-2

(a) its take-off setting was one of economic difficulty of working people with low wages making access to basic necessities of life a terrible struggle.
(b) This problem called for a solution which required some 'intelligence' and 'determination'.
(c) Such intelligence and determination gave birth to the wisdom of pooled thrift and savings.
(d) The pooled thrift and savings provided necessary capital for bulk-buying, and
(e) Bulk-buying provided greater economic benefits.

This means that a co-operative society comes into being from a combination of multiple factors and needs of man which include both social and economic necessities. It is social in the sense that it brings persons together in one unit. It is economic in the sense that these persons have a common goal which is usually one in the nature of meeting their economic and financial needs.

These factors and needs do not include political factors. Indeed, as shall be shown presently, a co-operative society must not be political. Was the Agege Planters Union a co-operative society? If it was, was it influenced by the Rochdale experience?

The concept of co-operation and its benefits, no doubt, have been known to the various peoples of Nigeria from a long time back in history. Muhammed S. Bello[3] observes that

> our forefathers practiced one form of mutual co-operation or the other either for social, economic, or community projects such as *ajo, aro, esusu, owe* in Yorubaland; *gayya*

3. Supra at p.6

and *adashi* among the Hausas; *isisie, isisie-ego, utu ummunna* and *oha* in Igbo-speaking areas.

The founding of the Agege Planters Union in 1907 is an indication that the concept of co-operation was not new to Nigerians. There is no evidence that Chief A. Coker was influenced by the Rochdale experience in founding the planters union.

However, if subjected to modern day criteria for determining what a co-operative society is, the Agege Planters Union would hardly qualify as a co-operative society seeing that one of its objectives was 'to serve as a means of furthering political agitation'. A co-operative society must be apolitical. Also a co-operative society strictly so called is required by law to have the word 'co-operative' as part of its name and should have the word 'limited' as the last word in that name.

The term "Co-operative Society" is a technical term legally speaking. Care must therefore be taken to distinguish between the concept of co-operation in the ordinary sense of the word and co-operative society in its technical legal sense.

It is to be conceded that the term 'co-operative society' is so fluid that it does not lend itself easily to a precise definition or even a description, but it is however now fairly settled that the purview of co-operative societies in the eye of the law is no longer that blurred. What a co-operative society is in the eye of the law is now fairly well-defined so that it will not be too difficult today for a court of law to identify what grouping of persons represent the concept of a co-operative society.

Defining Co-operative Society

The practice and operations of co-operative societies over the years since Rochdale have assumed such wide dimensions that it is difficult, if not impossible, to have a single definition capable of incorporating every facet of the idea and concept of co-operative societies. In the words of Strickland,

> '... there is no beneficial activity to which the co-operative method ... may not be applied'.

Co-operative societies today attract the interest of not only individuals and local organizations – corporate or unincorporated - but also of national and even international bodies due largely to the impact of co-operatives in the fight against poverty and in the creation of wealth. It is in this regard that the International Labour Organisation recognizes that a co-operative society is

> an association of persons who have voluntarily joined together to achieve a common end and through the formation of democratically controlled organizations, making equitable contributions to the capital required and accepting a fair share of the risks and benefits of the undertaking in which the members actively participate.

Even the United Nations Research on Social Development is interested in co-operative societies which it sees as being all organizations that are

> legally recognized as such which are subject to organized supervision and which claim to follow co-operative principles.

Another international organization[4] that is interested in co-

---

4. The Cody International Institute. See generally for these definitions Sofowora M.O. (1999) *General Principles of Business and Co-operative Law* (Soft Associates) at p.220.

operative societies considers co-operative societies as

> free associations of persons legally constituted for the purpose of conducting economic enterprises or businesses which they control and administer democratically according to established principles and techniques.

In a study entitled *The Co-operative Movement in Africa* commissioned by the Economic Commission for Africa, co-operative society was defined as a

> legally incorporated body with an economic purpose common to all its members; a society of persons and services rather than of capital open to all who may benefit by its activities and democratically controlled by its members, with provisions in the rules for roughly equal contributions of capital per member and for equitable distribution to them of any profits arising from the undertaking.

Muhammed S. Bello describes a co-operative society as essentially an economic system with a social outlook and that it is a reaction mechanism which gives birth to

> a voluntary association of people with similar socio-economic (survival) problems who come together to find solutions to their common problems using legal and democratic means.[5]

Another useful definition worthy of consideration is that of A. H. Calvert who defines a co-operative society as

> a form of business organization wherein people voluntarily associate together as human beings on the basis of equality for the economic interests of themselves.[6]

---

5. *Essentials of Co-operative Administration for Primary Societies in Nigeria* (CLERC Publications 1992) at p.6
6. Quoted ibid at p.2.

Describing co-operative society, C.F.Strickland states that it is

> a group of individuals who aim at an agreed object of social or economic betterment, and live in such circumstances of proximity, common language, and normal harmony...[7]

Folorunsho Omojola is of the view that a co-operative society is

> basically an association which persons voluntarily join and leave upon the basic principle of co-operation with themselves in order to enjoy mutual economic advantages[8]

adding that its principal aim is to further the economic interest of members while the underlying principles are co-operation, voluntariness, and collective responsibility.

A close look at the sundry meanings assigned to co-operative society shows that it is concerned with the coming together of persons legally to engage in some form of economic endeavour intended to solve their common problems, usually economic in the main, but which may include social problems under democratic and equitable arrangements. It is obvious that there are and there will always be as many definitions and descriptions as there are writers on the subject-matter of co-operative societies.[9]

---

7. Report on the Introduction of Co-operative Societies into Nigeria and the Cameroons under British Mandate at p.1
8. Omojola Folorunsho (2004) *Omojola's General Principles of Business & Co-operative Law in Nigeria* (Darkol Press and Publishers, Lagos) at p. 273.
9. The following other definitions and descriptions are as compiled by Helen E. O. Erhurun in her book: *Co-operatives – Principles, Practice and Field Administration* (P.A. Anigboro Prints, Asaba 2007) at pp. 17 - 21:

(i) '… an association of persons, usually of limited means, who have voluntarily joined together to achieve a common end through the formation of a democratically controlled business organization, making equitable contribution to the capital required and accepting a fair share of the risks and benefits of the undertaking' - per S.O. Owojuyigbe (1998) *Co-operative Administration and Field Work in Nigeria* (Anu Olu Publishers);

(ii) '… an economic system with a social content. Its idealism penetrates both its economic and its social elements. The economic ideals affect the business enterprise, its methods and operations. The social ideals have a direct bearing on the association of persons comprising the society, particularly as they affect the membership and personal relations' - per Professor Caselman (Primary source not stated);

(iii) '… voluntary organization of consumers into a society controlled as democratically as possible for the purpose of directly supplying their immediate needs by observing definite and generally accepted rules of action' - per Warbess I.P.(Primary source not stated);

(iv) '… an association open to all and granting equal rights and responsibilities to members, engaged in an economic enterprise on their common account and in which benefits are bestowed on members in proportion to their use of the enterprise itself, without regard to their share in the society capital' - per Prof. Standinger (Primary source not stated);

(v) '… an enterprise whose owners are at the same time the customers and users of the facilities, goods and services provided. It is governed by equality in social relations and equity in economic relations among members. (They) are structured in such a way as to exclude the profit in business, providing goods and services to owner-users at cost in a spirit of mutuality and self-help' - per Dr. Onuoha E.O. in (1996) *How to Organise a Viable Co-operative* (John Best Publishers, Enugu);

(vi) '… societies whose essential aims are to reduce for the benefit of their members and by their common effort, the cost price of, as the case may be, the selling price, of certain products and services by undertaking the services of middlemen whose remuneration would increase the cost price. To improve the market quality of products supplies to their members, or those produced by the members and supplied the consumers' – French Co-operative Societies Law 1964 as reproduced by Obodoechi O.O. in (2002) *The Cobwebs of Co-operation* (MaryDan Publishing Company, Enugu);

(vii) '... an organization for the purpose of joint trading originating among the weak and always conducted in an unselfish spirit on such terms that all who are prepared to assume duties of membership may share in its reward in proportion to the degree in which they make use of their association' – Fay Dr. C.R. (1908) as reproduced by Obodoechi O.O. Supra

This may be due to the varied and wide dimensions and purposes to which co-operatives may today be applied. For purposes of the law, the Nigerian Co-operative Societies Act has defined a co-operative society to mean

> a voluntary association of individuals, united by common bond , who have come together to pursue their economic goals for their own benefits.[10]

This definition is about the first statutory attempt to include some detailed explanation of what a co-operative society is other than the simple declaration that a co-operative society

> means a co-operative society registered under the provisions of the Co-operative Societies Act or under the provisions of this Law

as contained in all the regional legislations[11] before the enactment of the 1993 Co-operative Societies Decree now published as Cap. N98 of the 2004 Laws of the Federation. Unfortunately, the federal statutory definition is, like every other effort, inadequate in meeting the myriad of requirements that may come to be met under the concept, meaning and law of co-operative societies. For instance, the need to emphasize that an association is not a co-operative society if it is not registered under the law ought to be part of a statutory definition of the concept of a co-operative society.

10. Cap. N98 Laws of the Federation 2004. Reference will continually be made to this Act in this book for purposes only of elucidation despite the submission *infra* that this Act is unconstitutional and cannot be relied upon in courts in Nigeria.
11. See for instance, Co-operative Societies Law (Cap. 28 of Northern Nigeria 1956; Cap. 26 of Western Region 1959; Cap. 45 of Bendel State 1976 as applicable in Delta and Edo states; and Cap. 26 of Ogun State).

Also, to say that a co-operative society is 'an association of individuals' as in the definition, instead of an association of 'persons'[12] is to ignore the legal existence of secondary co-operative societies which of necessity and under the law must include other incorporated societies as members.

Universal Principles of Co-operative Societies and the Law

A principle has been defined as a guiding policy or policy, a practice regarded as valid and being independent of time and circumstances; a generalization accepted as true, having been deduced from facts empirically observed over time and verified by experience[13]. In relation to co-operative societies, Erhurun[14] sees principles as the basic ideas which constitute the fundamental concepts of co-operation which are independent of time and circumstances and have proved, in practice, to be essential orientation marks for the proper functioning of co-operative societies.

Co-operative principles are significant as guiding rules for the co-operative movement and they serve as part of the working document for co-operative societies in the course of carrying out co-operative businesses. The universal principles of co-operative societies differentiate co-operative societies from other forms of social and business organizations and serve as the binding chord of unity among all co-operative societies worldwide.

12. Section 18 of the Interpretation Act (Cap. 192) Laws of the Federation 1990 defines "person" to include "anybody of persons corporate or unincorporate" whereas there is no such definition for the word "individual" which must be given its ordinary meaning of 'natural persons'.
13. S.Y. Berko: an unpublished work (1989).
14. *Co-operatives: Principles, Practice and Field Administration* (P.A. Anigboro Prints, Asaba, 2007).

As a result of the success of the Rochdale example, co-operative societies have become so popular worldwide that it became inevitable to have regulations and guidelines for ensuring that they are not only properly managed, controlled and administered but also that they are not turned into what they should not be.

In the course of time, the International Co-operative Alliance was formed in 1895 with the principal aim of promoting a non-profit-making system of production and trade where productive and trading activities are democratically organized and carried on in the collective interests of the whole whose membership is voluntary. The Alliance then proceeded to formulate the first set of regulations and guidelines for the operations of co-operative societies which are now generally known as the Universal Principles of Co-operatives. These regulations include that every co-operative society must

(a) have open and voluntary membership
(b) have a democratic management
(c) pay interests and dividends to members not on the basis of shareholding but on patronage
(d) be religiously and politically neutral, and
(e) continually educate its members on co-operative principles.

These principles formulated from the Rochdale Rules of Conduct have over the years since 1844 undergone sundry modifications and reviews principally by the International Co-_operatives Alliance (ICA). The latest of such reviews was undertaken at the ICA congress of 1995 which produced what is now considered the current universal principles of co-operatives. They are:

(a) voluntary and open membership,
(b) democratic member control (same as democratic management),
(c) economic participation of members,
(d) autonomy and independence of society (replacing political and religious neutrality),
(e) education, training, and information,
(f) co-operation amongst co-operative societies, and
(g) concern for the community within which a society operates.[15]

In line with the above universal principles of co-operatives, every statute in Nigeria on co-operative societies has made specific provisions requiring that only societies which have, as their objects, the promotion of the socio-economic interests of their members in accordance with co-operative principles may be registered as co-operative societies.[16]

What the term 'co-operative principles' means or entails is however not stated as the term is no where defined in any of the statutes but perhaps may be gleaned from a panoramic consideration of the characteristics of co-operative societies as thrown up by the various definitions and descriptions and the ICA principles as presented above. These are that:

(a) Group of Persons – A co-operative society must consist of a group of 'individuals'. Individuals in the

15. For a fairly more detailed reading, see ibid at pp. 44 – 73.
16. Section 2 (b) Nigerian C-operative Societies Act (Cap. N98) Laws of the Federation 2004; Section 4 of the Co-operative Societies Law (Cap. 42) Laws of Delta State of Nigeria 2007. (Formerly Cap 45 Laws of Bendel State 1976 as applicable in Delta and Edo states).

context of the law must be taken to include corporate persons and not only human individuals. This has to be so as certain kinds of co-operative societies can only come into being when they have 'as members at least five registered societies'.[17] A registered co-operative society is a body corporate.

By Section 5 (1) of the Co-operative Societies Law (Cap. 42) Laws of Delta State 2007, a co-operative society must have as members at least ten persons.[18] In this regard, a co-operative society is different from a company which is required by the Companies and Allied Matters Act [19] to have at least two members.[20]

There is no provision in the law prescribing an upper limit in the number of persons which can make up a co-operative society. Accordingly, while there is a prescribed minimum number of individuals which can make up a co-operative society, there is no maximum number. Whereas Section 19 (1) of the Companies and Allied Matters Act prohibits any group of persons in excess of twenty from being formed for the purpose of carrying on any business for profit or gain without registering as a company, subsection 2 thereof provides that

> nothing in *(the)* section shall apply to
> (a) any co-operative society registered under the provisions of any enactment in force in Nigeria.

A co-operative society is therefore similar to the public company which has no upper limit in the number of

---

17. See Section 3 (3) of Nigerian Co-operative Societies Act 2004.
18. Section 3 (1) of the Act.
19. See Section 18 thereof
20. Same minimum number is required for partnerships.

persons who can be members but not the private company which has the maximum number of persons who can be its members fixed at fifty.[21] Similarly, a co-operative society is, in this respect, different from a partnership whose membership cannot exceed twenty.[22]

(b) Community of Interests – The group of persons which make up a co-operative society must share a community of interests. This sharing of interests is what Section 57 of the Act refers to as a 'common bond' which unites the individuals making up the group. The common bonds usually include:

(i) *Common problems* - which are usually economic or financial in nature.

(ii) *Common efforts* - by associating together, the persons in the group pool their efforts which are geared towards solving their aforesaid common problems.

(iii) *Common goals* – the goals which the efforts are aimed at solving must be common goals to all the members. Usually, these goals are economic and financial in the main. There are sometimes social goals also.

(c) Unity – It is of paramount importance that the individuals in the co-operative group be necessarily united in terms of purpose in order that they can achieve their common goals with minimum distractions arising from a want of unity of purpose. Strickland in his Report[23] observed that a co-operative society should be

> a group of individuals who aim at an agreed object of social or economic betterment, and live in such

---

21. Section 22 (3) Companies and Allied Matters Act
22. Section 19 (1) Companies and Allied Matters Act
23. Supra at pp.1 and 2.

circumstances of proximity, common language, and normal harmony.... (and that) ordinarily ... (it) will comprise a group of individuals living near to one another and familiar with each other's income, occupation, and personal character. They will be persons who feel a common need and believe that they can lawfully satisfy it if they combine for the purpose.

(d) Voluntariness – The characteristic of voluntariness is that nobody shall be coerced or forced into joining a co-operative society as this will take away the elements of unity and the community of interests. Voluntariness is synonymous with freedom which is an integral quality of democracy.

Accordingly, no member of staff of an organization may be compelled against his wish and desires to join a staff co-operative society – a practice very common in Nigeria whereby persons are automatically made members of co-operative societies upon their appointment sometimes without even informing the staff who finds out only on pay day that certain amounts have been deducted from his emoluments as co-operative thrift.

(e) Democracy – A very simple yet universally accepted definition of democracy is that it is a form of government for the people by the people and of the people. It is a definition which also coincides with the notion of co-operation. A co-operative society is an organization of persons managed, administered and controlled by democratic tenets[24] so that it is indeed an organization of people by people and for people. Democratic tenets dictate

24. See the definitions by the International Labour Organisation (ILO), Coady International Institute, and the Economic Commission for Africa.

that there shall be equality of all persons who are members of a co-operative society; they shall all be subject to the same set of rules and regulations in equal force; the set of rules and regulations shall be as accepted by all persons who shall also possess equal rights to vote and to aspire to leadership positions.

(f) Equality – Equality as a distinct characteristic of a co-operative society is that there is, as among members, equality of status. It is an element which forbids that any member be discriminated against but requires that every member shall be free to contribute to the capital of the society according to his ability without let or hindrance and that he shall also be entitled to participate equally in the surplus accruing to the society. It is also that every member shall have an equal right with other members to vote and be voted for.

The characteristic of equality is in the nature of fairness and justness. It is in the nature of equity and employs the equitable maxim of "equality is equity" which dictates that every member shall be entitled to equitably benefit according to his own equities. It recognizes also that while equality is equity, equity is not equality.

(g) Legality – A co-operative society is a legal entity. This is that it is a body known to and recognized by law. So also are its activities and operations; provided that such activities and operations are themselves lawful.

(h) Incorporation – Every co-operative society is required by the law to be incorporated. Incorporation means registration in accordance with the law. Such incorporation or registration confers upon the registered group or association corporate status. This is that the society becomes a legal person – an artificial person created by legal fiction which possesses almost all the rights and duties of a natural person. It has its own identity which is different and distinct from those of the individuals which constitute the membership of the society and can own property in its own name, sue and be sued. It also has perpetual succession and may never die as a natural person would. A co-operative society duly incorporated does not need to own and hold its property through trustees in view of its own legal personality which entitles it to own its own property in its own name.

The concept of corporate personality is usually associated with companies and is illustrated by the English case of *Salomon v Salomon*[25] where a Mr. Salomon who had carried on a one man business successfully for many years incorporated a company known as Salomon & Co. Ltd.

He thereafter sold his one man business to Salomon & Co. Ltd which soon went into liquidation at a time when the company was owing various persons about N14,000.00. The assets of the company were enough only to pay the secured debentures which were held by Mr. Salomon personally.

The creditors argued in court that Salomon & Co. Ltd. was the same thing as Mr. Salomon who was the principal of the company and that Mr. Salomon could not owe himself. They argued further that Mr. Salomon was liable to indemnify the company against the claims of the creditors who should be paid first from the assets of the company before the debenture holder.

25. (1897) A.C 22

The House of Lords disagreed with the creditors and held that Mr. Salomon was in law distinct from the company and that since the business of the company belonged to the company and not to Mr. Salomon, he was entitled to be paid first as debenture holder

Ordinarily, the Corporate Affairs Commission which is established pursuant to Section 1 (1) of the Companies and Allied Matters Act is statutorily invested with the functions of regulating and supervising the

> formation, incorporation, registration, management, and winding up of companies

and other business organizations in Nigeria.[26] But the registration, incorporation, registration, management, and winding up of co-operative societies are not regulated or supervised by the Corporate Affairs Commission.[27]

By Section 6 of the Co-operative Societies Law (Cap. 42) Laws of Delta State 2007 (Section 6 of the Nigerian Co-operative Societies Act (Cap. N98) Laws of the Federation 2004), a Registrar of co-operatives appointed pursuant to Section 3 of the Law either for the state is invested with powers or the function to register co-operative societies.

(i) Economic Goals – While considering the community of interests of members of a co-operative society, it was shown that these interests are usually economic and financial. Is a co-operative society an economic institution? Coady sees it as being involved in "conducting economic

26. Section 7 Companies and Allied Matters Act 1990.
27. Section 662 of Companies and Allied Matters Act provides that where any business name contains the word 'co-operative', the Registrar shall refuse to register the business name.

enterprises or businesses". The Economic Commission for Africa states that it is legally incorporated with "an economic purpose". Indeed, the Act in its definition of co-operative society states that the individuals who constitute a co-operative society do so "to pursue their economic goals".

It is safe, in the light of the above, to conclude that a co-operative society is an economic organization. But is a co-operative society *ipso facto* one which does business with a view to achieving its economic goals.

(j) Business Organization – A.H. Calvert defines a co-operative society as a "form of business". Coady states that a co-operative society conducts "economic **...** business"**.** Is a co-operative society a *business*? The answer to this question is crucial as it raises issues relating to the status of a co-operative society in relation to tax and the status of a public officer who is an officer of and is therefore engaged in the management of a co-operative society.

(k) Co-operatives and Public Officers: By paragraph 2 of the Code of Conduct for Public Officers contained in the Fifth Schedule to the 1999 Constitution of the Federal Republic of Nigeria, it is declared that:

> ... a public officer shall not ... engage or participate in the management or running of any private business, profession or trade ...

By this provision, if a co-operative society is a business, a public officer may only be a member but not be able to participate in the management thereof. If this position be correct, what happens to the elements of equality and democracy in co-operatives? Who manages a staff co-operative society where all the members are public officers as often happens in a federal or state ministry?

A public officer means any person holding any of the offices specified in Part II of the Fifth Schedule to the 1999 constitution and these are all persons holding political office including the President of the Federation down to the least person holding a political office and all persons in the civil service of the federation or of a state from the Secretary to the Government to the least person. It includes also chairmen, members and staff of local government councils, all staff without exception of universities and all government parastatals unless they are not on full time appointments.

All these persons, being public officers, are not to participate in the management of co-operative societies (i.e. if co-operatives are private businesses) of which they are members notwithstanding the democratic characteristic of co-operative societies which assures for all members free access to leadership.

But what is 'business' in this context? Does every activity of economic nature amount to business for the purposes of the prohibition contained in paragraph 2 of the Fifth Schedule? 'Business' is defined in Section 671(1) of the Companies and Allied Matters Act as including

> any trade, industry and profession and any occupation carried on for profit.[28]

Is a co-operative society any of these? Are the operations of a co-operative society carried on for profit? Paragraph 19

28. This definition is specifically for the purposes of Part B of the Companies and Allied Matters Act which deals with registration of business names.

of the Fifth Schedule has its own definition of 'business' to the effect that it means

> any profession, vocation, trade, or any adventure or concern in the nature of trade and excludes farming.

If a co-operative is not a "trade, industry and profession and any occupation" as listed in Section 671 of Companies and Allied Matters Act, it certainly must be one of either adventure or concern as contained in the Fifth Schedule. However, for the adventure or concern to qualify as business in the contemplation of the Fifth Schedule, it must be one in the "nature of trade" and must not be farming. So, what is trade?

There is no statutory definition of trade. The 1999 constitution does not define the word trade nor does the Companies and Allied Matters Act. However, the court in *Bank of America (National Trust and Savings Association) v Alexander*[29] adopted the following definition that trade is

> business especially mechanical or mercantile employment as opposed to a profession carried on as a means of livelihood or profit.

It must be submitted then that any adventure or concern including any of the things listed in Section 671 of Companies and Allied Matters Act and the Fifth Schedule which is carried on for profit will be trade. But there is the view worth considering that "all trades are businesses but not all businesses are trades" and that the "profit motive" in an adventure or concern or indeed in any of the listed activities in Companies and Allied Matters Act and the Fifth Schedule "is not sufficient to prove the carrying on of

29. (1969) ANLR 698, 701. Also *Marina Nominees Ltd v FBIR* (1986) 2 NWLR (Pt. 20) 48 for another view on trade.

a trade although it can be an indication".[30] Are the adventures or concerns in co-operative societies carried on for profit? The crucial answer to this question is unlikely to be in the affirmative.

(l) Co-operative Societies and Taxation – The answer as to whether the operations of a co-operative society are carried on for profit arising out of trade or adventures or concerns in the nature of trade is crucial for purposes of taxation. An answer in the affirmative means co-operative societies must be subject to assessment to tax.

In *Arbico Ltd v FBIR,*[31] counsel to the appellant contended that to make an income taxable, the profit must be shown to have been made as a result of trade or an adventure in the nature of trade. The court did not disagree with him. Therefore the answer to the crucial question as to whether a co-operative runs a business or whether its operations amount to trade or an adventure or concern in the nature of trade must be, legally speaking, in the negative. To answer otherwise is to mean that

(a) public officers are prohibited from engaging or participating in the management or running of co-operative societies and
(b) the results of the operations of co-operative societies are liable to taxation.

Generally, the words 'business', 'trade' and 'profit' in their ordinary usages are not appropriate for discussing co-operatives and except in few instances, the various enactments in Nigeria including the Act do not use these

30. Ogundele, E. Afe (1990) *Elements of Taxation* (Libriservice Nig. Ltd) at p.71.
31. (1966) ANLR 578

words in their ordinary contexts. For instance, in Section 34 of the Act, the words 'profit' and 'surplus' are used interchangeably. The word 'operations' is used in place of business and trade. This is not to say that these words may not be used sometimes for reasons of convenience but when used, their ordinary meanings must not be attached to them.

Because a co-operative society is not a business which is carrying on trade for profit purposes, it becomes necessary to make laws and put in place arrangements to effectively insulate it. Hence the registration, regulation, supervision, control, and incorporation of co-operative societies are expressly excepted from the jurisdiction of the Corporate Affairs Commission and the Companies and Allied Matters Act.[32]

Similarly, even though the Companies Income Tax Act uses the words 'profit' and 'company' in relation to co-operative societies, its provisions expressly exempts the results of the operations of co-operative societies from taxation. Section 19 (b) thereof provides that

> there shall be exempt from the tax, the profits of any company[33] being a co-operative society registered under any enactment or law relating to co-operative societies[34]

provided that the profits are not derived from any trade or business. Also, by Section 20 (2) of the Nigeria Co-operative Societies Act, it is provided that a co-operative

---

32. See Section 55 of the Act.
33. Which it defines as 'any company or corporation (other than a corporation sole) established by or under any law in force in Nigeria or elsewhere'.
34. See also Schedule III to the Personal Income Tax Act of 1993.

society

shall be exempted from payment of tax under Section 26 of the Companies Income Tax Act 2004.

These exemptions from taxation are conclusive that the law does not regard the operations of co-operative societies as trade or adventures in the nature of trade whose results are seen as profit assessable to tax. According to Rickland,[35] these exemptions are granted the co-operative society because the surplus which a co-operative society distributes to its members represents a sum saved by the members of the co-operative society by their co-operation and on their own transactions and is not profit gained from other people.

It is in this sense, perhaps, that the Economic Commission for Africa sees a co-operative society as a 'society of persons and services rather than of capital' and whose principal aim, in the view of the International Co-operative Alliance, is the 'promoting of a non-profit-making system of production' as an important characteristic of a co-operative society.

Co-operative Societies and other 'Business' Associations

In the strict technical sense of the word, a co-operative society is not, as we have established above, a business association. But it is difficult to completely avoid the use of such words as business, trade, and profit in relation to co-operative societies. When used, it is usually in the loose, non-technical and general sense.[36] Accordingly, comparing co-operative societies with other 'business associations' here is not intended to render co-operative societies as

35. See Report (supra) at p.2.
36. But A.H. Calvert's usage, it is submitted, is in the strict technical sense.

Businesses but to further accentuate that they are not, by contrasting them.

(a) Companies – A company may be defined as

> an association of persons with a distinct legal personality incorporated mainly for commercial or profit making purposes.[37]

A co-operative society is, like a company,

(i) an association of persons,
(ii) has a distinct legal personality, and is
(iii) incorporated.

However, whereas a company is incorporated mainly for commercial and profit making purposes, a co-operative society is not. In a company, the minimum number of members is two while that of a co-operative society is ten except in the case of a secondary or an industrial society where the minimum number of members is five and six respectively.

The maximum number of members in a private company is fifty while the co-operative society, like a public company, has no upper limit of number of members. A company may enjoy limited liability and usually does while every co-operative society is required by the Act to be of limited liability.[38]

Whereas a company declares a profit and pays dividends to its members as shareholders, a co-operative society declares a surplus and pays dividends to its members not as shareholders but as members simpliciter or as co-operators or as patrons.

---

37. Ezejiofor, Okonkwo & Ilegbune (1982) *Nigerian Business Law* (Sweet & Maxwell, London) at p. 258
38. See S. 3 (5) of the Nigerian Co-operative Societies Act (Cap. N98).

A company pays tax but a co-operative society does not pay tax and is also exempted from payment of other indirect taxes such as stamp duties and registration of instruments. Whereas a company is required by the law to file Annual Returns with the Corporate Affairs Commission, the Director of Co-operatives does not demand such returns from a co-operative society. In place of a company's memorandum of association and articles of association, a co-operative society is regulated under its bye-laws.

(b) Partnerships – A co-operative society is not a partnership but, as with a company, a co-operative society is similar to a partnership in some respects including basically that both are an association of persons with a common interest. A partnership is defined as the

> relationship which subsists between persons carrying on a business in common with a view of profit.[39]

Whereas the association of persons in a partnership is 'with a view of profit' arising from the 'carrying on (of) a business', the co-operative society is not. A partnership is required under the provisions of Section 656 (1) (a) of the Companies and Allied Matters Act to be registered if it trades under a name which

> does not consist of the true surnames of all partners without any addition other than the true forenames of the individual partners or the initials of such forenames,

but the co-operative society is forbidden from being

39. Section 1 (1) Partnership Act 1890 which is a statute of general application in Nigeria but may not be directly applicable in Delta, Edo, Lagos and all the states which make up the former Western Region which have enacted their own partnership laws. These Laws are substantially *impari materia* with the 1890 Act.

registered in the names of individuals. Accordingly, not every partnership may be registered but no co-operative society can operate without registration. Section 57 of the Co-operative Societies Law provides that

> no person, other than a registered society, shall trade or carry on business under any name or title of which the word 'co- operative' is part without the sanction of the director (and any) person who contravenes the provisions of this section (shall) be guilty of an offence … .

A partnership may consist of only two members but a co-operative society needs at least ten persons safe in the case of secondary and industrial societies whose minimum number of membership is less than ten but more than two. The maximum number of persons who can validly be partners in a partnership is restricted at twenty[40] while a co-operative society has no legal upper limit in number of members.

Except in the case of a limited partnership, a partnership does not enjoy limited liability but every co-operative society is per force of law required to be limited as Section 3 (5) of the Act provides that

> the word "limited" or its vernacular equivalent shall be the last word in the name of every society registered under this Act

This means that "every" society must be registered under the Act as a "limited" liability society albeit that the state laws do not contain this mandatory limited liability provision but provide[41] only that societies may be registered under the Law 'with or without limited liability

40. See Section 19 (1) Companies and Allied Matters Act.
41. Section 4 of the Law; Section 5 of Cap. C15 Lagos State; Section 4 of Cap. 26 Ogun State

as the registrar may decide'.

This limited liability concept is, again, one which is usually associated with companies and it means that the individuals who obtain shares of the company shall be liable for the debts of the company in the event of the company going into liquidation only to the extent of the amount of shares they obtain in the company. If at the time of the liquidation, the shares obtained by the individuals are fully paid up, then they shall not be required to contribute any more money to the debts of the company. But if the shares held by the individual are not all fully paid up, then the individual shall be required to contribute the amount remaining unpaid on his shares towards the paying of the debts of the company upon the liquidation.

In relation to co-operative societies, the concept means the same thing. In the event of a co-operative society going into liquidation, every co-operator shall be liable for the debts of the society only to the extent of the value of shares held by them. If the shares held are unpaid, the co-operator shall be called upon to pay up in order to meet the debts of the society.

Where the co-operator has part-paid his shares, he shall be called upon to pay only the part remaining unpaid on his shares. This is because the society is a limited liability society which means that the liability of the co-operator is limited to only that part of his shareholding remaining unpaid.[42]

A partnership is not a separate legal entity with distinct identity from those of the individuals who make up

42. See Section 55 (2) of the Law for a practical application of the limited liability doctrine.

the partnership because it is not a body corporate. A co-operative society is a body corporate[43] with a distinct identity from those of the co-operators.

The death of a partner dissolves a partnership but the death of a co-operator does not affect the life of the co-operative society. Where a co-operator dies, just as in the case with a public company, the existence or legal status of the co-operative society is unaffected. The same effect applies with the insanity or bankruptcy of a partner or a co-operator.

Whereas every partner in a partnership (except a limited partner) is an agent[44] of the partnership and his other partners for the purpose of the business of the partnership, a co-operator is not an agent of the co-operative society of which he is a member nor of the other co-operators who are members of the co-operative society with him. Every partner (except a limited partner) has a right to participate in the management of partnership but only a member of a co-operative society's committee may be involved with the administration and management of the co-operative society.

The document which contains the regulations of a partnership is the Partnership Deed or Articles of Partnership whereas that of a co-operative society is the bye-laws. A co-operative society pays dividends from its surplus but a partnership shares profits among its partners.

(c) Clubs and other Unincorporated Bodies - A co-operative society is not a club. Whereas a club is essentially

43. Section 8 of the Law; Section 6 (1) of the Act.
44. Section 5 Partnership Act 1890.

a social group of persons who may be under an obligation to make periodic payments of moneys into the coffers of the club in the form of levies and dues, it is fundamentally different from a co-operative society in many respects.

A club is usually not an incorporated body in which case it lacks juristic or legal personality but it may be registered under Part C of the Companies and Allied Matters Act. When so registered, it will still lack legal personality as the registration is done in the names of its trustees and can therefore only sue and be sued, and own properties in the names of its trustees. Section 673 of the Companies and Allied Matters Act provides that

> where one or more trustees are appointed by any community of persons bound together by custom, religion, kinship, or nationality or by any body or association of persons established for any religious, educational, literacy, scientific, social, development, cultural, sporting or charitable purpose, he or they may … apply … for registration as a corporate body (and), upon being so registered, … the trustee or trustees shall become a corporate body.

The reference to "community of persons" and "body or association of persons" bound together is a reference to clubs. The sundry purposes listed for which the community or association of persons is established are the usual objects for which clubs and such like associations are founded. Except for the social purpose, all the other purposes listed usually have no direct connection with a co-operative society.

Clubs and such like associations are usually not registered or incorporated as they are not under any legal requirement to be registered or incorporated. However, where a club's circumstance dictates that registration or incorporation is imperative, what it does is to appoint trustees who, in the words of Section 673 of the Companies and Allied Matters Act, "may … apply … for registration".

Registration or incorporation will become imperative for a club where such a club desires to take advantage of the benefits of the effects of registration as contained in Section 679 of the Companies and Allied Matters Act which are the usual consequences of incorporation and this include the benefit of owning property especially landed property in the club's name instead of holding such properties in the names of trustees who are human beings subject to death. These are the significant differences between clubs and co-operative societies. A co-operative society is mandatorily required to be registered or be guilty of a crime by its members.

While the objectives of clubs are as listed in the Act and which are not economic or financial, the objects of a co-operative society are in the main economic and must not be religious. Although a co-operative society may have social objectives, such social objectives are usually only consequential and incidental which arise from the reality of a co-operative society being a society of persons.

(d) Financial Institution – A co-operative society is an association of persons concerned with the economic interests of its members. Such economic interests are usually measured in terms of money or financial calculations. In effect, a co-operative society, especially a credit and thrift society, may well be described as a financial institution since it is an institution which deals with finance. But it is not!

The term 'financial institution' is a technical term which relates to what the Banks and Other Financial Institutions Act defines[45] as

> any individual, body, association or group of persons, whether corporate of unincorporated, other than the banks licensed under (the) Act which carries on the business of a discount house, finance company, and money brokerage and whose principal objects include factoring, project financing, equipment leasing, debt administration, fund management, private ledger services, investment management, local purchases, order financing, export finance, project consultancy, financial consultancy, pension fund management and such other businesses as the (Central) Bank (of Nigeria) may from time to time designate.

A co-operative society does non of the above listed 'businesses' as contained in Section 66 of the Banks and other Financial Institutions Act except perhaps the business of fund management in its loose, non- professional sense in the case of a credit and thrift co-operative society. Therefore a co-operative society is not a financial institution.

(e) Collective Investment Schemes – A co-operative society is very similar to a collective investment scheme but it is not. A collective investment scheme is any kind or arrangement with respect to any kind of property including money whereby persons become part-owners so as to participate in or receive profits or income arising from the

45. Section 66 Banks and other Financial Institutions Act (Cap. B3) LFN 2004

acquisition, holding, management, or disposal of the property or monies paid out of such profits or income.

Under the arrangement or the scheme, participants may pool their contributions for the purpose of sharing the profits or income arising from the management of their money or property solely from the efforts of a third party.[46]

The pooling of contributions and sharing of profits or income arising from the management thereof makes a collective investment scheme look very much like a credit and thrift co-operative society. But the difference between the two lies in the fact that whereas the management of a collective investment scheme has to be done by a third party, that of the co-operative society is done by the members of the co-operative through their elected management committee.

A collective investment scheme is strictly a business undertaking in the nature of trade. It is devoid of those characteristics of democracy, unity, equality, political and religious neutrality etc which are peculiar to co-operative societies. It is therefore not a co-operative society.

(i) Esusu – This is a form of collective investment scheme. It is very common with traders. Under the scheme, a person usually known as "collector" involved in his personal enterprise of itinerant collection of daily deposits of small savings from traders, promises the depositor safe custody of his deposit. He does this at an agreed fee which is paid to him or is deducted by him from total deposits at the end of

46. See generally Section 123 of the Investments and Securities Act No. 45 of 1999 for a fuller description of collective investment schemes.

each trading season, usually a month. This form of collective investment scheme is a curious one since the depositor who is obviously the investor does not participate in the profits or income which arises from the acquisition, holding, management or disposal of the monies pooled into the custody of the collector. Instead, it is the investor who pays a fee as it were for services rendered to him by the collector.

The service will be that of safe-keeping of the depositor's monies. But the Investments and Securities Act recognizes *esusu* as a form of investment[47] under its collective investment schemes provisions describing it as "falling within the category of community savings schemes".

Savings is a form of investment which usually pays interests. Therefore, notwithstanding that *esusu* does not yield any returns, profits, interests, or dividends to the depositor-investor, it is nonetheless seen as a form of investment by the Securities and Investments Act.

What the collector does with the funds he collects from his numerous customers is not for any of the depositors to question. The only duty the collector owes to the depositor is that at the end of the agreed trading season, the collector shall pay back to the depositor all his savings less the agreed fee for services rendered. The collector is therefore free to, and usually does, invest the funds he collects from his customers in usually unregulated investments of his choice including money lending and lodgments in fixed deposits with commercial bank. These

47. Section 146 (1) Investments and Securities Act.

further pay him some returns which he keeps exclusively for himself.

Esusu comes in different forms. Another variant of it which is popular with middle class Nigerians and different from the itinerant collector's form is one whereby a small group of persons, usually neighbours or workers in the same office organize themselves together and hold themselves bound to contribute each an agreed fixed and equal sum of money into a pool at a fixed date and which is paid to one of themselves in turns until everybody in the group is paid. This is what Strickland defined as

> a contribution society to which each member undertakes to pay in an equal amount of money in each month for a succession of months, and the whole of each monthly collection is handed over to a single member until every member has received the bonus in turn.[48]

Esusu is widely practiced in Nigeria and is known by different names in its variant forms. It is the same thing as what the Yorubas call *ajo* and such other names as has earlier been referred to. The Isokos call it *azoho*. The Urhobos call it *etoro ka ahwe.*

Whatever the form or name, and no matter the degree of similarity, *esusu* is not a co-operative. Also, even though the Investments and Securities Act provides for it under Part XI which deals with collective investment schemes, *esusu* of whatever kind is not an investment. At best, it is a collective savings scheme or, in the language of the Act, a community savings scheme which however does not yield any returns as regular savings. One of the advantages of a co-operative society is that it encourages

48. See the Report at p.13

and even compels savings. Such savings is more in tune with an investment in that it pays some benefits especially in the form of dividends arising from the holding and management of the pooled savings of members. This, *esusu* does not.

(ii) Unit Trusts – Another form of collective investment scheme which looks like a co-operative society is the unit trust in that it involves the pooling of resources by participants from the public and the sharing of profits or income therefrom. The unit trust scheme is also known as a mutual fund and it involves an arrangement for providing facilities for the participation of members of the public as beneficiaries under a trust in profits or income arising from the acquisition, holding, management or disposal of securities or any other property whatsoever.[49] Such property could include, and is usually, money.

Under a unit trust scheme, members of the public are invited to invest in a pool of funds for the collective acquisition of company securities which are held in trust by financial experts for the benefit of the participants. These financial experts are the trustees who hold the investment in broken units for the benefit of the participants who are the beneficiaries under the trust. The income or profit arising from the investment is shared to the beneficiaries according to the volume of units held by each participant.

Notwithstanding the pooling of resources for investment and the sharing of proceeds, a unit trust is not a co-operative. This is because the parties in the scheme are not in an association governed by any co-operative

49. Section 124 Investments and Securities Act.

principles. The scheme, unlike a co-operative, is strictly a business affair in the nature of trade.

(f) Co-operative Societies and Banks – A credit and thrift co-operative society operates in a manner that gives it some characteristics of a bank in that it receives deposits of monies from its members and grants loans to them. These are the essential characteristics of a bank – a term so imprecise in its definition.

The terms 'bank' and 'banker' can be very difficult to define but it will appear that it is now fairly settled in law that in Nigeria, 'bank' is any person who carries on banking business[50] while any such person is a 'banker'.[51]

Defining 'bank', the Nigerian Banking Act declares that the term means "any person who carries on banking business" and that this includes a commercial bank, an acceptance house, a discount house, a financial institution, and a merchant bank.

This list of 'persons' which can constitute a bank does not include an individual or a natural person. This is because for 'any person' to carry on banking business, the 'person' must be a company[52] duly incorporated in Nigeria and must be in possession of a valid banking licence granted by the minister authorizing it so to do.

A co-operative society is always an incorporated body. Where it is involved in the receiving of moneys as deposits and the granting of money loans, it is said to be a credit and thrift co-operative society but not a bank

50. Section 43 Banking Act (Cap. 28) Laws of the Federation 1990.
51. *Akwule v The Queen* (1963) ANLR 191, 198.
52. Section 1 Banking Act 1990.

notwithstanding that the Banking Act defines 'banking business' as

> the business of receiving moneys from outside sources as deposits irrespective of the payment of interest and the granting of money loans...[53]

A credit and thrift co-operative society is similar to a bank in that both are incorporated and with limited liability and are engaged in the business of receiving moneys as deposits and the granting of money loans. They are however different in that

(i) while a bank must be in possession of a valid banking licence before it can operate or carry on its business, a co-operative society does not need to possess a banking licence.

(ii) the bank receives its deposits from outside sources while a co-operative society receives its deposits only from members of the society who are not outside sources but inside sources. Section 43 (3) (a) of the Banking Act provides that receiving moneys as deposits means to accept deposits from the general public as a feature of the acceptor's business.

(iii) Banking business is a trade[54] and whose profits are chargeable to tax while co-operative 'business' is not.

iv. Deposits are withdrawn from the bank by means of cheques, drafts, or money orders drawn on the bank but this is not necessarily so with co-operatives.

---

53. Section 43 ibid.
54. See Afolabi, Layi (1999) *Law and Practice of Banking* (Heineman Books) at p. 5.

(v) Although co-operatives lend money to their members and charge interests thereon as banks also do in the ordinary course of their banking business, co-operatives are not thereby banks because whereas bank interest rates are largely a function of market forces and Central Bank regulations which are themselves adjusted from time to time in reaction to market forces, co-operative interest rates do not necessarily so fluctuate as the maximum interest rate chargeable by a co-operative society is fixed by its bye-laws and stated in all cases not to exceed fifteen per centum per annum.

(g) Co-operatives and Money Lenders – A money lender is any person whose business is that of money lending or anybody who carries on or advertises or announces himself or holds himself out in any way as carrying on the business of money lending. Such a person will be a money lender still whether or not he also possesses or owns property or money derived from sources other than the lending of money and whether or not he carries on the business as a principal or as an agent.[55]

A money lender is therefore a person who lends money to others as his lawful business. He must not be a body corporate but a natural person.[56] He must be in possession of a money lender's licence[57] otherwise he will be guilty of a crime and liable to be imprisoned for up to three months upon a second or subsequent conviction.

---

55. See Section 2 of the 1994 Lagos State Money Lenders Law (Cap. 133) or the definitions' section of the Money Lenders Law of any of the states.
56. Ibid.
57. Section 5 Money Lenders Law (Cap. 133) Laws of Lagos State 1994.

A co-operative society is not a money lender notwithstanding that a credit and thrift co-operative society also lends money. A co-operative society lends money usually only to its members and from funds contributed by the members whereas a money lender lends money to the general public and from his own personal funds.

A money lender is never incorporated. In defining a money lender, Section 2 of the Money Lenders Law expressly states that a money lender shall not include any society registered under the Co-operative Societies Law, or anybody corporate, incorporated or empowered by special enactment to lend money in accordance with such enactment.

Benefits and Advantages of Co-operatives – The practicability in the common saying that a problem shared is a problem half-solved plays itself out in co-operative societies. So also is the logic in the expression 'unity is strength'. A co-operative society is one organization known to law which enjoys so much indulgence from the law.

The benefits and advantages for which a sole-trader or a partnership desires to transform into a company[58] apply even more attractively to co-operatives. These include that a company

(a) has greater and better potentials for growth and, with growth, enjoys the benefits of the economies of scale,

(b) more easily attracts loans from banks and other financial institutions,

58. *Salomon v Salomon* (1897) AC 22.

(c) commands greater respectability and confidence with other corporate organizations including governments when it comes to dealings with each other especially in contractual relations,

(d) the attraction of corporate legal personality which distinguishes a company's liabilities from those of its members; its perpetual succession; its capacity to distinctly own its own property; its capacity to sue and be sued in its own name.

These benefits are also accruable to the co-operative society which a single individual confronted with the usual problems of finance and the economy and doing business as a sole-trader, or an individual employee of government or some other organization does not possess. Even the partnership does not possess these benefits and advantages.

The co-operative society enjoys these benefits and advantages like the company but without being subjected to the kind of legal demands to which a company is subjected. A company pays tax; the co-operative does not. The company is subjected to a cumbersome and expensive registration and incorporation requirements; a co-operative is not.

Also, a co-operative society enjoys certain protective rights under the Law which other organizations do not enjoy and which further make the co-operative society more attractive. Such protective rights include

(a) the exclusion of its members' shares and interests from attachment or sale in satisfaction of the judgement of a court[59] and

59. Section 17 of the Law.

(b) exemption from the travails of litigation in relation to contracts in restraint of trade.[60]

The benefits and advantages of co-operatives can be split into two categories. First is the advantage to society generally and, secondly, the benefits and advantages to the individual member of co-operative societies. To society generally, co-operative societies encourage economic growth, the creation of wealth and generally enhances the quality of life of the people.

To the individual who joins a co-operative society, the benefits to him are quite a lot. These include that

(a) he becomes both an owner as well as customer and user of the goods, services and facilities of the enterprise;
(b) he takes the benefits of pooled efforts and resources,
(c) he takes the benefits of buying cheaply in bulk;
(d) he takes the benefits of keeping the profits from his own purchases;
(e) he benefits from the sharing of interests and dividends accruing from his own loans and the loans granted other members;
(f) he enjoys the right to participate in the management of the society;
(g) his benefits in form of interests and dividends are bestowed on him not in relation to the volume of his shares in the capital of the society but in proportion to the level of his patronage of the operations of the society;

60. Section 14 of the Law.

(h) he enjoys the benefits of a direct supply of his basic and immediate necessities;
(i) he is entitled to a fair share of the benefits and profits of the undertakings of the society;
(j) he has the opportunity of relating economically and socially with other persons of like stations in life and is entitled to equal rights and responsibilities with his fellow co-operators within the society;
(k) he enjoys free ingress and egress in relation to his society;
(l) the benefits of the exemption from payment of tax on the earnings of the society rubs off on him;
(m) so also is he entitled to the benefits of the society's exemption from the payment of stamp duties and other taxes in relation to documents and other instruments;
(n) he is enabled, generally, to overcome his immediate and long term economic and financial problems;
(o) he is entitled to cheap and easy access to capital for investment purposes and or expansion of existing investments;
(p) has easy and cheap access to funds during emergencies;
(q) he is encouraged to save for the rainy day; and
(r) has a ready market for his products and at best market prices.

Chapter Two

Sources of Co-operative Societies Laws

The National Assembly shall... make laws ... with respect to ... incorporation, regulation and winding up of bodies corporate, other than co-operative societies ....[1]

Sources of Law

The expression 'sources of co-operative societies laws' is used in the context of locating the means through which a rule or rules of law become part of the general body of law on co-operative societies. In other words, the term is employed to mean the legal sources from which the sundry binding rules and regulations for the formation, running, and winding-up of co-operative societies can be obtained.

These binding rules and regulations can be found in the

(a) general provisions of the 1999 constitution of Nigeria,

(b) regional co-operative societies laws of the various states (persuasively including the federal enactment known and referred to as Decree 90),

(c) regulations made pursuant to the state laws,

(d) bye-laws as made by the individual society for itself in compliance with the Law and Regulations,

(e) judicial precedents, and

(f) the received English laws as applicable.

The Laws are the substantive statutory enactments by the appropriate and respective state legislatures containing the general legal framework for the formation and control of co-operative societies. They are the principal legislations

1. Item 32 Exclusive Legislative List pursuant to Section 4 (2) of Constitution of Federal Republic of Nigeria 1999.

pursuant to which the Rules and Regulations for the internal running of co-operative societies are made.

The Rules and Regulations are subsidiary legislations made under powers contained in the principal statute. For instance, Section 53 (1) of the Co- operative Societies Law (Cap. 42) Laws of Delta State 2007 provides that

> the governor may make all such regulations as may be necessary for the purpose of carrying out or giving effect to the principles and provisions of the Law'[2]

While the Regulations are made pursuant to the Law, the **Bye-laws** are usually made pursuant to the Law and Regulations hence, as in all other states' Regulations, Clause 4 (1) of the Delta State Regulations provides that

> a society shall make bye-laws in respect of the following matters - ...[3]

and by Section 6 (3) of the Law, the application for registration of a co-operative society

> shall be accompanied by three copies of the proposed bye-laws ....

Judicial Precedent - By judicial precedent, as a source of

2. All other states' laws contain this provision with substantial similarity. The more recent Lagos State law has it as *'The State Commissioner may make regulations for the purposes of this Law'* in Section 64 (1) while Section 56 of the Federal Government's Cap. N98 declares that *'the Minister or the Commissioner responsible for matters relating to co-operative societies may make all such regulations as may be necessary for the purpose of carrying out or giving effect to the provisions of this Act.'* See also Section 53 of the Ogun State Co-operative Societies Law (Cap. 26).
3. See also Regulation 4 Lagos State Regulations, Regulation 5 for Ogun State. The Federal Government's Cap. N98 has no Regulations but by its Section 11, it provides that *'a registered society may make bye-laws for such things as are necessary or desirable for the purpose for which the society is established ...'*.

law for co-operative societies, it is meant that with reference to the practice of the courts whereby the decision of a higher court of record on a point of law becomes binding on all other courts below it in the hierarchy courts. Such binding decisions become also binding on all persons who have anything to do with co-operative societies in relation to the particular point of law so decided. In other words, where the particular point of law is one touching and concerning co-operative societies, it becomes a source of law with respect thereto.

The doctrine of judicial precedent is inherited by or **received** into Nigerian law from the English common law. It consists of what is commonly referred to as 'case law' which is no more than 'law' as handed down by the courts in the process of interpreting the laws as made by the legislature.

A good example of a so-called court-made law is the Nigerian Supreme Court's decision in the case of *Oseyomon v* Ojo[4] that the provisions of Sections 51 (1) (a) and (b) and 51 (6) of the Delta State Co-operative Societies Law Cap. 42[5] which are state enactments must be regarded as void in so far as they purport to limit or oust the jurisdiction of the High Courts as therein provided contrary to the express provision of the 1979 constitution.

Accordingly, from the date of this court decision, it is no longer the law relating to co-operative societies that a decision of the registrar of co-operatives or of an arbitrator shall be final and shall not be called in question in any court as provided in Section 51 of the Delta

4. (1997) 7 SCNJ 365.
5. Formerly Cap. 45 Laws of Bendel State.

State Co-operative Societies Law.[6]

A discussion of the development of the legal framework of co-operative societies in Nigeria cannot be undertaken in full without the mention of C.F. Strickland – a British citizen who worked for the Colony and Protectorate of Nigeria. It was him who was commissioned by the colonial government of Nigeria to conduct a research and enquire into the possibilities of introducing co-operative societies into Nigeria. His research and enquiries led to the publication in 1934 of his *Report on the Introduction of Co-operative Societies into Nigeria and the Cameroons under British Mandate.*

In the Report, C. F. Strickland who is believed to be the first Registrar of Co-operatives in Nigeria[7] wrote:

> I have submitted to the Nigerian Government a draft Co-operative Societies' Ordinance and of Regulations under the Ordinance, based on the Tanganyika[8] Ordinance and that of several British Colonies and Dominions[9]

The 1935 Co-operative Societies Ordinance

Strickland's *draft Co-operative Societies Ordinance* was subsequently enacted as the Nigerian Co-operative Societies Ordinance (Cap. 39) of 1935 as the very first piece of legislation on co-operative societies in Nigeria. As

---

6. All other co-operative societies enactments in Nigeria contain this provision including even the Federal Government's Cap. N98 as in Sections 49 and 50 thereof.
7. But see Erhurun, Helen E.O (2007) *Co-operatives – Principles, Practice and Field Administration* (P.A. Anigboro Prints, Asaba) at p.14 for the position that Mr. E.F.G. Haig was the first Registrar of Co-operatives in Nigeria.
8. Present day Tanzania.
9. Page 28 thereof.

at the date of this enactment, Nigeria had a unitary system of government and, accordingly, the Ordinance had a national application.

In 1954, the Nigeria (Constitution) Order in Council was promulgated under which a federal constitution was introduced into Nigeria. By Section 57 of this Federal Constitution, any ordinance, including the Co-operative Societies Ordinance of 1935, which was in force as at the 1st day of October 1954

> was to be deemed ... a law made by the federal legislature or a law made by a regional legislature or a law made separately by the federal and regional legislatures, roughly in accordance with the distribution of legislative powers under the constitution[10]

Regional Co-operative Societies Laws

Under the above legal framework, all the regions[11] published their respective co-operative societies laws beginning with the Western Region Co-operative Societies Law of 1953 with its Rules which were published in 1959. The Northern Region Co-operative Societies Law with its Rules followed in 1956 while the Eastern Nigeria Co-operative Societies Law with its Rules came out in 1963.

Following the incursion of the Nigerian military into governance in 1966, the country reverted by implication to a unitary system of government until the military relinquished the reins of power in 1979 and then put in place a 'constitution of the Federal Republic of Nigeria 1979' which proclaimed in its Section 2 (2) that

10. See Obilade: The *Nigerian Legal System* (Sweet & Maxwell, London 1974) at p. 64.
11. There were three regions to wit Northern, Western, and Eastern Regions.

> Nigeria shall be a federation consisting of states and a federal capital territory.

By its Section 4, the 1979 constitution vested the legislative powers of the Federal Government in a National Assembly with powers to make laws on any matter in the Exclusive Legislative List. Item 30 of this Exclusive Legislative List provided thus:

> Incorporation, regulation and winding up of bodies corporate, other than co-operative societies, local government councils and bodies corporate established directly by any Law enacted by a House o Assembly.

This means that the Federal Government shall have legislative powers to make laws relating to the incorporation, regulation, and winding up of all bodies corporate except co-operative societies.

Also excepted from the federal legislative powers is the incorporation, regulation, and winding up of bodies corporate established by any Law enacted by a House of Assembly. Co-operative societies are bodies corporate established under co-operative societies laws enacted or deemed to have been enacted by state legislatures i.e. houses of assembly.

The meaning of Item 30 of the 1979 Constitution is clear and unambiguous. It is that the Federal Government was expressly precluded from making laws on co-operative societies. Anything done therefore in contravention of this constitutional provision will be invalid.

Decree 90 of 1993

In 1983 when the military again invaded governance, they did not suspend Section 2 (2) of the 1979 constitution and, although they suspended the legislatures, they did not suspend the legislative lists. However, in 1993, the Federal Military Government enacted Decree No. 90 of 1993 entitled the Nigerian Co-operative Societies Decree.[12]

Did the Federal Military Government possess the requisite legislative powers to promulgate this Decree? A military government nonetheless governs by laws known as Decrees. These were laws all the same notwithstanding that they were called Decrees.

In other words, the military government wanted to be and was taken to have intended *ab initio* to govern through laws and be bound by them. However, it might amount to overstretching an argument to expect a Federal *Military* Government as at 1993 to always respect the provisions of the unsuspended parts of the 1979 constitution or any law for that matter and to refrain from making laws which the constitution precluded it from making.

Even then, the making of Decree 90 of 1993 was clearly *ultra vires* the legislative powers of the Federal Government.

In 1999, again, the military relinquished governance to a democratically elected government under a 'constitution of the Federal Republic ...' which contains an Item 32 in its Exclusive Legislative List and providing that the Federal Government shall have exclusive powers to legislate on matters relating to the

> incorporation, regulation and winding up of bodies corporate, other than co-operative societies ....

12. Now published as Nigerian Co-operative Societies Act (Cap. N98) Laws of the Federation 2004.

Can the democratically elected government under the 1999 constitution retain the *ultra vires* Decree 90 of 1993 as its laws? A democratic government is a constitutional government. It may not possess the legislative rascality of a military government. But it has powers under the constitution to retain previously made laws validly made and subsisting as 'existing law'.[13]

Can an *ultra vires* piece of legislation survive as an existing law under the constitution? Is it not said that what is void *ab initio* is void for all times and that therefore you cannot place something on nothing and expect it not to fall?[14] Can the invalid Decree 90 of 1993 of the military government which was however 'in force' before the date of the coming into force of the 1999 constitution be deemed an Act of the National Assembly and thereby render it a valid existing law? An existing law is defined by the constitution as

> any law and includes any rule of law or any enactment or instrument whatsoever which is in force immediately before the date when this[15] section comes into force or which having been passed or made before that date comes into force after that date.[16]

The 1993 Decree 90 was a 'law' or an 'enactment' which was in force immediately before the date Section 315 of the 1999 constitution came into force on the 29th of May 1999. This ought then to qualify it as an existing law. But an existing law exists subject to the constitution itself and shall have effect with such modifications as may be

13. See Section 315 of the 1999 constitution.
14. *Mcfoy v UAC* (1961) 3 WLR 1405, 1409 – 1410 per Lord Denning
15. Section 315 of the 1999 constitution.
16. Section 315 (4) (b) ibid.

necessary to bring it into conformity with the provisions of the constitution.[17] It is doubtful if Decree 90 can be brought into conformity with the constitution no matter the amount of modification since the Decree was *ab initio* void for being ultra *vires* its maker.

Also, an existing law is only deemed to be an Act of the National Assembly and thereby becomes an existing law only to the extent that such an existing law is a law with respect to a matter on which the National Assembly is empowered by the constitution to make laws.[18] Item 32 of the 1999 constitution does not empower the National Assembly to make laws on co-operative societies.

The Nigerian Co-operative Societies Act (Cap. N98) Laws of the Federation 2004 being a 'law' made in 1993 as a Decree of the military government before the coming into effect of Section 315 of the 1999 constitution must be

(a) made subject to the provisions of the constitution,
(b) modified to bring it into conformity with the provisions of the constitution, and
(c) a law which the National Assembly is empowered by the constitution to make

before it can qualify as a deemed Act of the National Assembly and as an existing law. To make the enactment subject to the provisions of the constitution means and includes making it come under the provisions of Section 4 (2) thereof which is that it must be a law with respect to a matter included in the Exclusive Legislative List as set

17. Section 315 (1) ibid.
18. Section 315 (1) (a) ibid.

out in Part 1 of the Second Schedule to the constitution which is a list of matters over which the Federal Government exercises exclusive legislative powers and, as has been shown *supra*, Item 32 of this list expressly precludes the National Assembly from making laws on co-operative societies.

In effect, it has to be submitted and with due respect, that Decree 90 of 1993 was invalid as at the date it was promulgated as the Nigerian Co-operative Societies Decree since it offended Item 30 of the Exclusive Legislative List in Part I of the Second Schedule to the 1979 constitution which was the constitution[19] then in force. Although it was invalid, it was nevertheless 'in force' as it were, being a military enactment.

Decree 90 fails to survive the military government which promulgated it. Beyond the futile attempt to change its name from a Decree to an Act in the 2004 edition of the Laws of the Federation, nothing can legally be done to give life to this enactment. It is a 'law' which the maker thereof had and still has no power to make and it is *ipso facto* null and void and of no effect whatsoever.

Subsection 3 of Section 315 of the 1999 constitution provides that nothing in the constitution must be construed as affecting the power of a court of law or any tribunal established by law to declare as invalid any provision of an existing law on the ground of its being inconsistent with the provision of any other law including any provision of the constitution.

19. There are decisions of superior courts of records to the effect that Decrees are, under the military, superior to the constitution.

Therefore, even if the Nigerian Co-operative Societies Act (Cap. N98) survives as an existing law (which it does not as has been demonstrated *supra*), any court in Nigeria, especially any of the High Courts, will find no difficulty in declaring it and or all its provisions invalid on the ground of inconsistency with the provisions of Section 4 (2) of the 1999 constitution.

However, the Act may be invalid for being *ultra vires* the maker and its deemed maker but its usefulness in the comparative study of the law on co-operative societies in Nigeria cannot be ignored. This is because, it being a more recent modern day enactment on the subject, it reflects and addresses in some of its provisions current trends and problems associated with co-operative societies. It will therefore be difficult in a book such as this not to make references to it now and again at least for comparative analysis even though it does not represent the law on the subject in Nigeria.

The Nigerian Co-operative Societies Act (Cap. N98) ought to be the supreme source of law on the subject of co-operative societies in Nigeria in view of the constitutional provision that any law made by a state House of Assembly which is inconsistent with

> any law validly made by the National Assembly, the law made by the National Assembly shall prevail, and that other law shall to the extent of the inconsistency be void.[20]

But in view of the above discussion relating to the legal status of the Act, recourse and reliance will be had in this

20. Section 4 (5) 1999 constitution.

book to the regional[21] (now states) enactments as the valid sources of the law on co-operative societies in Nigeria. The provisions of these regional or state enactments are substantially *impari materia* as their respective provisions are influenced by each other which have all lifted from the 1935 Co-operative Societies Ordinance with slight modifications in section numberings and arrangements and minor differences in choice of wordings. Consequentially, a reference to the provisions of one of them is as good a reference to the others. Accordingly for the purpose of this book, references and reliance shall be to the Co-operative Societies Law (Cap. 42)[22] Laws of Delta State 2007 and which throughout this book , is referred to as 'the Law'.[23]

Regulations – All of the state enactments have Regulations made pursuant to them as subsidiary legislations. These Regulations, though as binding as law, are not law in the substantive sense. They are generally known as subsidiary law because they are made pursuant to the Law.

A subsidiary law is another term for delegated legislation which is sometimes also known as subordinate legislation. Under our laws in Nigeria, the constitutional powers to make laws is vested in the legislature which in England is known as 'parliament'.[24] Section 4 (1) of the

21. See supra at p. 45
22. Formerly Cap. 45 Laws of Bendel State 1976.
23. Which expression, except the context otherwise indicates, shall, throughout in this book, be a reference to the said Co-operative Societies Law of Delta State.
24. A term which has assumed general application to mean the legislature so that in Nigeria, 'parliament' is known as the 'National Assembly' at the federal level and 'House of Assembly' at state level.

1999 constitution specifically provides that

> the legislative powers of ... Nigeria shall be vested in a National Assembly ... which shall consist of a Senate and a House of Representatives.

Similarly, subsection 6 of this section vests the legislative powers of a state in the House of Assembly of the state. Therefore, only the National Assembly and a state House of Assembly have constitutional powers to make laws in Nigeria which are known as 'Acts' and 'Laws' at the federal and state levels respectively. Sometimes however, these parliaments make laws containing provisions of a general nature and creating powers therein and vesting same on named or specified authorities or persons to legislate necessary details thereto. Such necessary details are usually matters which may be open to frequent changes or which are adjectival in character and which cannot therefore be left to the tedious and time consuming procedures of parliaments for making laws. When made, these necessary details are known as subsidiary legislation.

The Co-operative Societies Law (Cap. 42) of Delta State provides that the Governor[25] may make all such

25. Section 53 (1) of the Law. All other co-operative societies enactments in Nigeria contain similar provisions but with the delegated legislative power vested in different persons or authorities from state to state. In Lagos state, it is the *'state commissioner'*. In all the states in the north, Section 58 (1) of the Northern Region Co-operative Societies Law of 1956 vests the power on the *'Governor-in-Council'* while the Law for the Eastern states enacted in 1963 vests it in *'the minister'* vide Section 54 (1) thereof. Under Cap. N98, it is *'the Minister or the commissioner responsible for matters relating to co-operative societies ...'*. This reference to the 'commissioner' in this federal enactment is because the Act purports to legislate also for the states. But see *supra* for the discussion on this Act.

Regulations as may be necessary for the purpose of carrying out or giving effect to the principles and provisions of the Law. But the governor of a state does not constitutionally have powers to make laws. By the above provision of Section 53 of the Law, he has nonetheless been invested with powers to make laws of some sort by the parliament. When he makes them, they are known not as substantive law, but as subordinate law or legislation arising from powers delegated to him by the parliament as contained in Section 53 of the Law.

Accordingly, the Governor in Delta State has made Regulations published as 'subsidiary legislation' immediately after the Law.[26] As with all the state co-operative laws, the Regulations made for the different states are substantially the same; the differences not being material but in semantics and numbering.

Prescriptions for the Regulations – The delegated legislative powers conferred on the state governor is one under which he may make all such regulations without let or hindrance or any form of restrictions as may, in his opinion, be necessary for carrying out or giving effect to the principles and provisions of the Law and, without prejudice to the generality of this delegated legislative power, he is, in making such regulations, particularly to provide for:

(a) standard forms which applicants for registration of co-operative societies are to use in applying for

26. This arrangement is applicable to all the other states. There are however no Regulations made pursuant to Cap. N98 despite the provisions of Section 58 thereof requiring the making of Regulations.

such registration; [27]

(b) conditions[28] to be met and complied with by the applying society in making its application;
(c) the procedure for making applications for the registration of a co-operative society;
(d) conditions to be complied with by persons applying to be members of a registered co-operative society;
(e) conditions for the election of members to the offices of a registered co-operative society;
(f) payments to be made and interest to be acquired by a member of a co-operative society before he can exercise his membership rights;
(g) limit[29] of interests capable of being acquired by a member (subject to Section 28 of the Law);
(h) limitation (if any) of number of members;
(i) appointment, withdrawal, or expulsion of members;
(j) payments, if any, to members who withdraw or are expelled;
(k) liabilities of past members;
(l) general meetings of members and procedure therefor;

27. No such forms have been provided for in the Regulations under the Law notwithstanding also the provisions of Regulation 2 (1) that applications shall be in the 'form' approved by the Registrar. But see the Ogun State Regulations for a prescribed form at Appendix C. It should be noted however that the use of prescribed forms in law is generally not a mandatory requirement provided that substantial compliance with the prescribed form is achieved.
28. Regulation 2 (1).
29. The Regulations made pursuant to the Law are silent on this as they are on many other items contained in Section 53 of the Law. But see Section 28 of the Law for this limit.

(m) power of Registrar to summon general meetings of members;
(n) powers of general meetings;
(o) appointment of representatives of affiliate societies and the voting powers of such representatives at meetings of a central society;
(p) appointment, suspension, and removal of management committee members or other officers of the society;
(q) procedure at management committee meetings;
(r) powers and duties of management committee and other officers of the society;
(s) content of bye-laws including procedure for making, altering, or rescinding bye-laws and conditions to be met before such making, altering, or rescission;
(t) qualifications and terms for granting loans;
(u) deceased member's interests, how ascertained, and succession thereto;
(v) insane member's interests, ascertainment, and succession thereto;
(w) formation, maintenance, objects, investment of reserve funds and other funds under a society's control; conditions for distribution of accumulated funds to members;
(x) maximum rate of dividend payable by a society;
(y) accounts and books to be kept by a society;
(z) periodic publication of balance sheet showing assets and liabilities;
(aa) audit of accounts;
(bb) entries in society's books – how and by whom certified;

(cc) formation and maintenance of register of members showing member's shareholding where liability of members is limited by shares;

(dd) inspection and issuance of documents and registers in the office of the registrar and fees payable therefore;

(ee) manner of determining breach of bye-laws or contracts relating to disposal of produce to or through a society; and manner of ascertaining or assessing liquidated damages therefore;

(ff) mode for appointing arbitrators and procedure for proceedings before registrar or arbitrators;

(gg) procedure to be followed by a liquidator, and appeals from orders of a liquidator;

(hh) forms for appeals, fees and procedure therefore;

(ii) all matters connected with or incidental to the presentation, hearing, and disposal of appeals.[30]

The above listed items on which the governor may by Section 53 (1) of the Law make regulations are not exhaustive. He has powers to make regulations on other matters not listed in the section since the section specifies that the governor may make all such regulations as, in his opinion, may be necessary for giving effect to the principles and provisions of the Law.

The Regulations as made under the Law are themselves silent on a number of items contained in the list. Some of such items are however provided for in the body of the Law thereby rendering regulations in respect thereto unnecessary. A good example of such an item can be found

30. See generally, section 53 of the Law.

in the profuse provisions of Section 52 of the Law on the division and amalgamation of co-operative societies. The whole of PART 10 of the Law is devoted to this item which, though dealt with in only one section, the section has twelve subsections! This must be the explanation why the Regulations are silent on division and amalgamation of co-operative societies.

The Regulations as Made – As stated above, the then military governor of Bendel[31] State made[32] and published a subsidiary legislation pursuant to Section 53 of the Law and in exercise of the powers conferred on him therein and which legislation is cited as the Co-operative Societies Regulations.[33] In it, the governor has made regulations for such issues as:

(a) The Application for Registration – Regulation for this is contained in Regulation 1 which provides that the application for registration of a co-operative society must be submitted to the Registrar of co-operatives in the form as approved by the Registrar and that if the Registrar declines registration, he shall write to the applicants informing them of his refusal and the reasons therefor.

(b) Name of Society – Every co-operative society is required by Regulation 3 to include in its name a word or words which clearly indicate the nature and situation of the society.

It is not clear what the lawmaker means or intends by 'nature' or 'situation' of the society which must be part of the name but is to be humbly submitted that by 'nature',

31. Now split into Delta and Edo states.
32. Same is applicable in all other states in Nigeria.
33. Regulation 1.

it is meant the type of co-operative society especially as to whether it is a limited liability society and as to whether it is, for instance, a farmers society, or thrift and credit society etc.

As for 'situation', a plausible interpretation will be what Erhurun describes in the classification of co-operative societies into their geographical location and operational areas.[34] If this interpretation is correct, then Regulation 3 must be taken to mean that the name of every co-operative society must include a word or words indicating the society's geographical location or its geographical area of operations. This may render the name rather unwieldy and too long. A tidier approach therefore must be to read 'situation' as used in the regulation together with 'nature' to mean the type of society.

(c) Compulsory Bye-Laws – Regulation 4 makes provision for the general matters in respect of which every co-operative society must make bye-laws.[35] There are thirteen such matters as listed in paragraph 1 of Regulation 4.

Where a co-operative society is of a type which has in its objects clause the creation and lending of funds to its members, such a society must, in addition to the thirteen general matters, make further bye-laws specifying the conditions on which loans may be made to members, the consequences of default in repayment, and how the annual surplus is to be disposed of.

34. *Co-operatives: Principles, Practice and Field Administration* (P.A. Anigboro Prints, Asaba, 2007) at p.89.
35. See Chapter Three on 'Co-operative Societies Bye-Laws' (infra) for a fuller discussion.

There is also regulation[36] permitting the making of new bye-laws and amending or canceling those already made specifying conditions and procedure for so doing.

(d) Membership – Regulations 6, 16 and 22 deal with admission, termination and register of members[37] respectively while Regulation 9 provides for the holding of general meetings by every co-operative society and the functions of such meetings.[38]

(e) Management Committee: Membership, Powers and Duties

These are provided for in Regulations 12, 13, 14 and 15 and are more fully discussed in the chapter on 'Management, Administration and Control of Societies'.

(f) Nominees – By Regulation 23, every person who is a member of a co-operative society enjoys the option of nominating at least one person on whom his interests in the society shall devolve upon his death.

If the society is one with a share capital, a member may not nominate more than one person as his personal representative unless such a member has more than one share in which case the amount to be paid to each such nominee or personal representative shall be specified by him at the time of the nominee's appointment.

A member is also at liberty to, from time to time, revoke, modify or change his nominee. The name of a member's nominee and other relevant personal details shall

36. Regulation 5.
37. See Chapter Five on 'Membership of Co-operative Societies'.
38. See Chapter Seven on co-operative societies meetings for a fuller discussion.

be entered in the register of members. Any change in the details or of the nominee must be recorded in the register of members.

Unless otherwise permitted and provided for in the bye-laws, a nominee or personal representative of a deceased member can only recover the actual amount paid by the deceased member to acquire the share or interest to which he is entitled in the society; and under no circumstance can such a nominee recover any amount if the society's balance sheet shows a net loss.

Where the nominee or personal representative is a minor, a receipt signed by him or his guardian shall operate as sufficient discharge in favour of the society for any sum of money paid to such a minor.

(g) Disputes – Regulation 21 makes profuse provisions in ten paragraphs for the presentation, hearing, and determination of disputes. Under the Regulation, whenever any dispute as described in Section 51 of the Law arises, a reference of it may be made to the registrar.[39]

39. See Chapter Nine on Co-operative Disputes for a fuller discussion.

Chapter Three

Co-operative Society Bye-Laws

Co-operative society bye-laws are therefore different from bye-laws in the usual ordinary sense - Infra

Every society seeking registration must have a set of proposed bye-laws which is to be submitted together with the application for registration. Prior to the registration and up to the time of making the application, these 'bye-laws' are but mere proposals which become registered bye-laws only upon their registration.[1]

Section 2 of the Law provides that in the context of the Law, the word 'bye-laws' means

> the registered bye-laws made by a society in the exercise of any power conferred by (the) Law, and includes any registered amendment thereof.

Bye-laws, strictly so called, are therefore bye-laws only when they are registered otherwise they remain only as mere proposals or proposed bye-laws.

Bye-Laws: What are they? The above quoted definition of the term 'bye-laws' as contained in Section 2 of the Law hardly explains what bye-laws are and their effect in law. A not-very-easy effort will here be made to expound on the legal meaning and effect of bye-laws. Litigation relating to co-operative societies is rare in Nigeria in view, clearly, of the ouster provisions in the Law. As a result, there are no direct judicial authorities to rely on in explaining and expounding on issues and matters in connection with co-operative societies except by analogy using strongly related concepts.

In general terms, bye-laws are, ordinarily, 'laws'

1. Section 6 (3) of the Law.

made as a form of delegated or subsidiary legislation usually by a local government or some other local authority empowered under law to so do. Bye-laws are made under a parent law which is the enabling statute that confers the power on the said local authority to make bye-laws. When made, such bye-laws have general application in relation to the public or a specified group within the public from the date[2] of their publication in the official government gazette or some other specified date therein. By Section 74 of the Evidence Act, such bye-laws are judicially noticeable.[3] They do not operate as agreements between individuals but as laws binding on all persons to whom they apply.[4]

The rules and regulations made by and for the regulation of social clubs and cultural associations known as their constitutions are also sometimes referred to as their bye-laws. These are not published in the official government gazette and they are strictly private documents[5] which relate to and concern only those persons who are members of the club or association.

In the case of co-operative societies, the bye-laws are made, in the first instance by a group of individuals with a common problem and who have voluntarily joined together to seek a common solution therefor and which, in the second instance, has been registered by a Registrar (or Director, as the case may be) of co-operative societies.

Co-operative society bye-laws are therefore

2. Tangale Traditional Council v Fawu (2001) 17 NWLR (Pt. 742) 293
3. See *Eagle Super Pack (Nig.) Ltd v ACB* (2006) 19 NWLR (Pt. 1013) 20, 46
4. See *London Association of Shipowners and Brokers v London and India Docks Joint Committee* (1892) 3 Ch. 242, 252.
5. *Omaliko v Awachie* (2002) 12 NWLR (Pt. 780) 1, 25.

different from bye-laws in the usual ordinary sense in that they are made not under powers directly conferred on some public authority by an enabling statute but by private individuals and which are applicable only to themselves.

Co-operative bye-laws are rules and regulations made strictly for the control and regulation of the internal organization, or internal matters of co-operative societies and matters relating to procedure in compliance with the provisions of the Law. They are therefore a set of self-made rules and regulations in conformity with the law for the internal regulation of the operations of co-operative societies. Bye-laws are in the nature of a constitution similar in effect to the memorandum and articles of association of a registered company.

By Regulation 5, as made pursuant to the Law, every co-operative society is required to, from time to time, make new bye-laws for the conduct of its business, or may amend or even cancel the bye-laws already made. In practice, all registrars of co-operative societies in Nigeria have printed standard-form or model bye-laws which they make available to all applicants for registration. These model bye-laws[6] have been settled by the registrars in

6. In Lagos State, for instance, the model bye-laws are entitled *'Bye-Laws of the ...... Co-operative Thrift and Credit Society Ltd. including appendices on Co-operative Credit Societies, Forms and Vital Notes'* while in Delta State they are entitled *'Bye-Laws of the ...... Multi-purpose Co-operative Society Limited'*. For Kaduna State, it is the *'Bye-Laws of the ...... Co-operative Society Limited'* with a footnote in parenthesis to the effect that *'(throughout the Bye-laws references should be made to the Nigeria Co-operative Societies Act Chapter 98 (Decree 90) of 1993 and Northern Region Co-operative Societies Regulations No. 9 of 1956)'*.

substantial conformity with the respective state co-operative societies law and the regulations made pursuant thereto.

The resort to these model bye-laws in standard form must have stemmed from the inability of most applicants for registration to draw up bye-laws which are in conformity with the Law and regulations on their own; and would be in no position or be unwilling to engage the services of professionals such as solicitors to assist them. These lead to avoidable delays and complications in processing applications. The model bye-laws therefore help to ease the process of registration.

Effects of Registered Bye-Laws – A registered co-operative society is a body corporate.[7] In this regard, it is similar to a company. The situation is not changed whether the society is a limited liability society or not.

Therefore, the consequences of incorporation as they relate to companies are, to a very large extent, persuasively applicable the co-operative society. Such consequences include that a body corporate is distinct from its members, has legal capacity to own its own property in its own name, and generally the capacity to enter into legally enforceable contracts.

When a corporate body publishes a document which it has registered as its constitution containing the terms by which it intends to deal with other juristic persons in the course of its operations, such a document must also be binding on it. A company, as a corporate body, usually publishes such terms in two documents known as the Memorandum of Association and the Articles of

7. Section 8 of the Law.

Association. The former has to do with those terms by which the company deals with third parties which are external to it while the latter deals with internal matters.

In current practice though, both the memorandum and the articles are published together in one volume as if they were one document and it is not uncommon to have certain terms which normally should be in one being published in the other such that the difference between the two are gradually becoming blurred and reference is now often made to both documents together than otherwise.

In line with this trend, Section 41 (1) of the Companies and Allied Matters Act[8] 1990 provides that

> the memorandum and articles, when registered, shall have the effect of a contract under seal between the company and its members and officers and between the members and officers themselves whereby they agree to observe and perform the provisions of the memorandum and articles, as altered from time to time in so far as they relate to the company, members, or officers as such.

The constitution of a co-operative society which contains the terms by which it deals with other legal persons both externally and internally is its bye-laws. It incorporates in itself all those terms in a company's memorandum and articles of association which are relevant to it as a co-operative society; and which have substantially similar legal effects.

It is therefore persuasively correct in law that the bye-laws of a co-operative society upon its registration has

8. This Act is not applicable to co-operative societies but is referred to herein for purposes of persuasive comparison and guide.

effect as a contract under seal between the co-operative society and its members and officers and between the members and officers themselves whereby they agree to observe and perform the provisions of the bye-laws, as altered from time to time in so far as they relate to the co-operative society, members, or officers as such.

This means, as has been explained in a number of judicial pronouncements in relation to companies, that by the bye-laws of a co-operative society,

(a) every member of the co-operative society, in his capacity as such member, is bound in contract to the society by the provision of the bye-laws.[9]

(b) In like manner, the co-operative society is bound to each member, in the member's capacity as member, by the provisions of the bye-laws.[10]

(c) The bye-laws constitute a contract under seal between each member and the other members, and

(d) That there is no contract under the bye-laws as between the co-operative society or the members and an outsider since the general position of the law of contract is that the doctrine of privity of contract will not permit any person who is not a party to a contract to exercise any rights or suffer any obligations under the contract.

With regards to the first two effects above, the wordings of Section 16 of the 1968 Companies Act is very explicit in that it makes a company's memorandum and articles of association a contract which binds the company (society) and the members thereof to the same extent as if they (the

9. *Hickman v Kent* (1915) 1 Ch. 881.

10. *Pender v Lushington* (1887) 6 Ch.D. 70.

bye-laws) respectively had been signed and sealed by each member, to observe all the provisions of the memorandum and of the articles (bye-laws), subject to the provisions of the Act (the Law).

Ashbury J. in the course of delivering his judgement in *Hickman v Kent*[11] explained the above provision in the following words:

> I think this much is clear, first, that no articles (bye-laws) can constitute a contract between the company (the society) and a third person; secondly, that no right merely purporting to be given by an article (bye-law) to a person, whether a member or not, in a capacity other than that of a member, as for instance, as solicitor, promoter, or director, can be enforced against the company; and, thirdly, that the articles (the bye-laws) regulating the rights and obligations of the members generally as such do create rights and obligations between them and the company (the society) respectively.

As for the third effect above on the issue whether the bye-laws create a contract between members *inter se*, i.e. between member and members, the words of Lord Herschell while deciding *Welton v Saffery*[12] are very helpful as he had declared that

> it is quite true that the articles (the bye-laws) constitute a contract between each member and the company (the society), and there is no contract in terms between the individual members of the company (the society), but the

11. Supra
12. (1897) AC 299, 315.

articles (the bye-laws) do not any the less ... regulate their rights *inter se.*[13]

Contents of Bye-Laws – Just as Section 53 of the Law makes prescriptions as to what particular matters the governor of a state may make regulations, Regulation 4 (as made by the governor pursuant to the Law) has made prescriptions as to what particular matters in respect of which a co-operative society shall make bye-laws.

These matters are divided into two categories the first of which lists all those matters in respect of which every co-operative society irrespective of type or kind must make bye-laws. The second category is in respect of matters which a society having in its objects the creation of funds to be lent to its members, that is, a thrift and credit society must make bye-laws.

The matters listed in these two categories can by no means be exhaustive and the lists are not closed. There is nothing in the Law or in the Regulations which precludes a co-operative society from making bye-laws to suit its peculiar circumstance provided that such bye-laws, though not in respect of matters listed in the Regulations, are not in breach of any express provision of the Law or the Regulations and are, generally, not illegal or unlawful.[14]

General Bye-Laws – By the said Regulation 4, every co-operative society's bye-laws must make provisions for the following:

(a) Name - In order to conform with the Law and the

13. This position is no longer as strict as Lord Herschell stated it to be in 1897 as, in appropriate cases, the articles may bind members *inter se* and their rights personally enforceable by action.
14. Section 7 (1) of the Law.

Regulations, the name of a co-operative society must be stated in the bye-laws.

The name must include the word 'co-operative' or some other word which has the same meaning as co-operative in any local language in Nigeria. If it is a society with limited liability, the last word in the name must be 'limited' or its vernacular equivalence.

A co-operative society's name must not include either the word 'bank' or 'banking' except where the society is a central financing society.[15] Also, a co-operative may not bear the name of a person or be named after a person but must include words which clearly indicate the nature and situation[16] of the society.[17]

(b) Registered Address – A co-operative society must have an address within Nigeria. This address must be indicated, usually in general terms, in the bye-laws and registered therewith. It must be an address which is traceable to a geographical location within the society's area of operations but must not be a post office box address.

(c) Area of Operations – The bye-laws of every co-operative society must state and define the society's area of operations. The Law does not define or delimit the extent of a society's area of operations. Therefore, every society is at liberty to define and delimit its area of operations – sometimes also known as the field of membership – as restrictively or as widely as it suits its peculiar circumstance.

However, a co-operative society's area of

15. Section 5.
16. It is not very clear what the lawmaker means by 'situation'.
17. Regulation 3.

operations may not be too extensively defined as to make managing and administering it difficult and unwieldy. It has been stated that a co- operative society should be an association consisting of individuals who live in such circumstances of proximity, common language, and normal harmony in that they ordinarily live near one to another and are familiar with each other's income, occupation, and personal character.[18]

Strickland wrote in 1934 at a time when the whole Nigeria was largely rural; and the state of technological development especially in telecommunications was still rudimentary. His expectation of members of a society living 'in such circumstance of proximity' and 'near to one another' must have been in terms of physical and geographical proximity and nearness.

Also, this Briton, who is reputed to be the first registrar of co-operatives in Nigeria, wrote at a time when Nigeria was a unitary state and he must have had the whole of Nigeria – a country of very wide expanse of land most parts of which were literally inaccessible - in mind. But times have changed.

The whole world is now regarded as a 'global village' arising from the monumental development in technology especially in telecommunications and transportation.

Today, Nigeria consists of comparatively smaller political and legislative units with powers separately to legislate on co-operative societies. The effect is that Strickland's concept of a geographical and physical proximity and nearness of the 1934 Nigeria must be now

18. Strickland C.F. – *The Report* at p.2

radically different.

In today's Nigeria, an individual living in Abuja may be regarded as being in circumstances of proximity and nearness to another individual in Asaba[19] than they were in 1934 if they lived in Benin City and Asaba[20] respectively.

It will therefore be correct to state that while a co-operative society's area of operations which, in 1934, extended beyond a town would be regarded as too extensive, in today's terms, even if the co-operative society's area of operations extends beyond a state, it may not be regarded as being too extensive.

Indeed there are in existence staff co-operative societies in large companies with branches spread all over the country and whose members work in these branches and whose area of operations must necessarily be defined to cover these branches. The result is that the whole country makes up their area of operations and yet not considered too extensive. One such society describes itself as having

> over 1,450 members consisting of all categories of staff (and that 47% of these) members are based in Lagos, 39% in Escravos, others in Warri, Port Harcourt, (and yet others in training overseas including the) United Kingdom, United States of America, Korea, Canada etc.[21]

This co-operative society has its headquarters in Lagos with branches in Warri, Port Harcourt, and Escravos with

19. A distance of not less than 400 kilometres by road.
20. Less than 140 kilometres by road.
21. See *2008 Diary: Chevron Employees Multipurpose Co-operative Society.*

'online connectivity to (its) members all over the world'. There are other such societies with widespread membership all over the country such as can be found in the military, the police force, the customs service, prisons and the like with nationwide spread in their operations and whose societies' areas of operations must necessarily be defined nationally and in some cases even beyond national boundaries.[22]

What matters, in all cases, is that the extent and size of a co-operative society's area of operations must not be stated to be or become too wide and too extensive as to make managing and administering the society become unwieldy and that every member is accessible with little difficulty and he, also, has access to the society with relative ease.

(d) Objects - Every co-operative society's bye-laws must contain a statement or statements indicating the purpose or purposes for which the society is set up. Known as the 'objects clause', this statement generally defines the type, functions and activities, extent, and the powers of the co-operative society to engage in the particular activities specified therein. The powers and or objects must be in respect of legal and lawful purposes as no court of law will enforce any illegal purpose or activity.

As under companies, the stated objects of a co-operative society delimits the society's scope of operations beyond which the society may not lawfully act. It announces to the world, especially to those who may have need to contractually deal with the society, the limits and

22. Provided that such societies have registered addresses within Nigeria.

types of activities the society is registered to lawfully engage in. It also enables persons seeking to become members of the society to know what kind of society they are joining. The objects clause assures the newcomer up-front that he is 'investing' his money in exactly where he intends to 'invest' it so that he does not end up finding out too late that he has invested in rotten grapes instead of in nutritious apples.

In current practice, most co-operative societies within a state have similar objects arising from the use by the Registrars of co-operatives of standard-form bye-laws or model bye-laws. The objects in the model bye-laws[23] include usually to:

(a) engage in thrift and credit operations;
(b) engage in arable and tree crops farming;
(c) engage in poultry farming;
(d) undertake simple processing and marketing of co-operative farm products;
(e) stock and distribute various kinds of farm inputs such as fertilizers and other farm chemicals to farmers;
(f) procure and distribute consumer commodities to the community (including members) at reasonable prices;
(g) to carry out any activities designed on co-operative principles which will encourage the spirit and practice of co-operation among members.

The model bye-laws under the Northern Region Co-operative Societies Regulations No. 9 of 1956 declares under its 'objectives' regulation that the:

23. See model bye-laws for Delta State.

objects of the society are to promote the economic and social interests of its members and especially to -

(a) provide facilities for deposits and savings by members;
(b) enable members to obtain loans for .... at reasonable interest rates;
(c) purchase and retail to its members .... as the management committee of the society may decide from time to time;
(d) to raise funds by issuing shares and contracting loans necessary for the attainment of these objectives;
(e) to take other measures designed to encourage in members the spirit and practice of thrift, mutual help and self-help;
(f) to promote co-operative spirit among the members, to work for the improvement of local educational and living standards and to encourage the development of the co-operative movement within the state;
(g) to participate actively as a member and or customer in organisations which are established to promote ....;
(h) to arrange for ....;
(i) to purchase equipment, machinery and implements needed to provide for ....;
(j) to provide for the increased production of ....[24]

Each society is at liberty to adopt these objects verbatim, add to, subtract from, or modify them to suits its particular or peculiar circumstances or requirements. If upon registration, these objects were registered as model bye-laws, the society shall be at liberty to amend them to suit its particular and peculiar needs.[25]

24. Each applying society is to fill in the blank spaces to suit its particular or peculiar circumstance and requirement.
25. Section 11 of the Law.

(e) Society Funds – Inescapably, every society must raise funds from whatever legitimate source which will include members' regular contributions either as periodic membership dues or savings, issuing of shares, surpluses arising out of the business of the society etc. Such funds must be deployed to appropriate purposes and properly kept. Therefore, every co-operative society's bye-laws must make provisions as to the purposes to which the society's funds may be applied, and as to the mode of custody and investment of such funds.

In this respect, the bye-laws must have regard to the provisions of Section 34 of the Law and Regulation 26 which require that a co-operative society

> may invest or deposit its funds
> (a) in the Post Office Savings Bank or with any bank or person[26] carrying on the business of banking approved for this purpose by the registrar; or
> (b) in any securities issued or guaranteed by the government of a commonwealth[27] country; or
> (c) with any other registered society approved for this purpose by the Registrar; or
> (d) in any other mode[28] approved by the Registrar.

---

26. It is doubtful if this provision in respect of a '*person carrying on the business of banking*' is still valid in the face of the provisions of Section 2 of the Banks and Other Financial Institutions Act (Cap. 133) Laws of the Federation 2004 to the effect that *'no person shall carry on any banking business in Nigeria except if it is a company duly incorporated in Nigeria and holds a valid banking licence issued under (the) Act'*.
27. Nigeria is a member of the Commonwealth of Nations.
28. These may include special reserve funds, insurance funds, assets depreciation funds, and such other funds for development, educational, or social propaganda purposes.

(f) Membership – A co-operative society's bye-laws must contain provisions relating to its membership specifying such details as to the qualifications a person must possess before he can become a member of the society; any other terms of admission to membership thereof including any entrance fees; withdrawal and expulsion of members.

(g) Officers – Another matter which every co-operative society's bye-laws must regulate has to do with the officers of the society. The provision in relation thereto must spell out the mode for electing or appointing the officers, their suspension and or removal.

(h) Powers and Duties of Committee Members – The elected or appointed officers of a co-operative society make up what is referred to as the management committee[29] of the society. This committee is charged with the responsibility of the executive administration and management of the affairs of the society. The society's bye-laws must therefore make provisions clearly specifying and delimiting its powers, functions, and duties.[30]

(i) Shares of the Society – Every co-operative society must provide in its bye-laws how its funds are to be raised; and if it is a society with a share[31] capital, how the share capital is to be raised including details as to the rights of members holding the society's shares

29. There is no express provision for this committee either in the Law or in any of the other co-operative societies enactments. But see Section 6 (2) of the Federal Cap. N98.
30. These duties must include those stated in Regulation 15. See also Chapter Seven on 'Management, Administration and Control of Societies' for a fuller discussion.
31. See Chapter Eight on Co-operative Society Funds and Assets for a fuller discussion on co-operative society shares.

relating to the transfer[32] of their shares or other interests in the society's funds and assets.

(j) Meetings – Also to be provided for in every co-operative society's bye-laws is the holding of general and other meetings[33] of the society clearly specifying the powers of such meetings and the procedure for summoning and conducting same.

(k) Signatories to Society's Documents – The persons or officers of the society authorized to sign documents for and on behalf of the society and to use the society's official seal must also be specifically provided for in the bye-laws. The signatories need not be trustees since co-operative societies, being corporate entities, do not need trustees to represent them in the signing of legally valid documents.

(l) Duration of Building Society – If the co-operative society is a building society, that is, one which has as its main object the building of houses or the supporting of its members in the building of their houses, then its bye-laws must indicate the duration of the society.

The exact meaning of this particular bye-law as required in Regulation 4 (1) (m) which is also contained in the co-operative societies enactments of other states including even the more recently reviewed law of Lagos State is not clear.[34] The ordinary meaning of the last leg of the paragraph is that the life span of a co-operative building society must be specified in the bye-laws. This is near

32. See Section 29 of the Law.
33. See Chapter Seven on co-operative society meetings for a fuller discussion.
34. Section 11 of the Federal Cap. N98, which is in all other respects a verbatim reproduction of Regulation 4, has advisedly omitted this provision.

absurd as it must be difficult if not impossible for a co-operative society to predict with any certainty how long it will take the society to accomplish its object even if the society has been established for a sole purpose which, in any event, is most unlikely.

Besides, every registered co-operative society becomes a corporate entity with perpetual succession as a consequence of its registration. Why would it then be necessary for such an entity to specify in its bye-laws a duration for its existence? The provision must be taken as now being undesirable.

Special Bye-Laws for Credit Societies – By Regulation 4 (2) as made pursuant to the Law, it is required that if the objects of a co-operative society includes the creation of funds to be lent to its members, then the society's bye-laws must contain additional provisions[35] in respect of the following matters:

(1) conditions for loans,

(2) consequences for default on shares and loans, and

(3) disposal of surplus.

1. Conditions for Loans – A thrift and credit society's bye-laws must contain provisions relating to the conditions on which it grants loans to its members. Majority of co-operative societies in Nigeria are thrift and credit societies. In practice, the only 'business' which these societies carry on is the business of lending money to their members at reasonable interest rates. The business of lending is very serious business as it is fraught with the risk of default in loans repayment.

35. Additional to the general matters.

The primary reason why persons join thrift and credit societies is the ease with which they can access co-operative loans and the relative cheap rates of interest chargeable thereon. The 'ease of access' to loans is encouraged by the fact that a co-operative society's membership is usually composed of, as Rickland[36] puts it,

> individuals living near to one another and familiar with each other's income, occupation, and personal character.

This engenders the building of trust between members which in turn reduces the risks of default in repayment of loans.

But man by nature is unpredictable and it must be appreciated always that he is, at best, a porridge of good and evil where the evil in him tends always to have the better of him. In every human society therefore, there are persons who as a matter of habit obey societal norms, rules and regulation because they are persuaded that doing so ensures the progress and the general good of society. In like manner, it is also true that in every human society, there will always be deviants[37] who will habitually break societal norms, rules and regulations.

Therefore, if society generally, including a co-operative society, is not to disintegrate, it has always been necessary to enact regulations coupled with sanctions to protect it from ultimate disintegration.[38]

Consequently, in order to curb the effects of the activities of deviants who inevitably will be members of

36. Supra.
37. There was Judas Iscariot among the twelve – a society established by Jesus the Christ Himself.
38. For further readings on the nature of man, see Dennis Lloyd (1983) *The Idea of Law* Penguin Books (N. Zealand) at p. 12

co-operative societies, especially thrift and credit societies, ever co-operative society must make adequate provisions in its bye-laws spelling out the conditions which regulate the grant of its loans.

Such conditions may not be as rigorous and strict as for loans by banks and other financial institutions, but must be such, in their very minimum, as would reflect prudence in the grant of loans and guarantee the safety and security of society's funds through the prompt repayments of loans as and at when due and in the ordinary course of the society's business.

It is in this respect that it is to be recommended to all thrift and credit society especially that notwithstanding the degree of trust which may exist among its members because of their proximity in residence, occupation and income, every applicant for a co-operative loan must be objectively appraised before co-operative funds are released to him.

In carrying out such objective appraisal, it is recommended that regards be had to what lending experts refer to as the five canons of lending which are:

(i) *Capital* – This has to do with how much economic interest the applicant is prepared to invest or has invested in the purpose for which the loan is sought. It is logical to expect that a person who has invested his money in a business venture would more likely devote more time and dedication to that business venture so as to ensure its success. The success of the business venture will in turn influence the prompt repayment of the loan.

(ii) Capability – The capability of a borrower relates to his ability to repay the loan and this involves a consideration of such factors as the borrower's regular source of income, the quantum of such income, the volume of the borrower's other indebtedness within and outside the society, whether he is standing surety for the debts of other members' loans and indebtedness within and outside the society. A person who has a high financial pressure on his regular resources is likely to find it less convenient to repay loans and therefore more certainly to be a risky borrower.

Other factors that may be considered in determining the capacity of a borrower to repay his loan as and at when due and in the ordinary course of business include the borrower's state of health, his level of education, his professional skill in the particular business which he carries on and to which the loan is to be deployed, the level of his industry and level of acumen, his social status and connections, the size of his family and lifestyle generally etc.

A member whose only source of income is his monthly salary of N100,000.00 but whose co-operative assets entitles him to a one million Naira loan arising from his over ten years regular thrifts and savings will be unable to repay the loan if, by the society's bye-laws, he has to repay the loan in 12 months. A loan of half a million Naira to him on those terms will still be a risky loan notwithstanding that he is entitled to double that amount. This is because he lacks the capacity to repay a loan of such exposure as he will have to pay almost half of his monthly salary to the society monthly if he is to meet up with the repayment schedule for the capital loan sum alone. He will require additional sums to pay the interest.

(iii) Character – This third canon of lending has to with the borrower's human attributes. If the borrower is a corporate person, a consideration of this canon might leave itself open to being one of those instances when the veil of incorporation may have to be lifted with a view to taking a peep at the human attributes of the natural persons who operate the corporation.

The attributes which will interest in relation to the borrower which include such attributes of integrity, honesty, reasonableness, objectivity, reliability, frankness, trustworthiness, consistency and such other attributes which would influence any reasonable person to consider the borrower a good person who can be entrusted with money that is not his own.

It must however be stated that personal attributes may not always be an objective yardstick for determining the credibility of a person deserving to be entrusted with a loan. A dealer in hard drugs, for instance, is a criminal. So also is a smuggler. The personal credibility of such persons is doubtlessly called into question without more. But the 'business' into which these kind of persons are engaged can be very 'lucrative' until they are caught. If such persons pay their debts promptly as they are likely to do, then they must regarded for purposes of lending as good persons notwithstanding their questionable character in some other respects.

(iv) Condition – This involves an assessment of the prevailing economic conditions and circumstances relating to the particular kind of business or source of income of the borrower. If he is a trader, for instance, who is involved in the importation of goods, the society should be interested in the degree of risks associated with the importation of the kind of goods he imports and to which he intends to deploy the loan.

Where the borrower is an employee, the society should be interested in the borrower's security of tenure with his employer.

If the co-operative society is satisfied that the conditions or circumstances of the borrower are such that he will not conveniently be able to repay the loan if granted, the application must be refused.

(v) Connection – This canon of lending relates to the public relations or goodwill effect which the granting of the loan or its refusal will have on the co-operative society. A well-connected member of the society who is granted a loan on generous co-operative terms is likely to attract his friends and business associates to the co-operative society and whose contributions would increase the assets base of the society. It will also boost the goodwill of the society as the news of the loan on such generous terms is certain to spread.

Of course, the converse will also be the case if the loan is refused. Hence the social, economic, and, perhaps the political, connection of a co-operator can be material consideration in the appraisal of an application for a co-operative loan.

Specific Provisions for Loans

Regulation 4 (2) (a) provides that the additional provisions which a thrift and credit society's bye-laws must make in relation to the conditions for granting loans to its members shall specifically include:

(i) Rate of Interest – The special provisions for credit society bye-laws must specify the rate at which interest is to be charged upon loans granted by the society to its members. The Law does not define the words 'loan' and 'interest'. However it must be taken that a loan may be legally understood as the principal sum of money actually lent by a lender, that is, the society, to a borrower, that is, the member, usually at an interest which term may legally be taken to mean the comprehensive charge in excess of the principal sum paid or payable to the lender by the borrower in consideration of or otherwise in respect of the loan.

Generally, no person may lend money to another person at an interest unless such a person is one:

(a) whose business, as registered under relevant laws, is that of money lending or who legally carries on or advertises or announces himself or holds himself out in any way as carrying on that business e.g. a money lender; or

(b) being a corporate body incorporated or empowered by special law to lend money in accordance with such special law e.g. a financial institution; or

(c) who is carrying on the business of banking or insurance or, in good faith, carrying on some other business not having for its primary object the lending of money but in the course of which business and for the purposes whereof he lawfully lends money.

In any of the above situations, the law under which the person carries on business expressly permits him to lend money and entitles him, in the course of such business, to charge interests on loans lent. A bank, for instance, is by usual banking custom entitled to lend money to its customers and to charge interests thereon at a reasonable rate.[39]

Co-operative societies enactments in Nigeria do not contain express provisions under which co-operative societies may be entitled to grant loans to persons and to charge interests; but it is submitted that, like banks, credit co-operative societies, are by usual co-operative credit customs and practices, entitled to lend money to its members and to charge interests thereon at reasonable rates.

It is therefore imperative, and the Law requires, that the bye-laws of every such credit co-operative society shall contain objects clause by which it is expressly provided that the society creates funds and grants loans to its members; and by Regulation 4 (2) (a) made pursuant to the Law, such bye-laws must provide for the rate of interest at which the society grants such loans.

In practice generally, the rate of interest on loans to members varies from society to society but usually does not exceed fifteen per cent per annum. This is because most of the model bye-laws with which new co-operative societies are registered contain a provision that pegs the maximum rate of interest at fifteen per cent. The provision is usually to the effect that

> interest on loans to members shall be charged at a rate to be fixed by the committee annually and approved by the general meeting but shall in no case exceed fifteen per cent per annum.[40]

Apart from this provision in the model bye-laws, there is no

39. See *Ayansina v Co-op Bank Ltd* (1994) 5 NWLR (Pt.347) 742, 763.
40. See, for instance, Bye-law 59 of the Delta State Model Bye-laws.

provision either in the Law or in the Regulations which pegs the interest rate, either as minimum or as a maximum rate, which a co-operative society may charge on loans.

The nearest to such provision in any enactment is to be found in the Moneylenders Law[41] where by Section 15 (1) thereof the interest which may be charged on loans shall not exceed a simple interest rate of fifteen per cent.[42]

A model bye-law is not law in any sense of the word. It has no binding effect. It is at best a suggestion made by the registrar of co-operatives to a society seeking registration as a co-operative society with a view to easing and facilitating the process of its registration. An applying society is therefore at liberty to accept, modify, or reject, in part or in whole, the suggestions as contained in the model bye-laws handed to it by the registrar.

The effect is that the present limit of fifteen per cent interest rate on loans as contained in most co-operative societies' bye-laws is not sacrosanct but must be taken only as a guide with every co-operative society retaining the right and liberty to fix and vary its interest rates downwards or upwards as it deems fit but bearing in mind that co-operative societies are never to be run as businesses with a view to profit.

Whatever the rate of interest a society fixes, it is to be advised that the interest be worked out and deducted up-front from the principal loan sum approved and the balance paid to the borrower. This eases the effort that may have to

41. Cap. 138 Laws of Delta State 2007.
42. This law is expressly stated to be not applicable to co-operative societies but the provision must have influenced the drafters of the model co-operative societies bye-laws.

be exerted in the recovery of and the risks of loans that may fall into difficult grounds. Current understanding and attitude towards the model bye-law-imposed maximum rate of interest is as though it were law is very helpful as otherwise some co-operative societies would have long imposed a higher rate on its loans. Excessively high rates of interests on co-operative loans cannot be in tune with co-operative principles.

(ii) Credit Limit – A credit society's bye-laws must also specify the maximum amount which may be lent to a member of the society. Generally in fixing this credit limit, regard is had to the availability of funds and the need to ensure that available funds are evenly spread so as to enable as many members of the society in need of loans, and are qualified, to have access to loans.

Most societies fix this maximum credit limit as a function of the amount of money standing to the credit of the member from his thrift savings and other assets multiplied by a number which varies between two and four from society to society.

A member needs not always be granted the maximum credit which his thrift savings and other assets entitle him to notwithstanding that it is his right to apply for it. In every case, the loans committee or whoever or whatever body has the responsibility for approving loans must have regard to the ability of the borrowing member to repay the loan within the prescribed period for repaying it. This is paramount. Therefore, the approving authority must take into account other factors relating to the borrower's actual income, and his other known liabilities within and outside the society and be satisfied with the borrower's ability repay.

A member who is a paid worker with no other source of income and who has consistently saved ten per cent of his monthly income over a period of five years before applying for his maximum credit level as loan which he has to repay in full within twenty-four months while he continues to pay his monthly ten per cent thrift will certainly be unable to repay the loan with the interest thereon within the time prescribed. An extension of time for him to repay will not be of much help as this can only come with an additional cost to him by way of further interests. Such further interests are most times at a higher rate being penal in nature.

A society with a large number of this type of borrower is bound to soon run into troubled waters with its funds tied up in a high number of unrepaid loans which situation will give rise over time to a real threat to the very existence of the society.

(iii) Duration of Loans – Another important provision which every credit co-operative society bye-laws is required to contain is the maximum duration of time for the repayment of its loans. This provision is very closely related in its effect with the provision as to the credit limit for members. It requires that the borrower must repay his loan in full within a fixed duration of time. A default in this respect usually attracts consequences.[43]

In practice, most societies fix this maximum period for the repayment of loans at between twelve months and thirty-six months having regard always to the convenience

43. See infra.

of the borrowing members to repay the loans with little stress on their incomes. The longer the period for repayment, the more convenient. But care must be exercised in fixing long repayment periods as this will have the effect of tying up funds in the hands of a few members and thereby denying other members access to funds.

A repayment period which is too short also has its problems as it is likely to put pressure on the borrower to repay within the period. If he is unable to meet the repayment schedule arising from the pressure on his finances, the loan then runs into difficulties and a situation is created whereby the society has to worry over its recovery. This is an unpleasant situation for any co-operative society. One way of avoiding stressful loan repayments is a periodic instalmental repayment scheme.

(iv) Extension and Renewal of Loans – As discussed above, repayment of loans may sometimes, and usually does, run into difficulties. So many factors and reasons may account for this.

Hence, by Regulation 4 (2) (a) (iv), every credit co-operative society must make provisions in its bye-laws to take care of situations where loans are not repaid within the duration of time scheduled for repayment in full. This is usually by way either of extending the term of the loan or the grant of an outright renewal thereof.

In practice, such extension or renewal is usually at an additional cost to the borrower in the nature of penalty which is calculated, in most cases, at no more than twice the normal rate of interest. This is a doubling of the interest on the balance remaining unpaid on the loan and it can amount to a huge burden on an already 'distressed' borrower.

Therefore, though each society is at liberty to decide on whatever method to impose a penal interest where there has been a default in loan repayment, care must be taken in fixing the penal interest at a reasonable rate so as not to over burden the borrower who may collapse under the weight of an excessive penalty and be pushed into completely avoiding the loan and thereby forcing the loan into the bad debts account of the society.

(v) Purpose of Loans – A credit society's bye-laws must make provisions relating to the purposes for which it may grant loans to its members and the modes for ensuring that its loans are strictly used for such purposes by the borrower. Generally, the purposes for which co-operative loans are granted must be such which, in the opinion of the management committee of the society or the society in general meeting, are productive or necessary, and in the best interest of the borrower.

The bye-laws of every thrift and credit co-operative society must therefore also provide for a monitoring mechanism for ensuring that loans are not deployed to unproductive uses or otherwise misapplied.

In practice, some societies maintain a standing loans monitoring committee while other societies make this the responsibility of the borrower's sureties who are required to promptly report any misuse or misapplication of loans to the society either at management committee level or the society in general meeting. Once such misuse or misapplication is proved, the society shall be at liberty to immediately recall the loan under a right reserved in its favour in the bye-laws or to take any other step which must have also been provided for in the bye-laws to ensure that the funds lent are not senselessly frittered away as to make recovery difficult or sometimes even impossible.

(vi) Security for Loans – By Regulation 4 (2) (a) (vi), every co-operative society which has, as part of its objects, the creation of funds to be lent to its members must include in its bye-laws provisions relating to the security or collateral security for which must be offered to ensure the repayment of the loans which it grants to its members.

Security is an asset which a borrower offers to a lender as a form of insurance in favour of the lender against unforeseen and undesired developments in relation to loans granted to the borrower by the lender. It provides the lender something of value to fall upon in recouping its funds when the borrower has become unable, has neglected or refused to repay the loan.

Nature of Co-operative Loan Security – Members of a co-operative society, as earlier pointed out, are generally persons who are bound together by certain common bonds or interests. They are usually persons who live in such circumstances of proximity, common language, and normal harmony in that they ordinary live near one to another and are familiar with each other's income, occupation, and personal character.[44]

As a result of this homogeneity of the co-operative society group, the members get to know each other somewhat intimately and which personal knowledge lead to trusting of each other and which in turn leads to a development of individual personal integrity within the

44. See footnote 17 supra.

group. This inevitably becomes the best and safest security available to co-operative societies.

Every lender of money, not excluding a thrift and credit society, relies heavily on the integrity of the person to whom he advances his funds by way of loans. Such integrity assures the lender, not only of the borrower's preparedness and ability to repay the loan, but also that it will be repaid as and when due in the ordinary course of business.

Collateral Security – Notwithstanding the above best security arising from personal knowledge, trust and integrity of a member, it is sometimes still necessary for a co-operative society to collaterally secure its loans given that, as pointed out earlier, man by nature is unpredictable and that in every human society there will always be deviants.

Also, repayment of loans is always a future undertaking which is fraught with uncertainties that no human is blessed with the capacity to predict. So many unpredictable factors may arise before the repayment of the loan which adversely affect the circumstances of the borrower so as to make even a *prima facie* safe and secure loan eventually turn bad and risky.

Such factors may include a sudden downturn in the business line of the borrower; he may suffer from accidents such as fire, flood or other forms of *viz majore*. He may experience increased competition in his line of business leading to decreased patronage and consequential reduction in cash-flow. There may be new inventions replacing the kind of items the borrower deals in and he may even fall ill and be incapacitated over a long period of time thereby exposing his business to dwindling fortunes. If he is a paid employee, he may lose his job and be unable to get another job in good time. He may even die. These are all possible intervening circumstances over which a borrower can certainly have no control over and which can render him unable to repay his loan.

Notwithstanding the above realities of life, a co-operative society which has advanced loans to its members will nonetheless be desirous of recovering such loans hence the need for collateral securities for its loans as further insurance against such occurrences.

Types of Co-operative Loan Security – A list of types of security open to the use of co-operative societies can be open-ended but the usual ones will include:

(i) guarantees,
(ii) liens over the borrower's shares and savings,
(iii) mortgages,
(iv) pledges,
(v) company stocks and shares,
(vi) insurance policies etc.

Qualities of a Good Co-operative Loan Security – A good security for co-operative loan is one which satisfies the requirement of being in the nature of an insurance against the risk of non-repayment of the loan in the ordinary course of business as and when due. In order that this expectation is not frustrated, a good security for a co-operative loan must possess the following qualities:

(a) Sufficiency in Value – The market value of whatever collateral security is offered by the borrower must be such as will equate in the least the value of the loan exposure. But it is usual to expect a prudent lender to insist on a collateral security of a value slightly in excess of the loan exposure for purposes of creating a buffer margin in respect thereof. This is especially so where the particular type of security offered by the borrower is one subject to the vagaries of fluctuating value.

(b) Valid Title - The borrower must have a valid legal title to the security he offers. In every case, the society must be satisfied that the security belongs to the borrower. This is accomplished by carrying out appropriate investigation into the borrower's title. This is fundamental since, if the borrower has a defective title or does not have title to the security he offers for his loan, no better title will move to the co-operative society. It is the legal principle of *nemo dat quod non habet*.

Therefore, if the security is, for instance, land, it should preferably be land in respect of which there has been issued a certificate of occupancy which becomes easily verifiable at the lands registry. Share certificates and insurance policies do not present much difficulty in the ascertainment of the owner's title as his name will usually be on them. Extreme caution must always be exercised with unregistered lands especially when the land is also vacant.

(c) Objective Value – A good security for a co-operative loan must be capable of being valued objectively. In other words, the value of the security should be such that can be ascertained by means which are not subject to the arbitrary personal opinion of the individual valuer or that the value should be such that it varies from one subjective valuer to the other.

In this respect, land, for instance, does not possess this requirement. Valuation of land is hardly ever objective. A good example of a security capable of being objectively valued is a life insurance policy the surrender value of which is fixed and readily ascertainable at any given time. Items such as gold, diamond, and silver which are valuable items of jewelry are usually valued sentimentally and the value placed on them at any given time largely depends on how much appreciation the valuer places on it and cannot therefore be valued objectively.

(d) Marketability – A good security for co-operative loan must be easily marketable to facilitate a quick and an inexpensive realization. Shares of a private company are a poor example of marketable security as they are not permitted by law to be traded in market overts such as the stock exchange. Accordingly, co-operative societies are to insist on publicly quoted stocks and shares of public companies as securities for their loans. Land is a common security for loans but not all lands are necessarily good security. Some lands are not marketable. This is because the marketability of land is dependent on a number of factors such as its location and user.

(e) Ease of Transfer – Another quality which a good security should possess is that it should be of a kind that can be easily and inexpensively transferred to the co-operative society and *vice versa.* A good example of this type of security is a bearer security the title to which can be transferred by mere delivery. Land is particularly cumbersome and expensive to transfer.

2. Consequences for Default on Shares and Loans – Regulation 4 (2) (b) requires that the bye-laws of a co-operative society whose objects include the creation of funds to be lent to its members must contain additional provisions spelling out the

> consequences of default in payment of any sum due on account of shares or loans and the consequences of failure to use a loan for the purpose for which it was granted.

This Regulation then is to the effect that every thrift and credit co-operative society must make provisions in its bye-laws for the sanction or penalty which must follow where there has been a failure on the part of a member to meet his obligations to the society with respect to default in (1) payment for shares, (2) loan repayment, and (3) failure to use loan for purpose.

(a) Default in Payment for Shares – Every member of a co-operative society is required by law to obtain and pay for a stated number of shares as a minimum being part of his interest in the co-operative society.[45] Whenever a person is admitted to membership of a society but he fails to pay to the society the value of the number of shares to which he is required by the bye-laws to subscribe as a minimum or he has voluntarily subscribed in excess of the minimum if the bye-laws so permit, he becomes indebted to the society.

Regulation 4 (2) (b) prescribes that the penalty to be imposed for such default by such a member must be specifically provided for in the society's bye-laws. In practice, the usual consequence for default in the payment

45. See Chapter Eight on Society Funds and Assets (*infra*).

for is to deny such a member the exercise of all his membership rights[46] including his right to loans.

(b) Default in Loan Repayment – Bye-law 59 of the Delta State Model Bye-Laws contains a second leg in words which are replicated in all other state's model bye-laws in substantially the same words thus:

> in case of default in repayment, penal interest shall be charged at twice the nominal rate.

The imposition of an interest at 'twice the nominal rate' of interest is a penal provision in consequence of a default in loan repayment. It is an example of what Regulation 4 (2) (b) requires that every thrift and credit society bye-laws must expressly make provisions for.

(c) Failure to use Loan for Purpose – In practice, an applicant for a co-operative loan is usually required to state in his application the productive or necessary purpose for which he requires the loan. This is usually to enable the society properly appraise[47] the application for loan with a view to determining the viability thereof.

If therefore a co-operative loan, having been granted on the basis of the information supplied by the borrower in his application as to the purpose of the loan, is proven to have been diverted to other purposes, especially risky purposes, the law requires that the society should not just fold its arms and allow the borrower to expose its funds on loan to risks.

For this reason, most societies will make it the duty of the surety or guarantor of the loan to personally take responsibility for ensuring that the loan is used by the

46. See Section 23 of the Law.

47. See *supra* at page 86 *et seq.*

borrower for the purpose it was meant for and to report any diversion or misuse promptly to the society.[48]

Regulation 4 (2) (b) requires that every thrift and credit society must expressly provide in its bye-laws what penalty or sanction shall be visited upon any such member who fails to use its loans for the particular purpose for which the loan was granted. In this respect, it is usual to provide in the society's bye-laws a right in favour of the society to be at liberty to immediately recall[49] the loan notwithstanding that the time allowed for its repayment has not become due.

3. Disposal of Surplus – As explained in Chapter One, a co-operative society is not a trading business and therefore does not make or declare profits. Instead, it declares a surplus. Therefore, where the society is one which has as part of its objects the creation of funds to be lent to its members, then it must provide in its bye-laws how its annual surplus shall be disposed of.

Such provisions must be subject to the provisions of Section 35 of the Law and with regards to the provisions of Regulation 29. Subsection 1 of Section 35 of the Law prohibits the payment of any sum from the net surplus of a co-operative society except as is provided in the society's bye-laws. Also such payments must have been approved by the registrar of co-operatives.

The net surplus of a co-operative society is the equivalence of a company's net profit and it is usually arrived at by deducting all the debts of the society from its gross surplus. The net surplus of a co-operative must be

48. See, for instance, Bye-law 64 of the Delta State Model Bye-Laws.
49. See, for instance, Bye-law 66 ibid.

ascertained by an audit[50] carried out by the registrar of co-operatives or caused to be carried out by him and which involves an examination of the society's overdue debts, if any, and a valuation of the society's assets and liabilities.[51]

Reserve Fund – Before the disposal of a co-operative society's net surplus as ascertained by the registrar's audit, at least 25% thereof shall first be charged thereto and 'carried to a fund to be called the reserve fund'.[52]

The creation of this reserve fund is mandatory for all co-operative societies. However, the Registrar is invested with powers under a proviso to Section 35 to exempt a limited liability society from further contribution to the said reserve fund from time to time; or to reduce the percentage rate of the contribution. Such exemptions or reduction may also be revoked by the Registrar at any time.

The Law does not specify the criteria or under what circumstance the Registrar may exercise his powers under Section 35 but it is humbly submitted that the Registrar's powers to exempt or reduce may be exercised by the Registrar upon an application made to him by a society showing strong and good reasons for such an exemption or reduction.

Strong and good reasons in the context would include where, for instance, there has become an accumulated huge sum of money carried into reserve over many years and which now lie idle in the reserve while the society itself is in some liquidity difficulties.

50. See Section 35 (2) of the Law.
51. Section 36 (2).
52. Section 35 (2).

By the second leg of Regulation 26, the sums of money in the reserve fund, no matter how huge, must remain idle in reserve as it

> shall not be utilized in the business of the society except with the written permission of the registrar.

The same kind of strong and good reasons of a starving society which has huge sums of money in reserve, it is humbly submitted, should persuade the registrar in granting his written permission to a society to utilize, in the ordinary course of its business, its funds in reserve.

Custody of Society Funds – The sums of money in a society's reserve fund must be kept,[53] by way of investment or deposit in any of the following places:

(a) Post Office Savings or other Bank – The Nigerian Postal Service operates a savings bank where co-operative societies can invest or deposit their funds. This bank is strictly a savings bank and its accounts carry with them the usual features associated with savings accounts.

Societies may also deposit or invest their funds in regular banks which operate accounts other than savings accounts. The wordings of the Law suggests that societies are also free to make use of specialized banks as appropriate to their operations since they are allowed to invest or deposit their funds in 'any bank'.

Section 34 (a) of the Law also permits societies to invest or deposit their funds with 'any person[54] carrying on the business of banking'. In this case, the Registrar's approval for the purpose of such depositing or investment

53. Regulation 26.

54. Under current laws, no person, not being an incorporated body, can carry on or be licensed to carry on banking business.

will be required. But it is humbly submitted that this provision can no longer be of any legal moment as no 'person' being an individual person and not a corporate entity can any longer be licensed to carry on banking business in Nigeria.

In summary, a co-operative society is free to invest or deposit its reserve funds in 'any bank' but especially in the Post Office Savings Bank. The last leg of the provisions of Section 34 (a) which requires the approval of the registrar refers only to a 'person carrying on the business of banking' but not the part of the provision relating to 'the Post Office Savings Bank' and 'any bank'.

The requirement that a co-operative society shall deposit or invest its reserve fund in a Post Office Savings Bank and the other places listed in Section 34 of the Law is an imperative requirement and leaves societies no options otherwise. This is because the words employed by the Regulation 26 is to the effect that

> the reserve fund of a society *shall* be invested or deposited as provided in Section 34 of the Law.

But Section 34 of the Law on its own does not employ the imperative 'shall' but is to the effect that

> a registered society *may* invest or deposit its funds[55]....

The section then proceeds to list the places where such funds *may* be invested or deposited which includes the Post Office Savings Bank or any bank as already discussed *supra*. The other places as listed in Section 34 of the Law are:

(b) Government Securities – By securities it is meant those

55. This refers to all the funds of the society. The reserve fund refers to only a part of the society's total funds.

forms investments using negotiable instruments such as bank notes, bonds and debentures which are classified as debt securities or company equity securities such as shares and stocks. Co-operative societies can invest in such securities provided they are either issued or guaranteed by the government of a commonwealth country.[56] They include government bonds which usually come in the form of medium and long term debt securities issued by the government of a sovereign nation or its agencies and are of high liquidity and believed to be of low risks.

Section 315 of the Investment and Securities Act 2007 which is the interpretation section of the Act interprets 'securities' to mean:

(a) debentures, stocks or bonds issued or proposed to be issued by a government;

(b) debentures, stocks, shares, bonds or notes issued or proposed to be issued by a body corporate;

(c) any right or option in respect of any such debentures, stocks, shares, bonds or notes; or

(d) commodities, futures, contracts, options and other derivatives,

and (that) the term securities in the Act includes those securities in the category of the securities listed in (a) – (d) above which may be transferred by means of any electronic mode approved by the Commission and which may be deposited, kept or stored with any licensed depository or custodian company as provided under the Act.

56. Nigeria is a member of the Commonwealth of Nations.

By the provision of Section 34 (b) of the Law, only the securities as listed in (a) of Section 315 of the Investments and Securities Act directly qualify for the investment and deposit of co-operative societies funds but it is to be humbly submitted that if any of the other forms of securities is guaranteed by the government, then a co-operative society may invest or deposit its funds thereat notwithstanding that it is not issued by the government.

(c) Approved Registered Societies – Section 34 (c) of the Law permits co-operative societies to invest or deposit their funds with 'any registered (co-operative) society approved' for the purpose of such investment or deposit by the registrar of co-operatives.

(d) Other Modes – The registrar of co-operatives is also with powers under Section 34 (d) of the Law to approve 'any other mode' for the investment or deposit of co-operative funds.

Distribution of Surplus: Prohibition of - By a further proviso to Section 35 (2) of the Law, the distribution of a co-operative society's surplus without an order of the governor of the state to that effect is prohibited where the society is one with unlimited liability.[57] This prohibition does not affect limited liability societies.

Donations to Charity – Whereas the prior creation of a reserve fund from the net surplus of a co-operative society before disposal thereof is an imperative requirement of the Law,[58] subsection 3 of its Section 35 provides that after setting aside the 25% reserve fund which is compulsory, a

57. For limited liability societies, see Chapter Four on Types and Formation of Co-operative Societies.
58. Section 35 (2).

co-operative society may contribute any amount but not exceeding 10% of the balance of the 'net surplus to any charitable purpose or to a common good fund'.

This contribution to charitable purposes or to the common good before the disposal of the surplus is not an imperative requirement of the Law. It is a donation and it is to be made at the option of the society but the option cannot however be exercised by the society without the sanction i.e. approval of the registrar of co-operatives. This is clear from the wordings of the subsection which is directed at 'any registered society' which 'may…' as against the wordings of subsection 2 thereof which is directed at 'every registered society' which 'shall'.

Charitable Purpose: What is? – In order to avoid creating situations which create avenues for fraudulent and other forms of sharp practices, it is necessary that a clear understanding of what 'charitable purposes' and 'common good' mean for purposes of making donations to them. Defining these terms as legal terms without references to the purposes or objects of certain types of organizations have always been a difficult undertaking.

A charitable purpose is therefore usually described as the purpose or object of a non-profit-making organization and which purpose or object must be in connection with such concepts as the prevention or relief of poverty, the advancement of education, religion or science, health or the saving of lives, the arts or culture, amateur sport, environmental protection or improvement, human rights, conflict resolution or reconciliation, animal welfare, and the promotion of religious or racial harmony, equality, and other purposes currently legally recognized as charitable purposes as well as any new charitable purposes which are similar to other known charitable purposes.[58]

Generally, every charity or charitable organization must have a purpose which provides a public benefit which is the same as saying every charitable purpose is one which benefits the public. A purpose which benefits the public is also one which serves the common good of society. Every charitable organization must:

(a) be engaged in activities and purposes which provide tangible benefits to the public

(b) have a benefitting public which is not a restricted group of persons or persons who share a private connection but members of the public as a whole or, at worst, a significant part of the public

(c) be engaged in activities which are not illegal and not contrary to public policy or in conflict with any law for the time being in force.

59. See Lord McNaughten in the English case of *Commissioner for Special Purposes of Income Tax v Pemsel* (1891) AC 531 and the 2006 Charities Act of the United Kingdom. Both references are persuasive.

Chapter Four

Types and Formation of Co-operative Societies

There is no beneficial activity to which the co-operative ...
may not legitimately be applied - C.F.Rickland

An exercise in classification of co-operative societies is an open-ended one as there can be no end in categorizing co-operative societies. As Strickland puts it,

> there is no beneficial activity to which the co-operative ... may not legitimately be applied'.[1]

He must have been thinking of a classification regime along the lines of the type of activity (i.e. the objects) engaged in by co-operative societies.

Co-operative societies can also be classified in terms of their membership i.e. whether they consist of only human beings or also of corporate persons; also as to whether they mono-purpose societies or multi-purpose. Indeed the classification of co-operative societies is not and can never be closed.

Erhurun[2] classifies co-operative societies as to their

(a) Position in a hierarchy of co-operative societies, that is to say, as to whether they are primary, secondary, or tertiary societies.[3]

(b) Legal Status, that is to say, as to whether registered,[4] in which case, they are formal, or they are unregistered, in which case, they are informal. An informal society, for the fact that it is not registered, is not strictly speaking, a co-

1. The Report at p. 2
2. Erhurun, Helen E.O. (2007) *Co-operatives: Principles, Practice and Field Administration* (P.A. Ainigboro Prints, Asaba) at p. 83
3. Section 5 of the Co-operative Societies Law (Cap. 42) Laws of Delta State 2007; Sections 3 and 4 of the Act (Cap. N98).
4. Section 57 of the Law.

operative society known to law. It is, at best, a society preparing to become a co-operative society - a 'pre-co-operative' society.

(c) Functions - The number or types of functions performed by a society is also a basis for classification. By functions, it is meant the objects[5] for which the society has been registered. Some societies are registered with single objects and are known as mono-purpose co-operative societies. Others are registered with multiple objects. These are poly-purpose co-operative societies and whose names, in practice, usually contain the word 'multi-purpose'.

The objects of a co-operative society, like those of a company, indicate the kind of business or businesses it can engage in beyond which the transaction would be *ultra vires* and therefore void. The Companies and Allied Matters Act[6] contains an express provision to this effect with regards to companies but there is no similar provision in this regard in the Co-operative Societies Law except the inference in Section 8 thereof that a society may not do anything which is not necessary for the purpose of its constitution.

Erhurun[7] sees the objects or functions of a co-operative society as a basis for identifying different types of societies such as consumers co-operative societies, thrift and credit co-operative societies, agricultural co-operative societies, building and housing co-operative societies, marketing co-operative societies, artisans co-operative

5. Regulation 4 (c) of the Co-operative Societies Regulations pursuant to the Law.
6. Section 39 thereof.
7. *Co-operatives: Principles, Practice and Field Administration* at p. 92.

societies, co-operative retail societies, and multi-purpose co-operative societies. This list cannot be exhaustive as the categories of co-operative societies can never be closed for as long there remains no beneficial activity to which the co-operative method may not be legitimately applied.

(d) Geographical Location – This is a reference to the operational area[8] of a co-operative society. In this classification are to be found rural co-operative societies, semi-rural or semi-urban societies, and urban[9] societies.

The significance of classification of co-operative societies under the law lies in the fact that the conditions for registration of a co-operative society vary slightly as to what type of co-operative society is sought to be registered.[10] In this connection, the various co-operative societies enactments including the Act create three main types of societies by reference. These are the primary society, the central society which is also known as the secondary co-operative society, and the tertiary or central financing society.[11]

Primary Society – Section 2 of the Law defines a primary society to be 'a registered society consisting of individuals as members'.[12] The Lagos State enactment uses 'persons' and not individuals as also used in the Act. Both usages however are a reference to human beings and will not

8. Regulation 4 (b).
9. See Regulation 6 (1).
10. Section 5 of the Law; Regulation 4 of Regulations.
11. Section 5 (1), (2) and (3) (c).
12. The Act and Cap. 26 of Ogun State have the same definition while Cap. C15 of Lagos State defines 'primary co-operative society' as a 'co-operative organization whose membership is up to ten persons'.

include corporate bodies or artificial beings.

Central Society – This is defined by the Law to mean a registered society established to facilitate the operations of other registered societies in accordance with co-operative principles and includes a central financing society. A central financing society is, on its own, defined as a registered society with the principal object of making loans to other registered societies.[13]

All other enactments on co-operative societies define central societies and central financing societies the same way to suggest that that both terms mean and refer to the same kind of society. The Act however does not have a provision for central societies and does not define the term.

Also, the Law makes no provision using the term 'secondary society' but all other enactments including the Act refer to secondary societies except the Lagos State law which appears to disagree with the view that there is such a thing as a secondary co-operative society because the law in Lagos State considers any co-operative organization whose membership is made up of primary co-operative societies not as a 'society' but as a 'secondary co-operative organization'.[14]

As for the Act, a 'secondary society' means the same thing as what the Law regards as a central society which is that

> a secondary society means a registered society established to facilitate the operations of registered societies in accordance with co-operative principles and includes a central financing society.

13. Section 2 of the Law.
14. Section 2 of Cap. C15.

In other words, a secondary society is the same thing as a

(i) a central society, and

(ii) a central financing society

Since, by the statutory definitions, a 'central society' includes a central financing society.

Industrial Co-operative Societies – As stated earlier, the categories or classes of co-operative societies cannot be closed. The Act refers to other types of co-operative societies one of which is the industrial co-operative society which the Act defines as a registered society whose principal objective is manufacturing, making, servicing or assembling of industrial goods and whose members are respectively manufacturers, craftsmen, artisans, industrial workers and apprentices.[15]

To get an industrial co-operative society registered, the Act provides that it must consist of six persons and must be economically viable.[16] This is the only other reference to this type of society in the Act.

School Co-operative Society – The Act also refers to a school co-operative society which it defines as a 'registered society whose members are pupils or students attending school or any institution of learning'[17] and the only other reference in the Act to this type of co-operative society is to be found in Section 22 of the Act relating to the age at which one qualifies for membership of a primary society and it provides that 'in the case of a school co-operative society, the age limit shall not apply'.

15. Section 57 of the Act.
16. Section 3 (2) of the Act.
17. Section 57 of the Act.

This provision suggests that a school co-operative society is a primary society and for purposes of its registration, there must be at least ten persons who must sign the application for its registration. Only the Act has provisions referring to or relating to industrial co-operative societies and school co-operative societies.

Limited Liability Co-operative Societies – There is some confusion relating as to whether a co-operative society can lawfully exist whose members' liability is not limited. Section 4 of the Law provides that

> subject to the provisions hereinafter contained, a society which has as its object the promotion of the economic interests of its members in accordance with co-operative principles, or a society established with the object of facilitating the operations of such a society, may be registered under this Law *with or without limited liability as the Registrar may decide*. Emphasis provided.

This provision clearly means that, apart from a limited liability society, a co-operative society 'without limited liability' can be registered into existence but subject only, in both cases, to what the Registrar may decide. It is not clear why it should be the decision (not advice) of the registrar[18] whether the society should be one with limited liability or not. This is usually and ought always to be the decision of those floating the society. The Ogun State law contains same provision which is absent in the Lagos State law.

Under the Act however, it would appear that a co-

18. The status and powers of the registrar is discussed in full infra at Pages 241 and 268 *et seq.*

operative society which is not a limited liability society may not be registered into existence. Section 2 of the Act provides that

> a society may be registered as a co-operative society under this Act if
>
> (a) it is a limited liability society and ....

Section 3 (4) thereof then goes on to provide that

> the word "limited" or its vernacular equivalent shall be the last word in the name of *every society registered under this Act*. Emphasis provided.

The state laws, including the Law, contain similar provision but in the following form:

> the word "limited" or its vernacular equivalent shall be the last word in the name of every society with limited liability registered under this Law.

What the above represents is that while societies registered under state laws, including the Law, may or may not be limited liability societies, societies registered under the Act must be limited liability societies.[19]

Therefore, it is possible to also talk about the limited liability co-operative society and the unlimited liability co-operative society as two types of co-operative societies.

Community Based Co-operative Society – A community based co-operative society is one which draws its membership from a community of persons generally and does not discriminate against any person provided the person belongs to that community and satisfies basic requirements for membership.

19. But see Chapter Two *supra* on the legal status of the Act.

Closed Co-operative Society – A co-operative society whose membership is open only to persons who belong to a class of persons e.g. by way of trade, employment, profession, vocation etc is a closed co-operative society. To belong to a closed co-operative society, a person must possess and share a particular common affinity with other members. A good example of a closed society is a staff co-operative society membership of which is closed to non-staffers of the organization under which the society is formed.

Staff Co-operative Society – This is a co-operative society whose membership consists only of persons who are members of staff or employees of particular organizations and no one who is not such a staff or such an employees can be admitted as member. It is a closed society.

Formation – No society is a co-operative society in the eyes of the law unless it is duly registered. It is a criminal offence to operate a co-operative society without registration. Section 57 (1) of the Law expressly prohibits trading or carrying on of business under any name of which 'co-operative' is part unless such trading or business has received the sanction of the registrar of co-operatives.

What this provision is saying is that no organization or society of individuals can carry on any activity or operations as a co-operative society under a name describing itself as a co-operative society without first being registered as such. To do so amounts to a crime the punishment for which is a fine[20] of N20.00 (twenty Naira)

20. It is N50.00 under the Act; N200.00 under Cap. C15 of Lagos State; and N5000.00 under Cap. 26 of Ogun State.

upon conviction.[21] For a continuing offence the punishment is a fine of N2.00 (two Naira) under the Law for each day during which the offence continues. The punishment is N5.00 (five Naira) for each day under the Act; N500 (five hundred Naira) per day under Cap. 26 of Ogun State; and N200.00 (two hundred Naira) per day under Cap. C15 of Lagos State.

Registration of every association or society of individuals or persons seeking to operate as a co-operative society under a name which includes the word 'co-operative' is therefore a legal imperative. However, by Section 10 of the Law, the governor of the state may, by writing under his hand and subject to conditions which the governor may impose, exempt any particular society from the requirement to register.[22]

Effect of Registration – The registration of a co-operative society renders it a body corporate[23] by the name under which it is registered. This means that the society becomes a juristic person under the law and thereby capable of enjoying and being subject to legal rights and duties which attach to it as such juristic person and which are distinct and separate from the rights and duties of the persons who are its members.

21. Section 57 (2) of the Law; Section 54 (2) of the Act; Section 57 of Cap. 26 of Ogun State; and Section 70 (2) of Cap. C15 of Lagos State.
22. Section 11 of Cap. C15 Lagos State and section 10 of Cap. 26 Ogun State. No such power is contained in the Act.
23. Section 8 of the Law; Section 6 of the Act; Section 9 of Cap. C15 Lagos State; and Section 8 of Cap. 26 Ogun State.

In *Okon v Ubi*,[24] the appellants had entered into an agreement with a registered multi-purpose co-operative society. Suing upon this agreement, the respondents as plaintiffs at the Cross River State High Court, Ugep Division sued in their personal names 'for themselves and on behalf of the entire members' of the co-operative society.

The 1st appellant entered a conditional appearance and filed a motion seeking dismissal of the suit on the ground, among other grounds, that the plaintiffs had no *locus standi* to bring the action since the agreement upon which they have sued was between the defendants and the registered co-operative society and not with the plaintiffs. The High Court per Akon Ikpeme J. in a considered ruling dismissed the application.

On appeal, the Court of Appeal, Calabar Division, per Omokri JCA allowing the appeal declared that

> by the clear and simple wordings of section 9 of the law, the moment a society is registered it becomes a body corporate with its registered name and all other features and attributes under the law flow automatically to the society. Thus it shall have perpetual succession and a common seal and power to hold movable and immovable property of every description, to enter into contract, to sue and be sued and to do all things necessary for the purpose of its constitution. All the above are donated to the society by law and it is a legal person, a juristic personality, a corporate personality

24. (2006) All FWLR (Pt. 328) 717.

clothed with the capacity to sue and be sued in its registered name without any further assurance.[25]

(a) Perpetual Succession – The rights which attach to the society as a result of becoming a juristic person or body corporate include one which entitles it to enjoy perpetual succession. This means that the society can exist permanently, *ad infinitum*, and beyond the lives of the persons who have formed it and its members. Unless it is dissolved in accordance with the provisions of Section 39 of the Law, or the registrar of co-operatives cancels its registration, where it is a primary society, in accordance with the provisions of Section 40 of the Law, a registered co-operative society never dies in the eyes of the law since it enjoys perpetual succession.

(a) Common Seal – Another effect of registration arising from the conferment of corporate status on a co-operative society is that the society becomes entitled to use a common seal with which it authenticates its legal documents.

(c) Proprietary Right – Corporate status entitles a co-operative society to own its own property in its own name. This right is vested in the society itself and directly. This means that every property acquired by the society belongs, not to the members of the society, but to the society directly because the rights of the society to acquire and own property, whether movable or immovable, is distinct and separate from those of its members.

In effect, a co-operative society does not need to acquire and hold property through or in the name of third parties such as trustees. The practice whereby co-operative

25. ibid at 741 per Omokri J.

societies make provisions in their bye-laws for trustees in whose names properties belonging to the society are acquired and held is thus not supportable in law. This is because a registered co-operative society is not an incorporated trustee and is different from incorporated trustees[26] which have to do with associations of persons bound together by custom, religion, kinship or nationality established for objects which are in the nature of religious, educational, literary, scientific, social development, cultural, sporting, or charitable purposes.[27]

The Companies and Allied Matters Act 1990 provides that where such associations appoint trustees, such trustees may apply to the Corporate Affairs Commission to be registered as a body corporate whereupon the trustees

> shall have perpetual succession and a common seal, and power to sue and be sued in its corporate name and … to hold and acquire, and transfer, assign or otherwise dispose of any property or interests therein belonging to, or held for the benefit of such association ….[28]

Under the provisions for incorporated trustees, it is clear that property is held by trustees on behalf associations which appoint them because of the want of capacity to hold property on the part of the associations not being juristic persons.

Here, the acquisition, holding or other dealing with property is done by registrars on behalf of the association which lack capacity. But a co-operative society, once duly

26. See Section 679 of the Companies and Allied Matters Act 1990. See also *Okon v Ubi* (supra)
27. Section 673 ibid.
28. Section 679 ibid.

registered, is vested with all requisite legal capacity to acquire, hold, and deal in and with property of every description whether movable or immovable.[29]

(d) Contracts – A contract is a legally binding agreement between persons or parties who possess the legal capacity or competence to enter into such an agreement. A contract entered into by persons or parties who do not possess the legal capacity or competence to enter into the contract is void. An unincorporated or an unregistered organization or association is a non-juristic person and cannot enter into a contract for want of capacity since it is unknown to law. A registered co-operative society, being a juristic person and a body corporate, possesses capacity to enter into contracts as a result.[30]

(e) Legal Proceedings – Also arising from a co-operative society's juristic personality status is its right to be able to institute and defend suits and other legal proceedings in its own name. This it does, not by or through trustees or any other persons under the incapacitation rules, but directly in its own name just like every other normal juristic person.[31]

Generally, the import of the registration of a co-operative society is to bring to the fore the truth in the *obitre* of Justice C. Oputa in *Fawehinmi v Nigerian Bar Association (No. 1)*[32] that 'there is therefore no distinction in law between a "natural" and "legal" person'. Registration makes a co-operative society a legal person

29. Section 8 of the Law; Section 6 of the Act; Section 8 of Cap. 26 Ogun State; and Section 9 of Cap. C15 Lagos State.
30. ibid.
31. ibid.
32. (1989) 2 NWLR (Pt. 105) 494

and, as a result, whatever a natural person can legally do, a co-operative society can do.

The only limitation to what a society can do is its own bye-laws or constitution as the provision in Section 8 of the Law concludes that a duly registered co-operative society can 'do all things for the purpose of its constitution'. Therefore, unless where a co-operative society engages in a transaction or does anything which is not necessary for the purpose of its constitution, it can validly 'do all things' as can every other juristic person.

Evidence of Registration – Upon registration, a co-operative society is issued a certificate of registration by the registering authority. The certificate must be signed and sealed by the registrar of co-operatives. Once issued, the certificate of registration becomes conclusive evidence at all material times that the co-operative society therein described is duly registered. Where it is proved however that the registration of the co-operative society described in the certificate of registration has been cancelled in accordance with the provisions of Sections 39 or 40 of the Law, then the aforesaid conclusive evidence of registration shall stand rebutted.

Procedure and Conditions for Registration – The registering authority for all co-operative societies within a state is the Registrar[33] of co-operatives. He is charged with the responsibility of regulating and supervising the registration or incorporation, formation, control, and winding up co-operative societies within the state. He is

33. Some states e.g. Lagos State and the Act use 'Director'.

appointed pursuant to Section 3 of the Law by[34] the state's public service commission[35] which may also appoint other persons to assist the Registrar.

The Law provides that the Registrar shall have a seal using such device as the governor[36] may approve and the impression of the seal shall be judicially noticed.[37]

The Application for Registration – An association seeking registration as a co-operative society is required by the Law to apply[38] in writing to the registering authority i.e. the Registrar (or Director as the case may be) of co-operatives.

Primary society: The application, in the case of a primary society, must be signed by at least ten persons who must be qualified to be members of a co-operative society.[39] The society will not be registered under the Law unless it consists

> of at least ten individuals each of whom is qualified under Section 22 of (the) for membership.

Except under the Ogun State Co-operative Societies Regulations (made pursuant to its Cap. 26) which contains a prescribed Form A pursuant to Regulation 2 (1) thereof, there are no prescribed forms[40] for the application under the

34. By the President or the Governor as the case may be under the Act.
35. Section 197 of the 1999 Constitution provides for the establishment of this commission for each state of the federation.
36. The President under the Act; the Commissioner in Lagos State.
37. Section 3 (2) of the Law and under Cap.26 Ogun State; Section 2 (3) of the Act; and Section 4 of Cap. C15 Lagos State.
38. Section 6 of the Law.
39. See *infra* at p. 142 on qualification for membership.
40. As with Incorporation Forms under the Companies and Allied Matters Act 1990. But Regulation 2 of the Regulations pursuant to the Law provides that applications shall be 'in the form' approved by the Registrar. See Appendix C for Form A of Ogun State.

Law and other co-operative enactments. A normal letter addressed to the Registrar and signed by at least ten qualified persons would therefore be sufficient in all cases.

The application letter must then be accompanied by three[41] copies of the society's bye-laws.[42] The proposed bye-laws should provide the Registrar with sufficient information regarding the nature, type and other relevant information relating to the society which is sought to be registered. This will enable the Registrar come to an informed decision whether to register the society or not.

Where the information supplied by the application for registration is inadequate and does not meet the above requirement to enable the Registrar make a decision, he may require the applicants or the persons on whose behalf the application is made to furnish further and better information in relation to the application and they shall be under a legal duty to furnish the Registrar with such further and better information.

Secondary Society: In the case of a central society or secondary society which is the same as the secondary society i.e. a society of which at least one of its members is a registered society, the letter of application shall be signed on behalf of every registered society which is a member thereof by a person being a member of that registered society who is duly authorized by that society so to do.[43]

The second leg of Section 6 (2) (b) of the Law provides that where the secondary society which is sought

41. Two copies under Cap. C15; and such number of copies as prescribed by the Director under the Act.
42. See *infra* at p… on Bye-laws, Rules and Regulations.
43. Section 6 (2) (b) of the Law.

to be registered consists of societies all of which are themselves not already registered, then the application for registration of the secondary society shall be signed by 'ten other members' after a duly authorized person shall have first signed on behalf of each of the societies. All the state enactments and the Act contain this provision which is difficult to explain in the light of the legal position that a co-operative society is not known to law unless it is registered.[44] The reference in the provision to societies which 'are not registered societies' must therefore be taken to mean societies which are not necessarily co-operative societies applying to form a co-operative society.

The Law requires that where the number of members making up the unregistered societies applying to form the co-operative society is 'less than ten other members', then the application shall be signed 'by all of them' i.e. all the members, being less than ten, consisting the unregistered societies.

The application for the registration of a secondary society must, as in the case for a primary society above, be accompanied, under the Law, by three copies of the society's proposed bye-laws[45] and the secondary society shall not be 'registered unless at least two registered societies are members thereof.'[46]

---

44. See Formation *supra* at p. 120 See also Section 57 of the Law where the word 'society' and not 'co-operative society' is used.
45. See footnote 39.
46. Section 5 (2) of the Law and of Cap. 26 Ogun State; Section 6 (2) of Cap. C15 Lagos State; but see Section 3 (3) of the Act that *'no secondary society which is established for the purpose of facilitating the operations of a registered society shall be registered unless it has as members at least five registered societies ...'*.

Registration – Prior to the grant of registration following the application, the registering authority carefully studies the proposed bye-laws; calls for necessary information as may be required by him and, if not satisfied, may make alterations to the bye-laws as he deems advisable especially so as to bring them into conformity with the Law. Where the alterations made by the registering authority are of material nature, the alterations shall be subject to the ratification of the applicants.

When the registering authority is satisfied that

(a) the applying society has complied with the provisions of the Law and the Regulations made pursuant thereto; and

(b) the proposed bye-laws do not offend any provisions of the Law or the Regulations,

he may then register[47] the society as a co-operative society and also register its bye-laws.[48] The newly-born co-operative society is then issued with a certificate of registration[49] indicating its corporate name and identity and duly sealed by the Registrar of co-operatives. In practice, a copy of the now-registered bye-laws is sealed by the Registrar and issued to the co-operative society with the certificate.

In Lagos State, Section 7 (3) of Cap. C15 requires that the state commissioner responsible for co-operatives shall first approve the application containing details of the objects of the applying society before the Director can register the society except where the objects of the applying

47. Section 7 (1).
48. Ibid
49. Section 9.

society are of a kind to which the commissioner had given his prior general approval.

Upon registration, Section 7 (2) of the Law requires that the society shall pay such fees as may be required by the Regulations which are in all the states currently silent on the amount of fees payable on registration.

Conditions for Registration – Section 5 of the Law makes provisions for certain conditions the existence of which the Registrar must be satisfied with before registering any society. These conditions are:

(a) Primary Societies: Before registering a primary society, the Registrar must be satisfied that the society seeking registration consists of at least ten persons who are qualified for co-operative society membership and as spelt out in Section 22 of the Law.[50]

(b) Secondary Society – Where the application is in respect of a central society or secondary society, the Law provides that registration shall be denied unless there are at least two registered societies as members.[51]

(c) 'Limited' as Last Word in Name: Another condition about which the Registrar must satisfy himself before registering a society is that the word 'limited' (usually abbreviated as "Ltd") or its vernacular equivalence[52] must be the last word in the name of the society, if it is a limited liability society.

50. Section 5 (1).
51. Section 5 (2) of the Law. But see Section 6 (2) (b) of the Law for the provision that 'where all members of the society are not registered societies …' and see also Section 3 (3) of the Act which requires 'at least five registered societies' for a secondary society.
52. Section 5 (3) (b).

This provision means that where the society is not one with limited liability, the word 'limited' needs not be part of the society's name. There is however no provision in the Law, as in Section 29 of the Companies and Allied Matters Act in relation to companies, requiring that the name of an unlimited co-operative society shall end with the word 'unlimited'.

(d) 'Co-operative' as Part of Name: One other condition which must be satisfied before registration is granted is that the word 'co-operative' or its vernacular equivalence must form part of the society's name.[53]

(e) Vernacular Equivalence: The provisions as to vernacular equivalence of words being part of the name of a co-operative society are hardly employed in practice but there is evidence of a handful of societies in the Yoruba-speaking West of Nigeria with names consisting of words such as *alajeseku* which literally means the one who eats today and leaves some for tomorrow approximating 'savings'; and *egbe alafowosowopo* which approximates more with the concept of co-operation.

It is to be observed that most of the vernacular words used in parts of Nigeria such as *ajo, aro, esusu, owe* among the Yorubas; and *gayya* and *adashi* among the Hausas; and *isisie, isise-ego, utu ummuna,* and *oha* among the Igbos as meaning 'co-operative' are hardly correct as they approximate more of the idea of savings or collection.

(f) Prohibition of 'Bank': Except in the case of a central financing society i.e. a registered co-operative society whose principal object is to grant loans to other co-

53. Section 5 (3) (a).

operative societies, no co-operative society is permitted to use the word 'bank' or 'banking' as part of its name.[54]

Registrable Societies – Societies must be deserving of registration as co-operative societies. Section 4 of the Law provides for the kind of society which is deserving of registration. This is the society which

(a) has as its objects the promotion of the economic interests of its members in accordance with co-operative principles; or

(b) is established with the object of facilitating the operations of other co-operative societies.

Registration may be Refused – The Registrar may not be satisfied with the application and may refuse to register the society. This is implied in the second leg of Section 7 (1) of the Law and in Regulation 2 (2) of the Regulations pursuant to the Law which is that

> if the Registrar refuses to register a society or its bye-laws, he shall inform the applicants in writing of the reasons for his refusal.

Time – None of the state enactments has made provisions for a time frame within which an application for registration ought to be disposed of except Section 5 (3) of the federal Act which contains the commendable innovation of a time frame in the following form:

> the Director shall within sixty days dispose of an application for registration by a society.

Appeal – An applicant who is dissatisfied with the refusal of his application has a right[55] of appeal to the appropriate

54. Section 5 (3) (c).
55. No such right of appeal exists in Lagos State under Cap.C15.

authority within one month[56] from the date of the refusal.[57] The appropriate authority to whom an appeal lies is the member of the state government who, for the time, being is charged with the responsibility for co-operative societies. This, usually, is a reference to the commissioner for the ministry supervising matters connected with co-operative societies.[58]

Neither the Law nor the Regulations makes provisions as to what the appropriate authority should do with the appeal or how he should deal with it and the status or effect of the outcome of his dealings therewith but it is humbly submitted that the lawmaker must have intended that the appropriate authority shall consider the appeal of the appellant and the reasons given by the Registrar for the refusal to register the society and to make a pronouncement thereon either upholding the Registrar's decision not to register or setting same aside and directing the Registrar to register.

56. 60 days under the Act.
57. Should read from the date of notification of refusal.
58. In most states, it is the ministry for commerce. Lagos State has a Ministry of Agriculture and Co-operatives.

Chapter Five

Membership of Co-operative Societies

... association which persons voluntarily join and leave ...

- Omojola Folorunsho

Membership of a co-operative society may be divided into two types namely:

(a) Original or founding members, and

(b) Members who join subsequently.

These members are either individuals i.e. human beings, or corporate entities i.e. artificial persons e.g. registered societies. Section 2 of the Law defines a member of co-operative society as including 'a person or registered society joining in the application for the registration of a society, and a person or registered society admitted to membership after registration in accordance with the bye-laws and regulations.

Founding Members - These are the members of a co-operative society referred to in the Law as joining in the application for the registration of a society. They are the persons or part of the persons who form a co-operative society and are like those known, in company law, as 'promoters'. A promoter has been defined as

> one who undertakes to form a company with reference to a given project and to set it going, and who takes the necessary steps to accomplish that purpose.[1]

Although this definition is in relation to the forming or 'promoting' of a company, it can safely be substituted for the promoter or founder of a co-operative society as one who undertakes to join in the formation of a co-operative society with reference to a given object and to set it going,

1. See Cockburn, C.J. in *Twycross v Grant* (1877) 2 C.P.D. 469, 541.

and who takes the necessary steps to accomplish that purpose.

Accordingly, a founding member or promoter of a co-operative society invariably includes all those who sign the application for the registration of the society as required under Section of the Law. It would include also all those who may not have signed the application but may have:

(a) taken part in the steps leading to the decision to form a co-operative society,
(b) identified, procured, or introduced potential members,
(c) contributed to the initial capital of the society or the expenses involved in forming the society and getting it going,
(d) attended pre-registration meetings,
(e) contributed to the drawing up of the society's bye-laws, submission and follow-up of the application for registration, and
(f) such other related sundry acts or steps in connection with the formation and registration of the co-operative society.

In the course of all or some of the above steps or acts which qualify a person as a founding member or promoter of a co-operative society, there might be need to engage the services of professionals such as consultants to prepare feasibility reports, legal practitioners to advise on and prepare the bye-laws, or even estate valuers or other kinds of valuers where the society is acquiring properties real and otherwise. These persons will not qualify, in their capacities only as such professionals, as promoters or foundation members of the co-operative society in respect of which they had been engaged to render professional services.

However, if, apart from rendering their professional services to the society, they also, as individuals sign the application for registration as members of the society or participate in any other manner in the steps leading to the formation of the society only as such individuals, then they would qualify as founding members or promoters.

Legal Status of Founding Members – A co-operative society is not a company.[2] But a co-operative society shares certain legal similarities with companies arising from the premise that both are corporate bodies with distinct identities, rights and duties which are separate from those of their members.

(a) Fiduciary Duties – One such area where a co-operative society is similar to a company is that just as a promoter of a company owes fiduciary duties to the company he is involved in forming, so also do founding members of a co-operative society must owe fiduciary duties to the co-operative society they are involved in forming. These fiduciary duties include that the founding members must

(a) not make secret profits for themselves in the process of the society's registration, and

(b) disclose any personal interest they may have in any transaction in relation to the formation of the society.

These duties are the usual duties which an agent owes to his principal under the general law of agency. The duties arise from the special relationship of principal and agent

---

2. See supra at p.25.

between them. But founding members of a society seeking registration or which is in the process of being registered cannot be and are not agents of the society they are forming just in the same way a company promoter cannot be and is not an agent of the company he is involved in forming.

This is because at this stage of its formation, the society, having not been registered into existence, is yet unknown to law and therefore lacks legal capacity to enter into legal relations such as that between a principal and his agent.

Being non-existent as yet, the co-operative society cannot appoint or have an agent hence the fiduciary duties a founding member owes do not arise from a relationship of principal and agent.

Nonetheless, the founding members owe these fiduciary duties not to make any secret profits and to disclose any personal interests they may have in any transaction relating to the formation of the co-operative society.

To be entitled to keep any profits made, a founding member must disclose the fact of the profits and the details thereof to all the members of the society. Similarly, where a founding member is interested in any transaction having to do with the formation and registration of the society, he must disclose this fact and the details thereof in the like manner.

Society's Remedy for Breach of Fiduciary Duty – Where a founding member is in breach of his fiduciary duties to his society, the society may recover by action any such secret profit from the member. Also, the society will be entitled to rescind any contract in which a founding member is interested and involved in without disclosing such interest. This right to rescind arises from the general principles of contract.

(b) Remuneration – Another legal effect on the status of a co-operative society's founding members is that as such founding member, he is, generally, not entitled to remuneration for his services which he renders to the society in the course of the society's formation and registration and cannot recover same from the society by action. Again, this is because there cannot be a legally binding contract between the founding member and the co-operative society which clearly did not exist in law as at the times material to the services he relies on for his action.

He may however be entitled to remuneration subsequent to the registration if the bye-laws make provision for such remuneration but such provision will still not entitle him to sue the society for the recovery of expenses incurred in the course of the formation and registration.[3]

(c) Pre-Registration Contracts – One other area of the law which founding members usually worry over is in relation to contracts entered into by or on behalf of the society prior to its formal registration. While a society is in the process of being formed and registered, it might be necessary for the founding members to enter into certain kinds of contracts necessary for realizing the purpose with third parties e.g. contracts with legal practitioners or with printers for the printing of the society's bye-laws.

3. In practice, such suits will be rare as the founding members are usually the first members of the management committee.

Such contracts cannot be entered into on behalf of the unregistered society which itself cannot so do nor can the founding members purport to do so as agents of a legally non-existent society. The reason for this is the same as has been pointed out earlier – an unregistered society lacks capacity to enter into a contract, and, being inexistent in law, cannot appoint or have an agent.

The society cannot, for the same reasons, subsequently ratify such contracts. It is also precluded from enforcing in its favour a contract purportedly entered into in its name prior to its registration.

The above position of the common law[4] of England in relation to companies which dates as far back in history as 1866 when *Kelner v Baxter*[5] was decided and which had over the years been echoed by decisions[6] of Nigerian courts including the Supreme Court, created a lot of hardship especially for promoters of companies. The need to relieve promoters of personal liabilities for contracts which they, in good faith, enter into on behalf of companies they are involved with in the process of their formation and the necessity of assuring third parties who enter such pre-incorporation contracts of their ability to enforce the contracts gave rise to the taking of deliberate steps to statutorily obviate the difficulties and hardships associated with pre-incorporation contracts.

---

4. Part of English law received into Nigeria by various reception statutes including the Law (Miscellaneous Provisions) Act; and the Law of England (Application) Law of 1959 W.R.N Laws.
5. (1866) L.R. 2 C.P. 174.
6. See, for instance, *Shonibare v Mansour* (1963) LLR 1; *Stephen v Buildco (Nig.) Ltd.* (1968) A.L.R Comm. 242.

The result is Section 72 of the Companies and Allied Matters Act of 1990 which is to the effect that

> any contract or other transaction purporting to be entered into by the company or by any person on behalf of the company prior to its formation may be ratified by the company after its formation and thereupon the company shall become bound by and entitled to the benefit thereof as if it has been in existence at the date of such contract or other transaction and had been a party thereto.

Subsection 2 thereof however provides that before the company ratifies a pre-incorporation contract, the person purporting to act in the name of or on behalf of the company shall be personally liable under the contract and be entitled to its benefit except there exists an agreement to the contrary.

These provisions are strictly in relation to companies but, as pointed out earlier, the logic and reasoning which informed the provisions stem from the principle of the legal personality or corporate personality of companies which same principle, logic and reasoning can be made applicable to co-operative societies which are also corporate bodies. While the provisions may not be relied upon and cited in proof of any legal point in co-operative societies, the logic and reasoning behind them are directly relevant to co-operative societies.

In the event, it is humbly submitted that the position of the law in relation to pre-registration contracts and co-operative societies ought to be that

(a) a co-operative society, prior to its registration, can enter into valid and enforceable contract subject to subsequent ratification;

(b) a founding member can enter into a contract with third parties on behalf of a co-operative society which is in the process of being registered subject to subsequent ratification;

(c) upon ratification, a pre-registration contract as in (a) and (b) becomes binding on the co-operative society as though it had been a party to the contract *ab initio*;

(d) upon ratification, a co-operative society shall also be entitled to the benefits of a pre-registration contract; and

(e) ratification relates back to the date of the pre-registration contract (and not the date of the ratification) as if the society had been in existence as at that date.

Membership by Admission - Upon its registration, a primary society will have at least ten[7] members while a secondary or central society will have at least two[8] members. These are the founding members and this is assuming that there were no other members outside those who signed the application for registration in the case of a primary society and that the society is only able to meet the minimum requirements in this regard. The society's bye-laws will however usually contain a provision per force of the Law relating to

(a) the terms of admission of new members,

(b) qualification for membership,

(c) entrance fees, if any,[9] and

7. Section 5 (1) of the Law.
8. Section 5 (2) of the Law; Five members under the Act.
9. Regulation 4 (e).

(d) sundry other matters

suggesting that, apart from the founding members, the society may admit other members after registration.

Qualification for Membership – A person must be a qualified person before he can be admitted as a member of any co-operative society and the Law makes specific provisions in this respect. Every society's bye-laws must accordingly contain provisions relating to these qualifications for admission into membership of such society in compliance with the provisions of the Law as contained in Section 22 to the effect that:

Primary Society – The law makes some minor differences in the qualifications for membership of a co-operative. With respect to primary societies, the following qualifications will apply:

(i) Age: To be qualified for membership of a primary co-operative society, a person must have attained the age of eighteen[10] years. The Act[11] provides for sixteen years while Cap. C15 of Lagos State provides in this respect that the

> person must be capable of entering into a legally enforceable contract'[12]

without attaching any age limit thereto.

The provisions as to age qualifications for membership show that a minor cannot be a member of a co-operative society. However, where the society is a school co-operative society registered under the Act, this age qualification shall not apply.

10. Section 22 (a) (i).
11. Section 22 (1) (a). Only the Act makes provisions for a school co-operative society.
12. Section 33 (1) (a).

A minor may however become a member of a co-operative society indirectly as when the bye-laws allow the personal representative of a deceased member to inherit a deceased member's rights and interests absolutely. Such succession is usually however at the discretion of the society.

(ii) Residence - Section 22 of the Law also provides that for a person to be qualified for membership of a co-operative society, the person must be resident within the area of operations of the society as described by the bye-laws. In the alternative, the person must be in occupation of land within the described area of operations.

A person is said to be in occupation of land if he resides in or carries on business of a kind which requires the use of land on the land. Such a person may live or be resident outside the society's area of operations but does business within. He may own a shop or an office within the area and be qualified to be in occupation of land. A farmer whose farm is within the area of operations is in occupation of land. A person who has built a house within the area but does not live therein is in occupation of land; so also is a worker whose place of work is within the area even though he lives elsewhere.

The Law does not, by this provision, require the person to own land. There is difference between being in occupation of land and being in ownership of land.[13] A person can be in occupation of land as a tenant. So also can

13. Consider the definitions of 'occupier' and 'owner' in relation to tenements in Section 51 of the Tenement Rates Law (Cap. 186) Laws of Lagos State 1994. See also M.G. Yakubu (1985) *Land Law in Nigeria* (Macmillan Publishers) at p.54 for a discussion on concepts of ownership.

a person be in occupation of land the title of which land resides in him as owner. The provision of Section 22 (1) (a) (ii) relates to a person who is 'in occupation of land' and not a person who is an 'owner' of land.[14]

Central Society – With regards to a central or secondary society, Section 22 (1) (b) of the Law provides that to be qualified for membership of a co-operative society, the applicant must

(a) have its registered address within the central society's area of operations as defined by the bye-laws – an equivalent provision to the provision of residence with respect to primary societies, and

(b) be a 'holder of property' within the central society's area of operations – equivalent to the provision for occupation of land for primary societies.

The section contains a proviso to the qualification in (b) which proviso empowers the Registrar to exempt a society with limited liability from the requirement to 'hold property'. Under the Act, this exemption is granted, not to a society with limited liability (as with the other enactments) but to a credit society.[15]

The use of 'holder of property' in Section 22 (1) (b) (ii) of the Law without more is capable of interpretative problems especially in the light of the discussion above relating to 'occupation of land' and 'ownership of land'. First, it must be taken that 'property' in the context of the provision is a reference to landed property and does not

14. But see Section 22 (1) (b) of the Act with a worrying reference to 'ownership or occupation of land' in the last leg thereof.
15. A term which the Act does not define but which must be taken to mean a reference to a society which lends money to its members.

relate to non-land property. This conclusion, though obvious, is put beyond debate by Section 33 (b) of the Lagos State Cap. C.15 which states that the person, 'in the case of a society of limited liability', must be 'a holder of landed property within the area'.

The other interpretative problem which 'holder of property' creates has to do with what the difference is between a person 'in occupation of land' and a person who is 'a holder' of (landed) property; and why the lawmaker used two different terms in paragraphs (a) and (b) of the same subsection (1) of Section 22 of the Law.

The lawmaker obviously did not intend to mean one and the same thing by the two different terms otherwise he would have been consistent in his choice of words. But there really is not much difference between he who 'occupies' land and he who 'holds' land. A lessee, for instance, is a person who 'holds' land as a tenant of a landlord or land owner. He can also be said to 'occupy' the same land where he is in actual occupation thereof.

The use of the two different terms suggests that while the lawmaker meant a 'tenant' by his use of 'in occupation of land', he meant 'owner' by his use of 'holder of property'. The exemption in the proviso lends credence to this conclusion as a strict enforcement of the requirement to 'own land' before a society can join in applying for the registration of a central society is sure to lead to hardship and discourage the formation of this type of society.

Residence within Nigeria – The above discussion in relation to a member of a co-operative society being resident or in occupation of land or being a holder of property 'within ... the society's area of operations' presupposes that the area of operation is an area within Nigeria. This is because a co-operative society should ideally consist of persons who live near to one another and familiar with each other's income, occupation, personal character, and generally live in such circumstances of proximity, common language, and normal harmony.[16]

Besides, Regulation 6 (2) pursuant to the Law provides that no co-operative society other than a thrift or building society shall admit or retain as a member a person who is not resident in Nigeria. Where a person, having been admitted to membership of a co-operative society, subsequently ceases to be resident within the sphere of the operations of the society in Nigeria and remains so resident outside the society's sphere of operations within Nigeria for one year, he shall cease to be a member of that society[17] and the managing committee of the society shall remove his name from the register of members.

A thrift or building society may accept or retain as a member a person who is not resident in Nigeria but such a person must possess or hold immovable property within the society's sphere of operations.[18]

The sphere or area of operations of a co-operative

---

16. See Rickland's Report at pp.1 and 2.
17. Regulation 6 (1).
18. Regulation 6 (2). Note that the Regulations use the word 'sphere' which must be taken to mean the same thing as 'area' as used in Section 22 of the Law. Note also that this Regulation uses the expression 'possessing or holding immovable property' which is again different from 'in occupation of land' and 'holder of property' as in Section 22 of the Law. Note further the use of 'immovable property' in the Regulations as against 'land' and 'property' in the Law.

society is usually as described in its bye-laws. This is one of the matters in respect of which a society must make bye-laws.[19]

This sphere or area of operations of a society must be within Nigeria. Where the society is an urban credit society, that is, a co-operative society which has as part of its objects the lending of money to its members and which society's sphere or area of operations is an urban area, the society shall not admit or retain a person as a member if the person resides outside the society's sphere or area of operations as prescribed by the society's bye-laws.[20]

An urban area is a place within a city or a town as different from a village or a rural area.[21] Therefore a registered society whose sphere or area of operations is within a city would be an urban society and if it lends money to its members, it would be an urban credit society. Such a society shall not admit or retain a person as a member if the person resides outside its sphere or area of operations.

Multiple Membership – An individual is free to be a member of more than one co-operative society at a time. A person may become a member of a society by implication of his involvement in some other group or organization or activity. Where he is involved in more than one such group or organization or activity which operates a co-operative society, such a person becomes, by implication of such

19. Regulation 4 (1) (b).
20. Regulation 6 (1).
21. Some states are delineated by statute into urban and non-urban areas for purposes of the Land Use Act 1978 e.g. the Designation of Urban Area (Order) 1987 vide B.S.L.N No. 14 of 1988 of Bendel State (now Delta and Edo States).

other membership, a member of more than one co-operative society.

This does not mean that he is compelled to be a member of these different societies. Every individual has a right to voluntarily join or refuse to join a society. A person who becomes a member of a co-operative society by implication of his membership of another organization operating a co-operative society exercises his freedom to voluntary join the co-operative society at the point of his becoming a member of that other organization which may be his place of work or place of worship or some other social or professional club or society.

However if a person has been a member of a co-operative society whose primary object is to grant loans to its members, he shall first obtain the sanction of the registrar of co -operatives before he can lawfully become a member of another co-operative society whose primary object is the granting of loans to its members. This is the provision of Section 24 of the Law ostensibly to prevent a situation where a person over borrows from the different societies of which he is simultaneously a member.

The Register of Members – Regulation 16 pursuant to the Law provides that 'every society shall maintain a register of members ...'. Therefore, upon admission to membership of a co-operative society, the name of the co-operator shall be entered into this register of members and the entry shall be *prima facie* evidence that the person is a member of the co-operative society.[22]

Other details which, by the Regulations, the register of

22. Section 20 of the Law.

members shall contain apart from the co-operator's name are:

(a) his address,
(b) his occupation,
(c) details of shares held by him,
(d) date of the entry of his admission i.e. the date he became a member,
(e) date he ceased to be a member (where applicable),
(f) details relating to his nominee (if any).[23]

Again, these entries are *prima facie* evidence of the particulars which they represent in the register especially those relating to the date the name of the co-operator was entered in the register as a member, and the date he ceased to be a member.[24] The evidence is only *prima facie* and not conclusive. Therefore, it is rebuttable.

The expression 'date at which the name of any person was entered in such register or list as a member' in the Law must be understood to mean not merely as the date of making the entry but as the date the person whose name was entered in the register became a member of the co-operative society.

Cessation of Membership – The Regulations make provisions for three ways by which membership of a co-operative society may be terminated. The member may withdraw his membership voluntarily; he may be removed if he ceases to possess the qualifications for membership as prescribed in the bye-laws; and he may be expelled for being in breach of prescriptions of the bye-laws.[25]

23. Regulation 16.
24. Section 20 of the Law.
25. Regulation 22.

(a) Voluntary Withdrawal - In line with the universal principle of voluntary and open membership of co-operative societies which allows for the freedom of ingress and egress of persons, the Regulations provide that any member of a co-operative society may withdraw from the society voluntarily.[26] The reason or reasons for such withdrawal will usually be personal to the withdrawing member who is not under any legal duty to disclose same.

But such a withdrawing member will be under a duty to comply with the prescriptions of the society's bye-laws in relation to the mode and procedure for withdrawing. Such prescriptions are usually in relation to the nature and length of notice to be served on the society by the withdrawing member and other conditions usually in relation to the withdrawing member's financial obligations to the society.

(i) Length of Notice - In practice, the length of notice for withdrawing is between three and six months and is usually required by the bye-laws to be in writing but it is open to individual societies to make peculiar provisions in this respect. It is important that sufficient notice is given to the society to enable it reconcile the financial records of the withdrawing[27] member. What time is sufficient will depend on the operational circumstances of the society.

(ii) Entitlements on Withdrawing – Although a withdrawing member is entitled to a repayment of the face value of his shares, this will be paid to him without interest and subject to appropriate set off against any debts owed the society by the withdrawing member either directly or as

26. Regulation 22 (a).
27. Regulation 22 (d).

a result of his being a surety for an unpaid loan granted another member.

Also, this repayment on account of shares will be forfeited by the withdrawing member and will not be paid to him if there is a net loss in the audited balance sheet of the society after the subtraction of the reserve fund and other undistributed surplus from the society's gross surplus for the period.[28]

(b) Removal for Want of Qualification – As discussed *supra*, Section 22 of the Law provides for the qualifications which a person must possess before he can become a member of a co-operative society.[29] These qualifications, in the main, are in relation to the person's age and residence or occupation or holding of land as the case may be.

The qualifications as provided for the Law and any other requirements or further qualifications as demanded by a particular society are required to be specifically provided for in the society's bye-laws.[30]

In Lagos State, the qualifications for membership of a co-operative society have been widened and expanded beyond the ordinary requirements of age and residence. Section 33 (1) (a) of the Lagos State Co-operative Societies Law (Cap. C15) of 2004 provides that

> to be qualified for membership of a registered society, a person must be
> (a) capable of entering into a legally enforceable contract …

Therefore, beyond the capacity of age to enter into a legally

28. Proviso to Regulation 22.
29. See page 142 *supra*.
30. Regulation 4 (e).

enforceable contract under the general laws of contract, all other legal rules relating to capacity for entering into legally enforceable contracts are now applicable with regards to the qualifications for membership of a co-operative society in Lagos State.

Under the general rules of contracts law, certain persons such as infants, persons of unsound mind, drunken persons (or drunkards), married women,[31] illiterates, and certain types of corporations[32] do not possess legal capacity or unqualified legal capacity to enter into legally enforceable contracts. Accordingly, by virtue of Section 33 of the Lagos State Co-operative Societies Law, any of these persons with contractual disabilities may not be admissible to membership of a co-operative society for being unqualified.

Also, any person who, having been admitted to membership of a co-operative society on the basis of his being qualified to be so admitted but subsequent to his admission loses the qualification to be a member of a co-operative society as provided for under the society's bye-laws, shall be removed as a member by the society's committee.[33]

Entitlements on Removal – On his being removed in the above circumstances, a member shall be entitled to a repayment on account of his shares under the same terms

31. There are now statutory exceptions or modifications to some of these common law rules of contracts law.
32. See Ezejiofor, Okonkwo & Ilegbune: *Nigerian Business Law* (Sweet & Maxwell, London 1982).
33. Regulation 22 (b) inclusive of the Lagos State provisions.

and conditions as discussed *supra* with regards to a withdrawing member.

(c) Expulsion for Breach of Bye-Laws – Regulation 22 (c) provides that

> a member of a registered society may be removed or expelled ... for such cause only as may be prescribed in the bye-laws.

As already stated, a co-operative society must make provisions in its bye-laws in respect of qualifications for admission to membership, withdrawal and expulsion of members and these must include those qualifications as provided for in Section 22 of the Law for admission and those as provided for in Regulation 22 for termination of membership. Nothing in these provisions restricts or prohibits a society from making other provisions which may be peculiar to particular societies in respect of these matters.

Hence it is not to be unexpected for particular societies to provide for cessation of membership if, for instance, a member:

(a) dies, or
(b) becomes permanently insane, or
(c) becomes physically incapacitated, or
(d) ceases to possess prescribed minimum share qualifications, or
(e) is adjudged bankrupt by a court of law in Nigeria or elsewhere, or
(f) repeatedly fails to make regular thrift savings as prescribed in the bye-laws, or
(g) repeatedly fails to pay instalments due on his shares, or
(h) is convicted of a criminal offence involving fraud or dishonesty or violence, or

(i) misconducts himself in relation to the stated objects of the society or engages in acts inimical thereto.

Where therefore, the bye-laws of a registered society contains these or such like prescriptions and a member falls in breach of them or any of them, he may be removed or expelled but such removal or expulsion shall be for such cause as prescribed only and never otherwise.[34]

Regulation 22 (c) does not indicate who or what organ of the society has the powers to remove or expel a member who has fallen in breach of bye-law prescriptions (as has been done in Regulation 22 (b)) and the procedure for arriving at such a decision which *prima facie* is punitive in nature. But it is to be submitted with humility that the organ to wield such punitive powers ought to be the management committee as has been done in (b). But this must be subject to a prior fair and objective investigation of specific allegations made against the member in writing to him with ample opportunity granted him to defend or explain himself.

Entitlements on Expulsion – Upon his removal or expulsion, a member shall nonetheless be entitled, as in (a) and (b) *supra*, to title repayments without interest of any money (not exceeding the face value of his shares) paid by him or his predecessor in towards the purchase of shares, after the period prescribed by the bye-laws but provided that no such repayment on account of shares shall be made if after subtracting the reserve fund and any other undistributed surplus, there is a net loss in the audited balance sheet of the society.[35]

34. Regulation 22 (c).
35. Regulation 22 (d) and proviso thereto.

Chapter Six

Consequences of Membership

Wo te rovwo edho, wo he rovwo ekwakwa rie
– Isoko proverb[1]

Upon becoming a member of a co-operative society, certain legal consequences follow. These consequences come in the form of rights, benefits, privileges, duties and liabilities. As for benefits, a co-operator becomes entitled and free to enjoy all those benefits[2] which a co-operative society ordinarily bestows on its members and according as to the type of co-operative society. He also becomes entitled to all those rights and privileges which attaches to a co-operator either directly or indirectly under the Law. He is, of course, also liable to all the duties and liabilities to which all members of co-operative societies are liable.

A right is direct where it attaches directly and personally to the person but is indirect when the person enjoys it only subsequently by virtue of his being a member of the co-operative society. In other words, the right attaches directly to the co-operative society affecting its operations advantageously before trickling down to each co-operating member of the society.

But no member of a co-operative society can enjoy any rights, benefits or privilege which the society confers unless he has made all such payments to the society in respect of membership fees, or he has acquired such interests, e.g. minimum share holding requirement, in the society as provided in the society's bye-laws.[3]

1. You cannot accept a deity without consequences.
2. See Chapter One (supra) for these benefits.
3. Section 23 of the Law.

However, the Law does not permit any individual[4] member to acquire or to hold interests in the share capital of the society in excess of twenty per cent. Also, notwithstanding the number, amount or volume of shareholding of any individual member in the share capital of the society, he shall have and exercise only one vote and no more in the conduct of the affairs of the society.[5] The chairman or the officer duly appointed to preside over a meeting of the society shall however have a casting vote in the event of an equality of votes.[6]

The twenty per cent limit restriction on shares imposed by Section 28 of the Law does not affect a registered society who is a member of a co-operative society. The section provides that

> no member, other than a registered society, shall hold more than one-fifth (i.e. 20%) of the share capital of any co-operative society.

This means that in any co-operative society in which a registered society is a member, the registered society may be permitted by the bye-laws to hold more than the twenty per cent limit of shareholding on the share capital of the society.

With respect to secondary societies, i.e. co-operative societies in which there is a registered society as member, the registered society shall have such voting

4. Section 28.
5. Section 25.
6. See proviso to Section 25.

powers as are provided in the Regulations.[7] This provision is a bit worrisome as it seems to suggest that such registered society may have more than one vote in the conduct of the affairs of the secondary society. This puts a question mark on the much avowed democratic principle of a co-operative society as the individual members of the secondary society will continue to have single votes in line with the main provision of the section as against the multiple votes of the registered society.

Section 26 of the Law goes on to provide that such a registered society which is a member of another registered society may appoint a proxy (who must be a member of a registered society) to represent it for the purpose of voting in the conduct of the affairs of the secondary society. By this provision, the person appointed as proxy need not be a member of the registered society which appoints him as proxy. The requirement is that the proxy must be a member of a registered society. Also, it is not provided that the registered society of which the person appointed as proxy is a member should be a member of the secondary society. This implies that such a proxy can come from any other registered society whether or not that registered society is a member of the secondary society.

This, it is humbly submitted, is not tidy as it is bound to permit mercenary proxies who may not be familiar with the operations of the secondary society let

7. See the further proviso to Section 25 but note that Cap. C15 of Lagos State does not have this further proviso while Section 25 of Cap. N98 provides that such voting power shall be as provided in the society's bye-laws and not in the Regulations as provided in the Law and the other state enactments whose Regulations, notwithstanding the provision in the laws, are silent on the society's voting powers.

alone have its interests at heart. But consider the provisions of Regulation 11 made pursuant to the Law which is to the effect that

> every representative of a society in a meeting of a central society to which it is affiliated shall be selected from among the members of the committee of his society.

The 'representative' described in Regulation 11 is clearly different from the 'representative' provided for in section 26 of the Law. Whereas the Regulations describe a representative of a registered society which is affiliated to (i.e. which is a member of) the central society, Section 26 describes a representative whose representation is by way of a proxy who is not necessarily a member of an affiliated society. The representative in the Regulations is not a proxy but a member. In the conduct of the affairs of the central society, he votes as a member voting in person and not as a member voting by proxy.

A proxy, with regards to companies, is defined as a person (not necessarily a company member) appointed by a company member to attend and vote instead of him at a company meeting. Such voting involves the casting of votes over a proposed motion at the meeting. In practice, the vote is first taken by a show of hands with each member either in person or by proxy exercising a one-vote right.

A member who is present in person or by proxy may however exercise a further right to demand a poll upon the announcement of the results of the vote by show of hands. At the poll, ballots are cast in accordance with the number of shares held by each member. Voting on the basis of the number of shares held by a member is statutorily forbidden with respect to co-operative societies as Section

25 of the Law provides that

> no member of any registered society shall have more than one vote in the conduct of the affairs of the society.[8]

The details and particulars of the voting rights of company members are usually contained either in the company's memorandum of association or the articles of association but more usually in the articles which is the company's constitution that regulates the internal workings of the company. It is the equivalence of the co-operative society's bye-laws and, since voting rights are essentially rights of members in relation to the conduct of the affairs of a co-operative society, their proper place ought to be in the bye-laws in agreement with the provisions of Cap. N98 and not in the Regulations as contained in the Law and the other states' laws.

It is therefore to be highly recommended that every co-operative society shall make adequate provisions in its bye-laws spelling out the voting procedures and voting rights of members which, in the case of a primary society, must be one-man one-vote[9] and, in the case of secondary societies, the voting rights of the registered-society-members shall be explicitly spelt out in such a manner as to preserve the democratic principles of co-operative societies.

Liability of Members – As pointed out already, no member of a co-operative society can take the benefits which the society offers unless and until he has paid up to the society his membership fees or has acquired such

8. But see the further proviso to the section and the discussion thereon *Supra* at p.157.
9. Section 25 of the Law.

other interests in the society as prescribed either by the regulations or the bye-laws.[10] This means that any member who is indebted to a co-operative society may be denied his rights until he has redeemed his indebtedness to the society.

Protective Provisions – All co-operative societies laws nationwide deliberately make certain provisions (as in Section 23 above) for the special protection of a co-operative society's interests especially in relation to its finances and other assets. They are provisions which create benefits in favour of the society but which at the same time are liabilities in relation to members since they make members forfeit an interest or hold them accountable to the society. These protective provisions include:

(a) First Charge on Crops - Hence, for instance, it provides for a first charge on the crops and trade assets of a member who is indebted to his society subject only to a prior claim of a government and a lien or claim of a landlord in respect of rent[11] with a proviso in favour of interests of a *bona fide* purchaser or transferee for value without notice.[12]

This proviso is in line with the general position of the law as an exception to the legal rule that no one can give a better title to a right or thing than he himself possesses – a rule generally represented by the Latin maxim of *nemo dat quod non habet.* The exception operates to protect commercial transactions involving innocent third party purchasers. It is that a person who

10. Section 23 of the Law.
11. Section 15 of the Law.
12. See Lord Denning in *Bishopsgate Motor Finance Corp. v Transport Brakes Ltd* (1949) 1 KB 332, 336.

takes in good faith and for value without notice of any defect in the title of the giver is entitled to a better title than that of the real owner. This is the common law rule which has been enacted in the proviso to Section 15 (a) of the Law.[13]

(b) Outgoing Member's Entitlements - One such other provision for the protection of the funds and other assets of a co-operative society is Regulation 22 pursuant to the Law under which a member or past member, in leaving the society, is liable to forfeit any repayments that may be due to him on account of his shares in the event of a net loss appearing in the audited balance sheet of the society. Regulation 23 contains a similar forfeiture provision in respect of entitlements to a deceased member's nominee where a net loss is shown in the balance sheet of the society.

(c) Intermeddling with Society Assets - Where, in the course of the winding up of a co-operative society, it appears that a member has intermeddled with any money or property of the society while he was involved, as an officer, in the conduct of the affairs of the society, he shall be liable to repay or restore such money or property to the society with interest.[14] This liability to repay or restore is enforced by the Registrar of co-operatives by order after an examination of the conduct of the member by him upon the

---

13. As has also been enacted in a number of other statutes such as in Sections 22 (1), 23, 24, and 25 (1) of the Sale of Goods Act 1893 and Sections 8 and 9 of the Factors Act 1889 both Statutes of General Application in Nigeria and as enacted for Lagos State in 1973; Delta and Edo states in 1976; and in 1958 for Ekiti,, Ogun, Ondo, Osun and Oyo states.
14. Section 48 of the Law.

application of the liquidator, or a creditor, or a contributor.

The Registrar's order carries with it the weight of law the breach of which gives rise to imprisonment for six months upon conviction with an option of fine of two hundred Naira only or to both such fine and imprisonment.[15]

(d) Mareva Directive – Section 49 of the Law provides for a kind of protection for co-operative societies which is very similar to the *mareva* injunction in equity. It is that when the Registrar of co-operatives is

> satisfied that any person with intent to defraud[16] *(the society)* or delay the execution of any order which may be made against him under Section 48 (1) or Section 51 (1) *(of the Law)* or of any decision given in a dispute referred to the Registrar or to any arbitrators under any regulations is about to
> (a) dispose of the whole or any part of his property, or
> (b) remove the whole or any part of his property from the local jurisdiction of the Registrar, the Registrar may, unless adequate security is furnished, direct the interim attachment of the said property or such part thereof as he thinks necessary; and such attachment shall have the same effect as if it had been made by a competent court and that any person who fails to comply with the directive *(or order)*

shall be guilty of an offence and shall be liable to imprisonment for six months on conviction or to a fine of two hundred Naira only or to both such fine and imprisonment.

15. Section 48 (2).
16. The Lagos State provision in Cap. C15 uses the word 'defeat'. See Section 44 (4) thereof.

The operative part of the provision is *'any person with intent to defraud* ('defeat' in Lagos State) *or delay the execution of any order which may be made ... '*.

The Registrar needs only to be satisfied of a person's 'intent' to defraud or delay execution. The provision then talks of an execution of an 'order which *which may be made'*. The order under Sections 48 and 51 etc is one which is yet to be made yet the registrar's directive or order of interim attachment can be made in anticipation thereof. This is unusual except reliance is placed on the 'is about to … dispose of … or remove' part of the provision.

Ordinarily, the law does not act to inflict pain upon a mere intention unaccompanied by some manifest act. Also, the law does not permit a court to make an order compelling a party to part with his property or assets pending the outcome of a trial.[17] As Megarry V.C. put it in *Barclay-Johnson v Yuill,*[18] the rule in law is that 'the plaintiff, like other creditors of the defendant, must obtain his judgement and then enforce it'

This has always been the position of the law even as at 1935 when the first legislation on co-operative societies[19] was enacted and as at 1959 when the Co-operative Societies Law (Cap. 26) Laws of the then Western Region[20] of Nigeria was made. Yet these enactments contain this

17. See the English decision in *Lister & Co v Stubbs* (1890) 45 Ch.D. 1.
18. (1980) 1 W.L.R. 1259, 1262.
19. The Co-operative Societies Ordinance of 1935 based on C.F. Strickland's recommendations from which all subsequent co-operative societies legislation have been copied.
20. The Law i.e. The Co-operative Societies Law (Cap. 42) Laws of Delta State 2007 is a subsequent direct copy from this 1959 Law.

protective protection as in Section 49 of the Law allowing the inflicting of pain by way of an 'interim attachment' of the property of a person following a mere 'intent'; and also compelling a party to be dispossessed of his property pending an examination of the conduct of the person.

These protective provisions as in Section 49 of the Law have turned out somewhat like a prophecy of what the English courts would subsequently do. This is because in 1975 (some sixteen years on) the English Court of Appeal in *Mareva Compania Naviera S.A. v International Bulk Carriers S.A.*[21] introduced what is now generally known as the *mareva* injunction permitting some restricted exception to the above stated position of the law and granting, by way of an *ex-parte* injunction, a restraint on a defendant from disposing of or dealing with or removing or disposing out of jurisdiction his property which may include funds to the credit of the defendant in a bank account pending the final determination of the suit.[22]

Guidelines for a *Mareva* Directive – Before the Registrar becomes satisfied that a person is with the requisite

(a) intent to defraud, or to

(b) delay the execution

of his order which he may make against that person under the Law, it is to be humbly recommended that the Registrar should allow himself to be persuaded by the following guidelines as laid down by the courts[23] for the grant of a *mareva* injunction:

21. (1975) 2 Lloyd's Rep. 509.
22. See the English decisions in *Mareva Compani Naviera S.A. v International Bulk Carriers S.A.* (supra).
23. *Third Chandris Shipping Corporation v Unimarine S.A.* (1979) Q.B. 645, 668-669.

***(i) Full Disclosure by Applicant*:** The Registrar must ensure that the applicant (in this case, either the liquidator, or a creditor, or a contributor) has fully and frankly disclosed all facts in relation to all matters within his knowledge and which will be material to the Registrar's decision.

***(ii) Statement of Allegations*:** Applicant must make a clear and concise statement as to the allegations upon which the application has been brought stating the part played by the respondent in the organization or management of the co-operative society or, where the respondent is a past or present officer of the society, details of any money or property which the officer has misapplied or retained or become liable or accountable for; or that the officer has been guilty of misfeasance or breach of trust in relation to the society.

If the respondent has made a defence in attack of the allegations against him, the applicant must also include a statement of such defence so as to enable the Registrar come to a balanced decision.

(iii) Property must be within Jurisdiction – The applicant for the directive of interim attachment must also show to the satisfaction of the Registrar that the respondent has property within the local limits of the jurisdiction of the Registrar and the grounds for believing that the respondent has such property and assets within the jurisdiction. The applicant may not be in a position to state precisely the value of the property but it will suffice if he shows that the respondent has a bank account within the jurisdiction whether or not the account has any funds in it.

(iv) Risk of Removal – Applicant must also satisfy the Registrar that there is a risk of the respondent disposing of or removing the whole or any part of the property from the Registrar's jurisdiction, the grounds for believing that there is such a risk, and the grounds for believing that the property will be removed before the demands of the Registrar's subsequent order or directive are met or satisfied.

(v) Undertaking as to Damages – A *mareva* order under the received English law is an order in equity. It is not obtained for the asking but in furtherance of justice and equity. Being an equitable order, it is subject to the grounds for granting such an order in equity. These grounds include that the applicant must enter into an undertaking as to damages. This is to the effect that should it turn out at the end of the proceedings that the applicant was not entitled to the order in the first place and the respondent has as a result of the order of interim attachment on his property suffered a loss (as he is very likely to suffer), the applicant shall upon his undertaking defray such loss by way of damages in favour of the respondent.

The provision of Section 49 of the Law is not equity but one of statute which must be strictly construed and applied. As pointed out earlier, this provision is not one for a *mareva* but one which is only a prophecy as to a *mareva* since as at the date of the enactment, *mareva* had not been born. The provision does not specifically provide for an undertaking as to damages, nor for any other guidelines as above. But it provides that the Registrar may make the directive for interim attachment only when 'adequate security' is not furnished.

The Registrar, having been satisfied of the sundry matters above, 'may, unless adequate[24] security is furnished, direct the interim attachment of the said property' as the Registrar thinks necessary.

The provision as to the furnishing of adequate security is similar to the entering of an undertaking as to damages except that an undertaking as to damages in equity is entered by the applicant for the order and not the respondent. But under the provisions of Section 49 of the Law, the furnishing of adequate security is by the respondent so as to prevent the order for the interim attachment of his property from being made.

As already stated, these kinds of provisions in the Law are designed to specially protect the assets of a co-operative society. The guidelines[25] for the making of a *mareva* directive, including that for the entering into an undertaking as to damages, are persuasively in the interest of justice.

It is therefore to be humbly recommended that in the event that the respondent is unable to furnish adequate security and the Registrar is to make the order for interim attachment of the respondent's property, the Registrar shall also require the applicant to enter into an undertaking as to damages so that if at the conclusion of the examination of the respondent's conduct, he finds the person not culpable and therefore ought not to have been subjected to the pains

24. There is no indication in the Law as to what will be 'adequate' except to assume that the Registrar is free to so determine as he 'thinks necessary'.
25. See generally for the *mareva* injunction P.V. Baker and P.St. J. Langan: *Snell's Principles of Equity* (Sweet & Maxwell, London, 1982, 28th Ed.) at p.648.

of having his property attached in the interim, his pains may be assuaged by way of damages even if he does not suffer any actual losses.

Effect of Violating a *Mareva* Directive - A violation of a *mareva* injunction made by a court would amount to contempt of court which will leave the contemnor open to imprisonment for as long as it takes the contemnor to purge himself of his contempt. Subsection 2 of Section 49 of the Law has also made provisions for a term of imprisonment for whoever fails to comply with an order or directive of the Registrar made under the section.

Liability for Society's Debts – Every member of a co-operative society is jointly and severally liable for the debts of the society. Accordingly, no member is entitled to be paid a bonus or dividend out of the society's funds until the entire expenditure of the society has been provided for.[26]

Reserve Fund to Meet Liabilities - It is for the purpose of meeting the demands of a society's debts that every society is compelled by the Law to set aside at least twenty five per cent of its net surplus into a reserve fund[27] which shall be indivisible and no member shall be entitled to claim a specified share in.[28]

The Regulations provide that in the event of the dissolution of the society, the reserve fund shall be applied to discharging the liabilities of the society beside the repayment of the share capital to its members. Hence it is without dispute that the liability of a society's members for the debts of the society is joint.

26. See Regulation 29 (4).
27. Section 35 (2) of the Law.
28. Regulation 27.

Limited Liability Societies - Notwithstanding the above general position of the law, the extent of the liability of members of a co-operative society with limited liability is fixed and determinate in relation to the number or value of the society's shares held by them. This is that members of such a society cannot be called upon, in the event of the society going under, to meet the demands of the society's debts beyond the amount of their shares except where the shares or part thereof had not been paid for by such members.

Where a member is owing on his share holding and the assets of the society are insufficient for meeting the demands of the society's debts upon its liquidation or its being wound up, then such a member will be liable to be called upon by the society or the liquidator to pay up whatever amount is outstanding against him and remaining unpaid in respect of the shares.

Duration of Liability – The liability of a member for the debts of his society is not extinguished when and if he ceases to be a member or dies. Section 30 (1) of the Law provides that the liability of a past[29] member for the debts of a registered society shall continue for a period of two years reckoned from the date he ceased to be a member. The debts for which he is liable shall be the society's debts as they existed in the books of the society as at the date on which the member ceased to be a member.

Similarly, where a member dies, his estate shall be liable for the share of such deceased member's liability for the debts of the society as they existed as at the date of his

29. A member can become a past member in any of the three modes as provided in Regulation 22.

death. This is because the death of a member does not *ipso facto* extinguish his liability for the debts of the society. The liability shall not become statute barred until after two years shall have elapsed reckoned from the date of his death.[30]

30. Section 30 (2) of the Law.

Chapter Seven
Management, Administration and Control of Societies

The committee shall exercise all the powers of the society except those reserved for the general meeting
– Regulation 14

A co-operative society is not a company; but like a company, it is an artificial legal entity which cannot function without relying on some other legal entities, persons or organs. As an artificial person, a co-operative society, like a company has no brains and limbs of its own. To carry out its legal functions and exercise its legal powers, it must and does depend on some organs composed of natural persons as its 'agents' or 'trustees'.

Generally, the functions and powers of a company are carried out and exercised by its board of directors and the general meeting as spelt out by the Companies and Allied Matters Act and the company's Articles.

In like manner, the management and administration of a co-operative society are entrusted to and vested in the society's management committee and its general meetings as spelt out in the Co-operative Societies Law, the Regulations made pursuant thereto and the Bye-laws of the society. Also, the Registrar of Co-operatives performs very far-reaching functions, duties and powers under the Law and Regulations in the control of co-operative societies and how they are managed and administered.

The Committee - The first of the organs for the running of a co-operative society is its management committee. This consists of the officers of the society who constitute themselves into a management body for carrying out the day-to-day activities and functions and exercising the powers of the society. There is no direct or express provision in the Law or the Regulations requiring that a co-operative society shall have such management committee or any such body by whatever name called. Section 246 (1) of the Companies and Allied Matters Act, Laws of the Federation 1990, provides specifically that

> every company ... shall have at least two directors

to whom the management of the business[1] of the company is entrusted. Also, a usual content of a company's Articles is that

> the business of the company shall be managed by the directors who ... may exercise all such powers of the company as are not ... required to be exercised by the company in general meeting....

There is no equivalent provision of this kind in the Co-operative Societies Law or in the Regulations. But by reference to certain provisions especially of the Regulations and to the nature of things generally, the existence of such a body for a co-operative society cannot be overlooked. Regulation 14 of the Co-operative Societies Regulations made pursuant to the Law, for instance, provides that

> *the committee* shall exercise all the powers of the society except those reserved for the *general meeting*

but nowhere has this committee been hitherto referred to either in the Law or in the Regulations before the reference in Regulation 14 except at the interpretation section where 'committee' is defined to mean

> the governing body of a registered society to whom the

1. Section 244 Companies and Allied Matters Act 1990.

management of its affairs is entrusted[2]

In effect, though the Law does not contain an express provision directly establishing or requiring that a co-operative society shall have a committee to manage its affairs, there is a definitional provision implying its existence and a provision in the Regulations which also infers the existence of the committee.

The absence of a direct provision for the creation of this committee is obviously a legislative lacuna present in all other co-operatives enactments in Nigeria except the unconstitutional[3] federal enactment which positively provides that

> the affairs of a registered society shall be administered and managed by a committee appointed by the members for that purpose.[4]

This provision of Cap. N98 is express, direct and commendable. It talks of the affairs of a society being *administered* and *managed* by *a committee*. This committee is to be appointed by the members of the society. The provision introduces the committee into being with the indefinite article 'a' unlike the use of the definite article

2. Section 2 Co-operative Societies Law (Cap. 45) Laws of Bendel State 1976 as applicable to Delta and Edo states and published as Cap. 42 in the Annotated Laws of Delta State 2007. All other states enactments have similar provisions and the federal Cap. N98 has it as meaning *'the governing body, by whatever name called, of a registered society to which the management of its affairs is entrusted'*.
3. See the discussion on Decree 90 i.e. Cap. N98 in Chapter Two especially the reference to the usefulness of this Decree in comparative study.
4. Section 6 (2) of the Nigerian Co-operative Societies Act (Cap. N98) Laws of the Federation 2004.

'the' in Regulation 14 which falsely infers a previous or an earlier introduction or establishment of the committee.

The provision talks of the committee being "appointed" by the members. This is a drawback as it offends the democratic principles requirement of a co-operative society. It also fails to spell out by what mode the members are to "appoint" the committee. This is untidy and bound to create problems in implementation.

In practice, this committee is referred to by different names which include 'executive committee', 'board of directors' (in which case, the members of the committee are also known as 'directors'), 'management committee', 'management board' etc. This must explain why the definition of 'committee' in Section 6 of Cap. N98 has appropriately included the phrase 'by whatever name called'.

The Committee – How Constituted – As has been pointed out, all the co-operative enactments in Nigeria except the federal Cap. N98 are silent on the creation of the co-operative management committee. Consequentially, there is also no statutory provision (not even in Cap. N98) as to the committee's composition or how it is to be constituted. Sundry readings however seem to suggest that membership of the committee is usually by election. S.O. Obeng suggests so much when he declared that

> management of every co-operative society is entrusted to a committee *elected* at its annual general meeting.[5]

The model bye-laws for Kaduna State made pursuant to the

5. *Business and Co-operative Law* (Nigerian Business Examinations Series) Vol. 3 at p.192.

Northern Region Co-operative Societies Regulations No. 9 of 1956 contains similar provisions in the following manner

> president (if any), treasurer, the secretary and not more than seven ordinary members, who shall be *elected* from among the members of the society[6]

M.S. Jatto holds similar views that the 'management board' of a co-operative society is composed of members *elected* at an annual general meeting or at any other general meeting.[7]

Section 6 (2) of Cap. N98 provides however that the 'committee' shall be 'appointed' by the members. Also, Regulation 10 infers that officers of the society are appointed in the following words:

> an officer ... shall not be *appointed* ... for an indefinite period or for a period exceeding one year.

The second leg of this same Regulation however goes on to provide for a *'re-election'* of a retiring officer, suggesting that the retiring officer was initially elected but not appointed.

There is a difference between an election and an appointment. An appointment by members as provided in Cap. N98 will practically be awkward which an election by members will not be. An election is also in line with the democratic principles of the co-operative movement.[8]

In the absence of an express statutory provision as to how the management committee of a co-operative society is to be constituted, the more democratic approach

6. Bye-law 40 (1).
7. *Key Points in Co-operative Movement and Management* at p. 11. See also Erhurun Helen E.O: *Co-operatives: Principles and Field Administration* (2007) P.A. Anigboro Prints (Asaba) at p. 117.
8. See the discussion at Chapter One.

by way of election is to be preferred and recommended. This has obviously influenced the positions of the sundry readings considered above which is that the committee members are to be elected notwithstanding the express provisions of Section 6 (2) of Cap. N98.

For instance, whereas Obeng based his entire discussion of co-operative societies on this Act as a prevailing federal enactment, he nevertheless states that the management committee of a co-operative society is 'elected at its annual general meeting' notwithstanding that the Act provides that members of the committee shall be 'appointed'.

Composition of Co-operative Committee - Members of the management committee of a co-operative society are the persons, as Cap. N98 put it, who administer and manage the affairs of the society just in the same way as the Companies and Allied Matters Act provides in respect of company directors as the persons who are 'to direct and manage the business of the company'[9] and that therefore 'every company … shall have at least two directors'.[10]

A member of a co-operative society's management committee is therefore, in terms of functions, like a director of a company. But whereas the companies Act makes provision for the minimum number of directors who shall constitute a company's board of directors i.e. two, there is not a similar provision in any of the co-operative society enactments in Nigeria prescribing the number of persons either as minimum or maximum who may constitute the

9. Section 244 of the Companies and Allied Matters Act 1990.
10. Section 244 ibid.

management committee of a co-operative society. The Regulations made pursuant to the various laws are also silent on this issue.[11]

Berko[12] S.Y. in a critique of the South Eastern states Regulations is of the view that 'there must obviously be' seven members in the management committee consisting of a president, vice-president, secretary, treasurer, at least two other members and 'may be, a financial secretary'.[13] Erhurun[14] is of the view that a large co-operative society could have a management committee consisting of a president or chairman, vice president, general secretary, financial secretary, treasurer, social/welfare secretary, and two or more ex-officio members but that for a small society, a president or chairman, general secretary, treasurer, and two ex-officio members will do.

Legally, except for the prescription for 'at least four members' on the South Eastern Regulations, there is no

11. But see Regulation 24 (8) of the South Eastern States of Abia, Ebonyi, Enugu and Imo made pursuant to Cap. N98 which is said to provide for *at least four members* and Bye-law 40 (1) of the model bye-laws for Kaduna State made pursuant to the Northern Region Co-operative Societies Regulations No. 9 of 1956 which specifically provides that *the management shall consist of the president, vice president (if any), treasurer, the secretary, and not more than seven ordinary members.* It is to be noted that this is only a suggested bye-law and does not carry the force of law.
12. Head of Department, Co-operatives and Rural Development, Enugu State University of Science and Technology, Enugu.
13. *The Co-operative Societies Decree and the Consequent Regulations: The Case of the New Regulations of the South Eastern States* (NJCS Vol. 2 No. 2) at p.40, 51.
14. Supra at footnote 7.

statutory provision prescribing the number of officers which shall compose the management committee of a co-operative society. This means that every co-operative society shall, in tune with its peculiar circumstances and nature of affairs elect for itself any number of officers who shall make up its management committee.

Eligibility for Committee Membership - The Law and Regulations may be silent on the creation, constitution and composition of co-operative society management committees but are not silent as to who cannot be a member thereof. Section 14 of the Law provides that the following persons are not eligible to serve as members of the management committee of a co-operative society:

(a) Minor: A person who is under twenty-one years of age, being a minor, [15] is ineligible to serve as a member of a co-operative society's management committee.

(b) Paid Staff – A person who is entrusted in his individual and personal capacity and not in his capacity as a member of a co-operative society with the secretarial or managerial duties of the society and receives a pay or an honorarium for performing such duties shall be ineligible to serve on the management committee of the co-operative society.

(c) Money Lender – Where a society is a credit society and a member of the society is a money lender on his own account, such a money lending member of the society cannot be a member of the co-operative society's management committee. By the provisions of the Money Lenders Law, any person

> whose business is that of money lending or who carries on or advertises or announces himself or holds himself

15. The current age of a minor in recent legislations is under 18 years.

> out in any way as carrying on that business, whether or not he also possesses or own property or money derived from sources other than the lending of money and whether or not he carries on the business as a principal or as an agent

is a money lender.[16] However, if he is a body corporate incorporated or empowered by special law to lend money in accordance with such law, or he is a person bona fide carrying on the business of banking or insurance or bona fide carrying on business, not having for its primary object the lending of money, in the course of which and for the purposes whereof he lends money, he is not a money lender.[17] A person who lends money to another in consideration of a larger sum being repaid is deemed a money lender until the contrary is proved unless such a person is a licenced banker, insurer, or a person who does not have for its primary object the lending of money.[18]

(d) Society Products – A member of a marketing co-operative society who on his own deals in the type of commodities which the society markets cannot serve on the society's management committee.

Cessation of Committee Membership – The Law makes provisions[19] for situations where a person who is already a member of a co-operative society's management committee

---

16. *Ajao v Ademola* (2005) 3 NWLR (pt. 913) 636. Section 2 Money Lenders Law (Cap. 138) Laws of Delta State 2007. All other state enactments on money lenders define the term in like manner.
17. ibid.
18. *Veritas Insurance Co. Ltd. v Citi Trust Investments Ltd.* (1993) 3 NWLR (Pt. 281) 349. Also *Nwankwo v Nzeribe* (2004) 13 NWLR (Pt. 890) 422.
19. Section 13 of the Law.

will cease to be such a member. These situations include (b), (c), and (d) discussed above for ineligibility and the following:

(a) Loss of Shareholding – A member of a society's management committee shall cease to hold the office if he ceases to be a holder of the society's shares. This is only natural as it is usually rare for a person to be a member of a society without holding at least a share of the society.

(b) Insolvency – Regulation 13 (a) provides that a member of a co-operative society's management committee must cease to hold office if he is declared insolvent. The provision does not expatiate but it is understood as the law that an insolvent person is a person in respect of whom an adjudication order has been duly pronounced by a court of competent powers – usually the Federal High Court under the Bankruptcy Act.

An adjudication order made pursuant to the provisions of the Bankruptcy Act 1979[20] effectively renders a person a bankrupt which is the same thing as the person being declared insolvent.[21] But a person cannot be declared insolvent unless prima facie evidence of his insolvency has been presented before the court.

Such evidence flows from proof that a debtor has committed one or other of three acts of bankruptcy as provided in Section 1 of the Bankruptcy Act which is to the effect that:

A debtor commits an act of bankruptcy in each of the

---

20. Published as Cap. 28 in the Laws of the Federation 1990.
21. In modern usage, only an individual can be bankrupt being a term consistent with the Bankruptcy Act but not insolvent even though both terms mean the same thing the latter usually used for corporate entities.

following cases –

(a) if a creditor:

(i) has obtained a final judgement or final order against him for any amount, and execution thereon not having been stayed, has a bankruptcy notice served on him, and

(ii) does not, within fourteen days after service of the notice, comply with the requirements of the notice or satisfy the court that he has a counterclaim, set-off or cross demand which equals or exceeds the amount of the judgement debt or sum ordered to be paid, and which he could not set up in the action in which the judgement was obtained or the proceedings in which the order was obtained ...; (or)

(b) if execution against him has been levied by seizure of his goods under process in an action, or proceedings in the court, and the goods have either been sold or held by the bailiff for twenty-one days; (or)

(c) if he files in the court a declaration of his inability to pay his debts or presents a bankruptcy petition against himself.

In effect, the requirement of Regulation 13 (b) pursuant to the Co-operatives Societies Law compelling a person declared insolvent to cease to hold office as member of a co-operative society management committee is only met when:

(a) the person is guilty of a bankruptcy act; and

(b) an adjudication order has been made against him in consequence of (a) and thereby rendering him insolvent under the Law.

(c) Insanity – A person who, being a member of a co-operative society's management committee, becomes of unsound mind shall cease to hold the office. The insanity must be certified by way of a declaration by a court of competent jurisdiction upon credible medical evidence.

(d) Conviction and Sentence – No member of a co-operative society's management committee shall continue in office upon his conviction of a crime by a competent court involving dishonesty. Similarly, a person who has been sentenced to a term of imprisonment of not less than three months shall vacate his office as a member of the management committee of a co-operative society.[22]

Duties and Powers of Committee Members – As has been observed, a co-operative society's management committee is similar to a company's board of directors. Having been elected to 'the governing body of a registered society to whom the management of its affairs is entrusted', a member of a society's management committee comes under certain duties which he owes to the society and its other members. These duties stem from his legal position, in relation to the society, as trustee and agent of the society. A trustee is a person who is

> compelled in equity to hold property, whether real or personal, and whether by legal or equitable title, for the benefit of some persons (of whom he may be one and who are termed *ces tuis que* trust) or for some object permitted by law, in such a way that the real benefit of the property accrues, not to the trustee, but to the beneficiaries or other objects of the trust.[23]

Accordingly, a member of a co-operative society's management committee, having been entrusted by his election with the management of the affairs of the society,

---

22. See generally, Regulation 13 pursuant to the Law.
23. Keeton, Prof.: *The Law of Trusts* (8th Ed.) p.3.

becomes a trustee of the society in that he now must hold the society's properties and manage the affairs of the society in such a way that the real benefit of his holding and management accrues not to him as such committee member but to the members of the society generally as beneficiaries, of whom he is one.

As trustees, all members of a co-operative society's management committee, hold and control the society's properties which they must apply for the purposes of the society's objects as specified in the bye-laws and in the general interests of the society.

The powers conferred on them by the Regulations must be exercised by them bona fide in the interest of the society and must not be used for acquiring or promoting personal interests.

Duties of Committee Member as Trustee – A member of a co-operative society's management committee is a trustee of the society and not for the individual members of the society. As such trustee, the usual duties of a trustee are relatively imposed on him. This is to say that the usual duties of a trustee, under a settlement for instance, are, though not in absolute terms, binding on him relative to his peculiar circumstances and status as a member of the management committee of a co-operative society.

He is not a trustee in the strict sense of the term in relation to his duties as a trustee but, at best, what may be termed a quasi-trustee. This is because, in the nature of things, a breach of his trust as a member of a co-operative society management committee may not necessarily lead to the same kind of consequences as can be contemplated when it is said that a trustee of a settlement has committed a breach of his trust.

Fiduciary Duties – The duties of a co-operative society management committee member are in the main fiduciary in nature. This is because they hold their positions as positions of trust and of confidence which is that the society and its members trust the management committee members and repose confidence in them to manage the affairs of the society and the powers conferred in them in good faith first for the purposes for which they have been conferred and for the benefit of the society and, secondly, not to place themselves in relation to their duties in such a position that their personal interests will conflict with their duties.

(a) Best Interest of Society – Specifically, the fiduciary duties of co-operative society management committee members require them, among other standards, to manage the affairs of the society and exercise their powers honestly and in the best interest of the society so that if they do anything under their given powers which is for a purpose other than that for which the powers have been given, such an act or thing as done will be void.

(b) Secret Profits – Also, a co-operative society management committee member, being under fiduciary duties, is forbidden from making secret profits as a result of the use of his office. It will not be a defence that he acted in good faith. He is under a duty to disclose to the society all profits made by him outside his agreed remuneration, if any, in full by virtue of his position as management committee member.

(c) Conflict of Interests – As stated above, a management committee member should not place himself in a position whereby his personal interests become in conflict with his duties as a management committee member or the interests of the society. For instance, he is precluded from dealing on behalf of the society with himself or entering into deals in which he a personal interest which conflicts or may conflict with the interests of the society to which he owes fiduciary duties.

Such deals may however subsequently be ratified by the society. The ratification must be obtained by fair and proper means. A personal enrichment by a management committee member from such deals must be accounted for to the society. A cause of action exists in favour of the society for the recovery of the amount involved in such unjust enrichment.

Care and Skill: Generally, a co-operative society management committee member is under a duty to use reasonable skill and care in the discharge of his duties. This duty does not require him to exhibit any special skills or a greater degree of skill than is reasonably expected of a person of his station, personal circumstance, knowledge and experience.

Committee Members as Agents of Society – The duties of a society's management committee member also arises from his status as an agent of the society. An agent has been defined variously including as being a person appointed by another person called the principal to act on behalf of the principal often to negotiate a contract between the principal and, not himself but, a third party.[24] In other words, an agent is a

> person who is authorized to act for a principal (who has agreed so to act) and who has powers to affect the legal relations of his principal with a third party.[25]

The concept of agency has also been described as the

> relationship that exists between two persons when one, called the agent, is considered in law to represent the other, called the principal, in such a way as to be able to affect the principal's legal position in respect of strangers to the relationship by the making of contracts or the disposition of property.[26]

A co-operative society management committee member represents the society in such a way as to be able to affect the society's legal position in relation to persons who are not party to the relationship of principal and agent which subsists between the society and the committee member. He is the agent and the society is his principal.

In this regard, the general principles of the law of agency apply to regulate his relationship with the society and which also impose certain duties on him as agent. These duties include the duty to:

(a) Obey Principal's Instructions - By this it is meant that the management committee member as agent of the co-operative society must carry out the instructions of the society as his principal in compliance with the society's bye-laws, the Regulations made pursuant to the Law and

---

24. See Ogboghro I. Vincent and Emiaso Miakpo (2006) *Banking Laws and Regulation in Nigeria* Krisbec Publications, Asaba at p.101.
25. Powell: *Law of Agency* (2nd Ed.) at p.7
26. Fridman (1971)*The Law of Agency* (Butterworths, London) at p.8.

the Law including any instructions or restrictions duly laid down by the society in general meeting.[27]

(b) Perform Agency with Skill and Care - Here it is expected that the committee member will perform his duties as an agent with the standard of care and skill which will be expected of a reasonable man in the particular station of the member.

He is not expected to exhibit a standard of skill and care which is beyond him or which is to be expected of an expert in specialized skills. But if he possesses or professes any specialized skill or calling such as that of a banker, legal practitioner, architect, an accountant etc., the degree of skill and care which will be required of him will be that to be reasonably expected of persons of such profession or calling.

(c) Perform Agency in Good Faith - This means that a management committee member must display absolute honesty and sincerity in the performance of the functions of his office. Again, the duty of utmost good faith imposed on him as an agent precludes him from allowing his personal interests to conflict with his duties and functions as a management committee member. This is because the relationship between him as a committee member and the society is a fiducial one and all fiduciary duties are binding on him.

(d) Render Accounts - This also is a duty which arises from the committee member's fiduciary relationship with the society. It forbids him from making any secret profits. He is also under a duty to hand over or pay over all monies

27. Regulation 14.

and properties received by him on behalf of the society and being monies and properties belonging to his principal.

(e) Personally Perform his Duties - An agent is a person to whom powers have been delegated to act on behalf of his principal. Under the law of agency, he is precluded from further delegating the powers so delegated to him to anyone else. This rule is expressed in the Latin maxim: *delegatus non potest delegare*. Accordingly, a co-operative society's committee member is required to personally perform the duties of his office since the personal qualities and capabilities of the agent would have informed the appointment in the first place.[28]

Duties of the Committee – The above discussion is on the personal duties which members of a co-operative society's management committee owe to their societies as individual members of the management committee. There are further provisions in Regulation 15 made pursuant to the Law as to the duties of the committee as a body to whom the administration and management of the affairs of a co-operative society has been entrusted. These duties, some of which are more in the nature of functions than duties, are as follows:

(a) Compliance with the Law and Regulations – In managing the affairs of a co-operative society, the management committee has a duty to comply with the

28. For further readings on duties and rights of agents, see Ogboghro and Emiaso: *Banking Laws and Regulation in Nigeria* (supra); Oyeneye O.O (2002) *Notes on Agency Relationship* Olabis Production, Lagos at p.25.

Law,[29] the Regulations made thereunder, and the society's bye-laws.[30]

(b) Proper Conduct of Business – Regulation 15 (a) also imposes a duty of conducting the business of the society properly on the management committee. It is to be humbly submitted with due respect that the law-maker's naked use of 'properly' without more in the Regulation is rather vague and somewhat subjective notwithstanding that a properly run outfit may be self-evident.

Regulation 15 lists other items under 'duties of the committees' but which items are more in the nature of things which a properly run outfit will ordinarily be expected to do. These include that the committee shall

(i) maintain true and accurate accounts,
(ii) keep true account of the society's assets and liabilities,
(iii) keep a correct register of its members, and to
(iv) lay before the annual general meeting a profit and loss account and a balance sheet.[31]

Where the society is a credit society i.e. a society which gives loans to its members, it is the duty of the management committee to monitor such loans with a view to ensuring that the loans are applied to the purposes for which they were approved and granted.[32] Similarly, the committee has a duty to monitor the produce marketed by a marketing society with a view to ensuring that the

29. i.e. the Co-operative Societies Law.
30. Regulation 15 (a).
31. These terms are not used in the context of trading enterprises. See supra at Chapter One for the discussion on co-operatives and public officers.
32. Regulation 15 (h).

produce are of good quality and that they are graded.[33]

Management committees are under duty to obtain adequate security from officers and employees of the society[34] and to assist the inspection of the society's books by any person authorized to see to the books.

Tenure of Committee Members – Officers of a co-operative society who, as has been shown, are appointed by election cannot hold their office for an indefinite period or for a period exceeding one year.[35] One year in this context means any period of twelve calendar months and not January to December.

The regulation against indefinite tenure is not absolute. The language of the second leg of Regulation 10 is to the effect that

> a retiring officer shall, unless the bye-laws otherwise provide, be eligible for re-election.

This means that a society may by its bye-laws allow for perpetual eligibility for re-election of a retiring officer. In other words, unless the bye-laws prohibit it, any officer who has held office for the statutory period of one year shall nonetheless be routinely eligible for re-election for a new period which shall not exceed one year.

Meetings – The second organ through which a co-operative society is administered and managed is its meetings which is the gathering or coming together of the members of the society either in whole or in committees at a place and at specified or agreed times for purposes of discussing the society's affairs and taking decisions in relation thereto.

---

33. Regulation 15 (i).
34. Regulation 15 (g).
35. Regulation 10.

There is no direct and express provision in the Law for the holding of meetings but this is, in the nature of things, to be inferred. Section 25 of the Law makes such necessary inference in providing that no member of a society shall have more than one vote in the conduct of the affairs of the society. Furthermore, Regulation 9 made pursuant to the Law provides the express enactment for the holding of meetings by co-operative societies. The Regulation declares that

> every society shall from time to time hold general meetings as provided in the bye-laws for the disposal of necessary business.

The requirement to hold meetings is therefore mandatory given the use of the imperative 'shall' by the law-maker in the Regulation 9 but the details as to how and when such meetings are to be held shall be 'as provided in the bye-laws' of the society.

Types of Meeting – The Regulations provide for only two types of meetings. These are the general meeting[36] and the special general meeting.[37] In practice however, there are other types of meeting e.g. the committee meeting which could either be of a standing committee such as the management committee or an ad hoc committee There is also the requisitioned meeting referred to in the Regulations as 'special general meeting'.

The General Meeting – As has been observed, Regulation 9 (1) pursuant to the Law expressly provides for the general meeting. This is the meeting of all members of the society whereat matters relating to the affairs of the society are

36. Regulation 9 (1).
37. Regulation 9 (2)

discussed and decisions thereon taken.

The general meeting is generally regarded as the supreme organ of the society since it consists of all members of the society who have equal rights thereat. The model bye-laws for Delta State describes it as 'the ultimate authority under the law in all the affairs of the society' and 'shall consist of the general body of members...'[38]

This model bye-law may have been influenced by the provisions of Regulation 20 of the Northern Region Co-operative Societies Regulations (Cap. 26) of 1956 to the effect that

> the supreme authority in a registered society shall be vested in the general meeting of members at which every member has a right to attend and vote on all questions ...*where* each member shall have one vote only which shall be exercised in person and not be proxy[39]

The Annual General Meeting – The general meeting as described above is, in practice, of two kinds. The first kind is the monthly general meeting held, usually, once a month while the second kind is the annual general meeting.

Regulation 9 appears to provide more for the annual general meeting and not for the monthly general meeting given the nature of the business the 'general meetings' can attend to under the Regulation which include the

(a) fixing of a maximum liability which the society can incur towards non-members,
(b) fixing of a maximum credit to which a member can be entitled,

38. Bye-law 16. See also Erhurun (supra) at p.16.
39. Rule 14 of the Eastern Nigeria Co-operative Societies Rules (Cap. 28) contains the same provision word for word.

(c) election of officers of the society and of members of committee,

(d) consideration of the society's audited balance sheet and disposal of surplus,[40]

(e) consideration of audit reports and of any inspection reports by the Registrar of Co-operatives or by an Inspector.

These represent some of the necessary businesses which a general meeting may attend to as being specifically reserved for the general meeting and therefore not open to the management committee to exercise powers over.

By Regulation 14, a co-operative society's management committee shall exercise all the powers of the society but is precluded from exercising any powers in relation to the sundry businesses listed in (a) to (e) above being businesses specifically reserved under Regulation 9 for the general meetings. In particular, the general meeting exercises the sole right to decide the disposal of the surplus. This Regulation specifically provides that a society's management committee

> shall exercise all the powers of the society except those reserved for the general meeting.

However, every society is at liberty to provide for itself other businesses as the society may desire which its management meetings may attend to provided such additional businesses do not relate to the businesses specifically reserved for the general meeting. Such additional businesses, for instance, may include the

40. Balance sheets are usually prepared and audited in the corporate world annually and not monthly although in some situations, half-yearly interim accounts may be raised but never monthly.

(a) consideration of any communications from the Registrar of Co-operatives,
(b) suspension or removal from office of any officer or committee member,
(c) amendment or repeal of any existing bye-law or the enactment of an entirely new set of bye-laws,
(d) fixing of or approving the rate of interest to be charged on loans to members,
(e) ratification or dismissal of the society's employees, and
(f) disposal of any proper business duly presented before it.

Although the Regulation does not use the word 'powers' in relation to the sundry matters contained therein as 'businesses' for the disposal of 'general meetings', the context in which the 'necessary business' has been used therein cannot be far from meaning the same thing as 'powers'.

Regulation 24 of the Northern Regulations expressly provides for an Ordinary General Meeting which shall be held at such intervals as the society's bye-laws may specify. Under this Regulation, the society can hold its monthly meetings as distinct from its Annual General Meetings which by Regulation 22 shall be convened by the committee as soon as the annual accounts have been approved by the Registrar or as soon as the report on the audit of the accounts by the Registrar or person authorised by him is received by the committee.

By Regulation 23[41] thereof, the functions of the Annual General Meeting are spelt out as being to:

(a) confirm the minutes of the previous Annual General Meeting and of any intervening Special General Meeting,

(a) consider the reports of the committee and the annual accounts and balance sheet as approved by the Registrar together with the report on the audit of the accounts for the previous year as prepared by the Registrar or the person authorised by him,

(b) elect its officers, and

(c) transact any other general business.

It is to be observed that the Regulation describes the above matters listed (a) to (d) as 'functions' of the Annual General Meeting but in its Regulation 25, it lists the matters[42] which the Ordinary General Meeting shall attend to as 'business' and which business include the:

(a) fixing of a maximum liability which the society may incur in loans or deposits from members or non-members,

(b) fixing of maximum credit limits for members where applicable e.g. as in credit societies,

(c) consideration of the audit report and the registrar's comments thereon if not already done at a previous Annual General Meeting,

41. Rule 16 of the Eastern Nigeria Rules.
42. Rule 17 (3) ibid.

(d) consideration of inspection reports and communications from the Registrar, and consideration of members' complaints.

By the nature of the above listed businesses which a society's general meeting can attend to, whether as specifically reserved for it under the Regulations or otherwise, it is to be humbly submitted that the law envisages more of the Annual General meeting than the monthly or other type of periodic meetings.

Section 214 of the Companies and Allied Matters Act of 1990 provides for businesses which a company's Annual General Meeting may attend to. They include:

(a) declaration of a dividend,
(b) presentation of financial statements,
(c) presentation of directors' reports,
(d) presentation of auditors' reports,
(e) election of directors to replace retiring directors,
(f) appointment of auditors,
(g) appointment of members of audit committee, and
(h) fixing the remuneration of auditors.

These are described by the section as 'ordinary businesses' of a company's Annual General Meeting and, in comparison, are similar to the businesses listed in Regulation 9 (Delta, Edo and Lagos states), Regulations 23 and 25 (North) and Rules 16 (2) and 17 (3) (East) which are specifically reserved for the general meetings of a society.

By direct analogy therefore, it would appear that the law envisaged and provided more for the Annual General Meeting than for any other kind of meeting but for the freedom allowed the society to 'from time to time hold general meetings' and which general meetings shall be held 'as provided for in the bye-laws'.

This means that apart from holding an Annual General Meeting to deal with the businesses specified in the Regulations and Rules, a society may also hold other kinds of meetings as it shall have provided in its bye-laws at any other time from time to time either monthly, bi-monthly, or quarterly as the society sees convenient.

The Monthly General Meeting – The above therefore creates room and allows a society to hold a Monthly General Meeting or any other kind of periodic meetings as it suits the society provided the holding of such a meeting has been provided for in its bye-laws.

Such a periodic meeting, not being an Annual General Meeting, shall be free to attend to sundry matters of routine nature concerning the affairs of the society a list of which can only be open-ended but may not include any of those matters listed in the Regulations and Rules which are specifically reserved for the general meetings and which, by their very nature, can only come up for consideration at the end of a 'trading' season which is usually at the end of the year or of a period of 12 calendar months e.g. a consideration of the society's audited balance sheet and the disposal of the net surplus.

However, whether a society provides for itself the holding of a monthly or other kinds of periodic meeting not being an Annual General Meeting will depend on a number of factors including, to a large extent, the type, nature. And character of the society especially of its membership.

Where membership of the society is widespread over a large area of operations which would require long-distance travel by members to attend meetings, a monthly meeting would be too frequent and very cumbersome as it will be expensive and will also raise worries as to safety connected with travelling. These factors will make a monthly general meeting unwise.

A monthly meeting can however be very useful where membership is closely-knit and where, especially, the society is a credit society as the frequent meetings will provide a useful platform for monitoring the performance of the loans the society has given to its members.

By the provisions of Regulation 9 as applicable in Delta, Edo and Lagos states, every co-operative society in these states and other states having the same provision in their Regulations or Rules as the case may be, has the freedom to organise its general meetings as it suits its peculiar circumstances. Such peculiar arrangement must be provided for in the society's bye-laws. For instance, Bye-law 16 of the Delta State model bye-laws can be modified to give effect to such peculiar arrangement as follows:

> The ultimate authority under the law in all the affairs of this society shall be the general body of members who shall meet from time to time and at least once in every month at a Monthly General Meeting and once in a year at an Annual General Meeting and at an Extra-ordinary General Meeting called in accordance with the provisions of these bye-laws to review and direct the work of the society.

Formalities in Respect of Co-operative Meetings – As has been pointed out supra, the Delta State Co-operative Societies Law (Cap. 42) which is *impari materia* in all particulars material with most other state co-operative enactments is silent on co-operative society meetings. Except Regulation 9 which contains some direct but inadequate provisions, these states enactments make no provisions for regulating the holding co-operative society meetings.

This is a fundamental draw-back. For instance, the whole of Part VIII of the Companies and Allied Matters Act consisting of 33 sections some of which have up to ten subsections is devoted to meetings of companies and the procedure for summoning and conducting them. The sections make profuse provisions in respect of types of meetings, notices of meetings, court powers in respect of meetings, voting at meetings and the procedure therefor, proxies, quorum, resolutions, minutes etc. In contrast, most co-operative societies' laws in the country are painfully laconic in respect of co-operative societies meetings.

However, the Northern Region Co-operative Societies Regulations (Cap. 26) of 1956 and the Eastern Nigeria Co-operative Societies Rules (Cap. 28) contain somewhat profuse provisions in substantially the same wordings regulating co-operative society meetings.

The Northern Regulations, for instance, devotes all of its Regulations 20 to 30 to meetings.[43] Regulation 21 thereof provides for a 'first meeting of members'[44] which must be held immediately after the receipt by the society of the certificate of registration or not later than one month thereafter.

43. The Eastern Nigeria Rules does substantially the same in its Rules 14 to 20.
44. Regulation 15 Eastern Nigeria Rules.

By its Regulation 27, the Northern Regulations makes provisions for the quorum of a co-operative society's general meetings which the Regulation puts at 50% of the total number of members or ten members whichever is less where the total number of the members of the society does not exceed forty members. Where however the total number of the society's members exceeds forty, then 25% thereof shall form quorum.

When the meeting is one summoned by the Registrar of Co-operatives in accordance with and under powers conferred on him under the Law and or the Regulations or Rules, the above rules relating as to quorum shall not apply. Any number of members present at such a meeting shall be deemed to form a quorum.[45]

Under the Eastern Rules, the provisions as to quorum differ somewhat from the Northern provisions as, under it,

> one quarter of the members or delegates of a society shall form a quorum, provided that, where the total number of members or delegates exceeds one hundred and twenty, thirty members or delegates shall form a quorum.

If within one hour after the time fixed for any meeting of the society other than a meeting convened by the Registrar the members present are not sufficient to form a quorum, such meeting shall be considered as dissolved if convened on the demand of members (that is if it is a requisitioned meeting); in all other cases, it shall stand adjourned to the

45. See also Rule 18(2) of the Eastern Rules which contains a proviso that at least four days notice shall have been given by the Registrar for such a meeting.

same day in the next week at the same time and place and a notice to that effect shall be posted by the secretary within twenty-four (24) hours, and if at the adjourned meeting a quorum is not present within one hour from the time appointed for the meeting, the members present shall form a quorum.

Notices of Meetings – In most states including Lagos, Delta, Edo, and Ogun, the Law and Regulations made thereunder do not make provisions as to notices of co-operative society meetings. The giving of notices for meetings is a fundamental requirement for conferring validity on the decisions at such meetings. For instance, Section 218 (3) of the Companies and Allied Matters Act provides, in respect of company meetings, that no business may be transacted at any general meeting of a company unless notice of it has been duly given.

In practice, most co-operative societies have fixed dates, times and venues for holding their meetings whether they are monthly or annual general meetings. These dates, times and venues are usually well known by every co-operator and so renders the giving of formal notices for the meetings unnecessary. This is all right with small societies but may create legal problems with big ones as, in the event of litigation or some co-operative dispute, whether notice was formally given or not may became an issue and might just be the point upon which the dispute or suit will be decided.

Although there are no direct provisions in the Law

and Regulations of most states, Section 52 of the Law[46] requires that at least seven clear days' notice must be given to members of a society where the meeting is called for the purpose of resolving to divide itself into two or more societies or for the purpose of two or more societies resolving to amalgamate into one society. Also, by Section 43 (h) a liquidator appointed for the purpose of liquidating as co-operative society is required to give at least fourteen (14) days notice in calling any such meeting as may be necessary for the proper conduct of the liquidation.

Notwithstanding the silence of the Law and the Regulations in these states, a large society with scattered membership over a wide area of operations might be better advised as to the imperative of formally giving written notices to its members in summoning its meetings especially of the Annual General Meeting.

Length of Notice – Where it has become wise or expedient to formally give notices, and since there are no specific and direct provisions in the Law and Regulations as to the length of the notices, it can only be respectfully submitted that a reasonable length of time shall be sufficient. What length of time is sufficient in each case will be dependent on the peculiar circumstance of each society in relation to its membership.

A society with a highly homogeneous membership may require a shorter length of time than a society with a varied collection of members located in far-flung places

46. i.e. the Co-operative Societies Law (Cap. 42) Laws of Delta State 2007 which is *impari materia* in almost every material particular with all other co-operative laws in the country especially those of the old Western Region which is used as guide in this book.

and the ease or otherwise with which the society can communicate with its members.

Section 217 (1) of the Companies and Allied Matters Act[47] provides that the notice required for all types of general meetings in respect of companies shall be 21 days from the date on which the notice is sent.

The Northern Regulations in its somewhat relatively profuse provisions require by its Regulation 22 that at least 14 days notice shall be given before any general meeting is held. Under the Eastern Rules, the length of notice required for summoning a general meeting is eight days.[48]

Societies in states without provisions can take a guide from the above provisions and provide in their bye-laws appropriate length of time for notices suitable to their individual circumstances.

Contents of Notice – Generally, the notice of a meeting must specify the exact physical venue where the meeting is to hold. It must also specify the date and time of the meeting as well as the general nature of the business to be transacted at the meeting in some detail.

Where the notice is to summon an Annual General Meeting, a statement therein to the effect that the purpose or agenda of the meeting is to transact the ordinary business of an Annual General meeting and which statement will generally be understood to mean that those businesses which are specifically reserved for the general meeting as

47. The references to this Act throughout this book are only for comparative purposes only as the Act does not apply to co-operative societies.
48. See Rule 16 (1).

contained in Regulation 9 (Delta, Edo and Lagos states), Regulations 23 and 25 (North) and Rules 16 (2) and 17 (3) (East) shall be attended to thereat.

Persons Entitled to Notice – The notice convening a co-operative society meeting shall be sent to the following persons as of right:

(a) every member of the society who shall have only one vote each as provided for in Section 25 of the Law. Such a member could be another co-operative society which may appoint a person as proxy to attend and vote on its behalf at the meeting.[49] The person so appointed by the society must himself be a member of that co-operative society.

(b) every person upon whom the ownership of the society's shares has devolved by reason of the person being a legal representative,[50] receiver or trustee in bankruptcy[51] of a member.

(c) every management committee member as such management committee member

(d) every auditor for the time being of the society

(e) the society's accountant, and

(f) the Registrar of Co-operatives who may be represented by any of the persons appointed by virtue of Section 3 of the Law to assist him.

49. Section 26 of the Law

50. The term would, in the context, relate more to a personal representative being a person entitled to deal with a deceased person's estate in accordance with his Will or in accordance with rules relating to intestacy either under customary law or otherwise. He could be either an executor under the Will or an administrator pursuant to a grant of letters in that respect.

51. See the Bankruptcy Act of 1979 Laws of the Federation of Nigeria 1990 (Cap. 30)

Decisions at Meetings – At every general meeting of a co-operative society, decisions are reached by a majority[52] of members present[53] at the meeting with a valid quorum. In so deciding, every member present shall have and exercise only one vote each as required by Section 25 of the Law provided that where there is an equality of votes, the chairman or any person presiding shall have a casting vote which he is expected to exercise in good faith and in the best interest of the society although he would naturally be entitled to also consider his personal interest.

Minutes of Meetings – Every society shall ensure that the minutes of all its meetings are properly recorded in minute books kept for the purpose. The minutes are usually recorded by the society's secretary personally or, in the case of large societies, by an employee of the society under the direct supervision of the society's secretary.

At subsequent meetings of the society, the minutes are read and adopted. Upon their adoption, the minutes are signed by the chairman whereupon they become *prima facie* evidence of the proceedings at such meetings and of the fact that the decisions taken are duly taken and deemed valid.

The Northern Regulations make provisions for these and other matters in connection with minutes of co-operative societies in the following words:

> Minutes of general meetings shall be entered in the minute book and shall contain –
>
> (a) the number and names of the members or delegates

---

52. Usually a simple majority except otherwise provided in the bye-laws.
53. See Regulation 9 (3) and Section 25 of the Law.

present at the meeting unless the names are recorded in an attendance register and the name of the person who presided at the meeting,

(b) the time fixed for the meeting and the time at which the meeting commenced,

(c) all resolutions passed or decisions made at the meeting.

At each general meeting the minutes of the previous general meeting shall be read and after confirmation with or without amendment shall be signed by the presiding officer and secretary.[54]

Conduct of Meetings and Powers of the Chairman – At the meeting of a co-operative society, the president of the society shall preside and in his absence, the vice chairman where the bye-laws provide for a vice chairman and there is one or where the is no vice chairman in his absence, any other person duly elected by a majority of those present shall preside at any general meeting.[55]

However, a meeting summoned and convened by the Registrar of Co-operatives or upon his requisition shall be presided over by him or any person appointed by him.[56]

The secretary or in his absence any other person nominated in writing by the presiding officer shall act as secretary at a general meeting and the presiding officer , if necessary, may nominate other officers to assist at the meeting.[57]

---

54. Regulation 30. See also Rule 21 of the Eastern Rules
55. Rule 19 (1) East. Compare Regulation 28 (1) North
56. See Regulation 28 (1) North
57. Regulation 28 (2) North; Rule 19 (2) East

The presiding officer or the chairman may by the decision of the meeting adjourn the meeting from time to time and from place to place but no business shall be transacted at any meeting so adjourned other than the business left unfinished at the meeting from which the adjournment took place.[58]

The Eastern Rules make provisos for an adjourned meeting to entertain new businesses at the adjourned meeting thus:

(a) a special resolution of the meeting to accept new business is passed by at least two-thirds of the members present; or

(b) at least eight days' notice has been given of the new business to be transacted.[59]

The presiding officer or chairman shall have the right to order the closure of a discussion and to put the matter to vote.[60] Other powers and functions of the person presiding over the co-operative society general meeting as chairman include to:

(a) preserve order with powers to take necessary measures reasonably required to achieve such order,

(b) See that proceedings of the meeting are conducted in a regular manner,

(c) ensure that all questions arising are fairly resolved, and

(d) generally act in good faith in the interest of the society.

---

58. Regulation 28 (3) North;
59. Rule 19 (3)
60. Regulation 28 (4) North; Rule 19 (4) East
61. All other state enactments invest this power on the Registrar

The Special General Meeting – By Regulation 9(4) made pursuant to the Law, the Registrar of Co-operatives has powers to summon a meeting of a co-operative society in such manner and at such a time and place as he may direct.[61]

Such a meeting can also be summoned at any time and by any person authorized by the Registrar. The meeting of a co-operative society summoned in these circumstances is known as a Special General Meeting. Regulation 26 of the Northern Regulations provides for the Special General Meeting thus:

> A Special General Meeting of members may be convened at any time by the committee; and on receipt of a demand stating the object of the proposed meeting signed by not less than one fifth of the members of the registered society, if such society is composed of less than one hundred members, or by twenty-five members if such society consists of more than one hundred members, it shall be the duty of the chairman of the committee to convene such a meeting giving fourteen (14) days' notice. If the chairman of the committee fails to convene a meeting within twenty-one (21) days from the receipt of a demand as aforesaid the members applying for such a meeting will have a right to convene the meeting by notice which must contain the object of the proposed meeting and a statement to the effect that the meeting is convened on the failure of the chairman of the committee to convene the meeting demanded:
> Provided that the Registrar or a person authorized by him may at any time summon a Special General Meeting of the registered society in such manner and at such time and place as he may direct. He may also direct what matters shall be discussed at the meeting. Such meeting

> shall have all the powers of a meeting called according to the Regulations.[62]

The Regulation invests the Registrar, whenever he calls a Special General Meeting, with powers to direct what matters shall be discussed at such a meeting and which meeting shall have all the powers and be subject to the same rules as a meeting called regularly and in accordance with the bye-laws of the society.

The provision of Regulation 9 (4) and those of the other states is one of the numerous provisions in the various co-operative societies enactments which confers excessive powers on the Registrar of Co-operatives in relation to the affairs of co-operative societies.[63] The provision does not specify the circumstance or circumstances in which the Registrar may be compelled to summon a Special General Meeting. This leaves it to the whims and caprices of the Registrar who is seemingly seen as a saint who would at no time be in want of uprightness. This is too subjective to be safe and it can be employed to cause harm to the societies.

Under the Companies and Allied Matters Act, similar powers are conferred on the court but in conferring the powers, the provision[64] specifically states the circumstances in which the court may order a meeting of the company. The section provides that

> If for any reason it is impracticable to call a meeting of a company … in any manner in which meetings of that company … may be called, or to conduct the meeting of the company … in the manner prescribed by the Articles

62. See also Rule 17 (2) East
63. See the discussion on Registrar's Powers (infra)
64. Section 213

> or this Act, the court may either of its own motion or on the application of any director ... or of any member ... order a meeting of the company to be called, held and conducted in such manner as the court thinks fit, and where any such order is made may give such ancillary or consequential directions as it thinks expedient.

Conferring a power of this nature on the court is to be preferred as against conferring same on individual regular civil servant with no constitutionally valid judicial powers.

The present anomalous situation as contained in Regulation 9 (4) and the other state provisions must have arisen by reference to the numerous ouster clauses contained in the co-operative societies' laws especially such as is contained in Section 51(5) of the Law to the effect that

> any decision given by the Registrar under subsection (2) or under subsection (4) shall, save as otherwise provided in subsection (6), be final and shall *not be called in question in any court.*[65] (italics supplied).

Of course, these ousters no longer represent the law in view of the provision of Section 4 (8) of the 1999 constitution expressly prohibiting the exercise of legislative powers to oust or purport to oust the jurisdiction of courts. Also, the Supreme Court's decision in *Oseyomon v Ojo*[66] is direct and specific in declaring void the provisions of Section 51 (5) of the Bendel State Co-operative Societies Law (Cap. 45) as applicable in Delta state.

Extra-Ordinary General Meeting – An Extra-ordinary General Meeting of a co-operative society is a meeting of

65. All other co-operative societies enactments contain this provision.
66. (1997) 7 SCNJ 365

the society not being a regular meeting and not called in the usual manner. It is usually summoned for the purpose of attending to some urgent and important business concerning the affairs of the society which cannot wait till the next regular meeting.

An Extra-ordinary General meeting could also be described as one summoned to attend to urgent and pressing business of the society by persons who, ordinarily and in the usual course of the society's business, do not and are not the ones to call the society's meetings. This can be so only where the society has made provisions in its bye-laws for it or under the provisions of Regulation 9 (4).

Requisitioned Meeting – A requisitioned meeting is an Extra-ordinary General Meeting summoned validly by demand of a person or persons who, in the ordinary course of the society's business, do not call or are not the persons who call meetings of the society. In effect, a meeting called by the Registrar of Co-operatives under Regulation 9 (4), for instance, is a requisitioned meeting.[67] In other words, a Special General Meeting demanded either by the Registrar or by members is an Extra-ordinary General Meeting.

Under the Regulation 9 (4), there can be a requisitioned meeting not called by the Registrar but by members. This is possible only where the bye-laws of the society make provisions for it. In the North and the East, Regulation 26 and Rule 17 (2) already create the right in favour of members hence whether the bye-laws further incorporates the right or not will not be material.

In practice, the provisions of Regulation 9 (4) can

67. See Regulation 26 North; Rule 17 (2) East.

be expanded in the society's bye-laws to include the right of members who meet certain requirements or criteria to call meetings in the following manner:

> An Extra-ordinary General Meeting may be called at any time by a simple majority of the members of the management committee or on a request in writing from the Registrar of Co-operatives or from not less than 25% of the total number of members of the society.

A Requisitioned Meeting or an Extra-ordinary General Meeting or a Special General Meeting may, in effect, be called

(a) any time (i.e. other than the usual times for the holding of the society's regular meetings) and
(b) by a simple majority of the management committee members, or
(c) on a request in writing from the Registrar of Co-operatives, or
(d) on a request in writing from not less than 25% of the total number of members of the society.

The Registrar of Co-operatives – In the management and administration of co-operative societies, the Registrar of Co-operatives performs certain far reaching functions and duties that he cannot be ignored in a discussion of how co-operative societies are run.

The Registrar[68] of Co-operatives is a civil servant regularly appointed by the Public Service Commission[69] of

68. In Lagos State and under Decree 90, he is referred to as Director of Co-operatives.
69. In Lagos State, the appointing authority is not stated in Section 3 of its Cap. C15. The 1956 Cap. 26 of the North has it as the Minister (now Commissioner) with responsibility for co-operative societies.

his state. In all the enactments, the enabling provision for the appointment of the Registrar is in Section 3 with substantially the same wordings. It runs thus:

> The Public Service Commission may appoint a person to be Registrar of Co-operative Societies, and may appoint persons to assist such registrar, and may, by notice published in state gazette, confer on any such persons all or any of the powers of a registrar under this law.

Qualification for Appointment – Section 8 (1) of the Companies and Allied Matters Act provides that

> There shall be appointed ... a Registrar-General who shall be qualified to practice as a legal practitioner in Nigeria and has been so qualified for not less than 10 years and in addition, has had experience in company law practice or administration for not less than 8 years.

None of the enactments on co-operative societies in Nigeria contains a provision such as the above specifying what ought to be the minimum qualification of the person who is appointed as Registrar of Co-operatives. This is an obvious legislative lacuna which ought to be urgently filled.

Powers and Duties of Registrar – The powers and duties of the Registrar are scattered all through the Law as there is no specific provision thereat which lists or enumerates what his functions under the Law are supposed to be. However, his duties and powers as can be gathered from a global consideration of the Law are quite similar to the functions of the Corporate Affairs Commission[70] which are contained in Section 7 of the Companies and Allied Matters Act thus:

> The functions of the Commission shall be to –
> subject to Section 541 administer this Act including

70. Established under Section 1 (1) of the Companies and Allied Matters Act.

(a) the regulation and supervision of the formation, incorporation, registration, management, and winding up of companies under or pursuant to this Act;

(b) establish and maintain a companies registry and offices in all the states of the Federation suitably and adequately equipped to discharge its functions under this Act or any other law in respect of which it is charged with responsibility;

(c) arrange or conduct an investigation into the affairs of any company where the interests of the shareholders and the public so demand;

(d) perform such other functions as may be specified by any Act or enactment; and

(e) undertake such other activities as are necessary or expedient for giving full effect to the provisions of this Act.

Registration of Societies – The application for the registration of every co-operative society within a state is made to the Registrar by virtue of section 6 of the Law. If he is satisfied that the applying society has complied with the provisions of the Law, he then registers the society.[71]

Registries and Offices – The Registrar maintains a central office[71] usually in the state capital where all records of co-operative society activities are kept and zonal offices[72]

71. Section 7 (1) of the Law.

72. These offices are not called registries like the companies registry but they perform substantially the functions of a registry

usually at the headquarters of every local government within the state.

Investigating Societies' Affairs – The Registrar of Co-operative Societies may of his own motion, and shall on the application of a majority of the committee, or of not less than one-third of the members of a registered society, hold an enquiry or direct some person authorized by him by order in writing in this behalf to hold an enquiry into the constitution, working and financial condition of a co-operative society.[73]

Where the Registrar decides to hold an enquiry as above, all officers and members of the society shall be under a duty to furnish him with all such information as regard the affairs of the society and shall produce the cash in hand and such books, accounts, papers, and securities of the society as the Registrar or the person authorized by him may require.

Indeed, the whole of Part 6 of the Law dealing with *audit, inspection and inquiry* confers on the Registrar extensive powers to take over a co-operative society and to audit the accounts, and inspect the books of the society with unimpeded access thereto.

In the course of exercising the powers conferred on him under this part, any officer, agent, servant or member of the society who neglects, fails or refuses to co-operate with the Registrar or any person authorized by him does so at pains of imprisonment for six months or a fine of two hundred Naira or to both such imprisonment and fine.

These powers and duties of the Registrar are so far-

73. Section 38 of the Law; Section 47 Cap. C15 Lagos; Section 42 of the Law (East); Section 41 of the Law (North).

reaching that they are to be considered excessive in the hands of an individual officer no matter the number of assistants appointed to assist him. Besides they tend to offend democratic tenets which is one of the universal principles under which co-operative societies are organized and run.[74]

This arrangement which personalizes such excessive powers may be justifiable in 1935 when the first co-operative enactment came into force and a time when capably trained personnel for running a co-operative registry would be hard to come by.

At the time, co-operative societies were regarded as small time business meant for poor struggling persons who were also mostly illiterate and uneducated. But times have changed and the business of co-operative societies is no longer small time business but a multi-billion Naira affair with highly educated and sophisticated persons involved.

With governments at almost all levels running poverty alleviation schemes and micro-credit programmes employing the machinery of co-operative societies for disbursing loans, nobody needs a prophet to predict that, before long, co-operative societies will be at the centre of vigorous litigation in Nigeria. To be proactive, the duties, functions and powers of the Registrar of Co- operative Societies need be depersonalized, better defined and well packaged for a greater efficiency geared towards a more satisfactory service delivery organization. It is humbly recommended that an arrangement similar to the Corporate Affairs Commission with a Registrar in charge as the accounting officer for co-operative societies will be ideal.

74. See Chapter One (supra).

Chapter Eight

Co-operative Funds and Assets

A co-operative society ... does not ... own and hold property through trustees in view of its own legal personality - supra

In Chapter One, the concept of co-operative societies was discussed and a number of definitions and descriptions considered whereat a co-operative society was seen as a special form of business organization. Every business organization must of necessity have capital.

A business organization in the strict sense is one set up for the purpose of trade and which has profit as its main and ultimate goal.[1] Its capital is part of the resources it deploys into the business in order to actualize its ultimate goal of profit. It is therefore a factor deployed for the production of wealth. In other words, capital is wealth used in the creation or production of further wealth.

Although an accountant will professionally define capital as the amount by which the value of a company's assets exceeds the value of its liabilities, capital is used in this chapter in the sense in which an economist will define the term which is that it is a stock of resources or stock of wealth which is set aside and put into the production of further wealth and this may be in the form of material non-material and human input.

In business terms, capital is the consideration which a business man or an investor furnishes for the benefit, interest, dividend or profit which he derives from a given venture.

---

1. See Section 671 (1) of the Companies and Allied Matters Act 1990 as published in the Laws of the Federation 2004 as Cap. C.20. See also Chapter One (supra) at p. 24 *et seq*.

The various co-operative societies enactments do not make direct provisions for co-operative capital safe for references to the term here and there within the Law. The term is to be found however in some of the definitions and descriptions of co-operative societies[2] and in the story of the Rochdale Society[3] where 'twenty-eight poor but intelligent weavers' were said to have been engaged in a

> severe struggle to give two pence a week to raise some capital.

In other words, it is on record that members of the Rochdale Co-operative Society, which is said to be the model for thousands of other co-operative societies, had to set aside parts of their earnings by way of weekly savings in order to raise the capital which they needed for realizing their co-operative business and objectives.

In the context of this chapter, co-operative capital refers to all that stock of resources or stock of wealth set aside and which a co-operative society is able to raise for the purpose of deploying same towards the attainment of its declared co-operative objectives. This involves the pooling of resources by the society's members for the meeting of the stated objectives.[4]

Nature of Co-operative Capital – The nature of a co-operative society's capital depends on the type[5] of society. An agricultural co-operative society may accept agricultural produce as capital in lieu of cash whereas a thrift and credit society would very unlikely be willing to

2. See pp. 9 – 10 *supra.*
3. See penultimate paragraph at p. 3 *supra.*
4. These are usually contained in the bye-laws as objects of the society.
5. See Chapter Four *supra.*

accept anything other than cash as capital. Section 135 of the Companies and Allied Matters Act makes provisions for payments for company shares in cash or by valuable consideration other than cash or partly in cash and partly by a valuable consideration other than cash.[6]

Although the co-operative enactments do not make direct provisions relating to co-operative capital, a society's capital, like for companies, can be in cash or valuable consideration other than cash or partly in cash and partly by valuable consideration other than cash.

By Regulation 4 (1) (i), it is however required that every co-operative society must make provisions in its bye-laws as to the manner of raising its share capital. Therefore, every society shall be free to prescribe in what form or the manner by which its capital shall be raised including as to whether it shall exclusively be payment of cash or by valuable consideration other than cash or partly in cash and partly by valuable consideration other than cash.

Sources of Co-operative Capital – By Regulation 4 (1) (i), every society is required to make provisions in its bye-laws as to the manner of raising its share capital while Section 23 of the Law provides that

> no member of a registered society shall exercise the rights of a member unless or until he has made such payment to the society in respect of membership or acquired such interest in the society as may be prescribed by the Regulations or bye-laws.[7]

In effect, every member of a co-operative society owes the society the duty to:

6. See Chapter Five *supra*
7. See also Section 26 of the Law (East).

(a) pay to the society a fee in respect of membership or
(b) acquire an interest in the society

both as may be prescribed by the Regulations made pursuant to the Law or as prescribed in the particular society's bye-laws.

In other words, a co-operative society shall be free to prescribe in its bye-laws the payment of membership fees or the acquisition of interests in the society by its members. Such prescription may also be as contained in the Regulations made pursuant to the Law. Consequently, in practice it is commonplace to have co-operative society bye-laws contain a bye-law to the effect that

> the funds of the society shall be composed of
> (i) an undetermined number of shares of the value of N1.00 per share;
> (ii) entrance fees as fixed by the management committee from time to time;
> (iii) savings of members as defined in these bye-laws;
> (iv) deposits and loans from non-members as provided for in these bye-laws;
> (v) surpluses arising from the business of the society and
> (vi) miscellaneous sources as approved by the director of co-operatives or the management committee.[8]

8. See also Bye-law 15 of the Northern Model Bye-Laws and Bye-law 37 (Delta).

Membership Fees – As already stated, by Section 23 of the Law, a registered society can raise its capital by way of membership or entrance fees which must have been prescribed either by the Regulation or the society's bye-laws.[9]

The amount to be paid as such entrance fee is usually fixed from time to time by the management committee of the particular society or the society at general meetings. The amount raised as capital from this source is usually very insignificant.

Shares – A good example of what Section 23 of the Law refers to as an 'interest in the society' is shares. The Law does not define the term shares nor does it contain any direct provision requiring the raising of shares by co-operative societies by way of shares[10]. The capital of a company is usually expressed in shares except where the company is not one with a share capital. By section 79 (3) of the Companies and Allied Matters Act1990,[11] in every company having a share capital,

> each member shall be a shareholder of the company and shall hold at least one share.

A share in the above context has been defined as

> the interest of a shareholder in a company measured by a

9. It is more realistic to have this prescription in the bye-laws and not in the Regulations since Regulations are not made by individual societies.
10. But see Rule 11 (1) of the Eastern Rules which provides that *'a society's bye-laws may provide that every person admitted as a member shall be deemed to have subscribed to a stated number of shares by virtue of his admission'*. See also Section 28 of the Law for a reference to *'share capital'*.
11. As published in the 2004 Laws of the Federation of Nigeria as Cap. C.20.

> sum of money for the purpose of liability in the first place, and of interest in the second, but also consisting of a series of mutual covenants entered into by all the shareholders *inter se* in accordance with the *provisions of the Companies and Allied Matters Act*

and that a share

> is not a sum of money ... but is an interest measured by a sum of money and made up of various rights contained in the contract, including the right to a sum of money of a more or less amount.[12]

To say therefore that one has a share in a co-operative society, as in a company, is to refer to the interest that person has in that co-operative society which interest is measured by a sum of money for the purpose of that person's liability towards the co-operative society on the one hand and for the purpose of interest (i.e. benefit) on the other hand. When therefore a society's bye-laws provide that

> the funds of the society shall be composed of (i) an undetermined number of shares of the value of N1.00 per share,

it is stating in effect that the capital of the society, being one with a share capital, shall be divided into units of the value of N1.00 each which members can acquire subject usually to a minimum and a maximum.

Minimum Shareholding – As shown above, the Companies and Allied Matters Act provides in relation to

12. *Borland's Trustee v Steel* (1901) 1 Ch. 279, 288 per Farwell J. See also Section 650 of the Companies and Allied Matters Act 1990 which defines a share as *'the interests in a company's share capital of a member who is entitled to share in the capital or income of such company'.*

companies that every member of a company shall 'hold at least one share' in the company of which he is such member. Neither the Co-operative Societies Law nor the Regulations contain similar provisions in relation to co-operative societies specifying the minimum number of shares which a member of a co-operative society must hold as such member.

But by Section 23 of the Law, no member can exercise the rights of a member of a co-operative society

> unless or until he has ... acquired such interest in the society as may be prescribed by the Regulations or Bye-laws.

The Regulations are silent as to the 'such interest' which a member should acquire before he can exercise the rights of a member. This means that the minimum interest which a member must acquire to be entitled to the exercise of rights of membership of a society may be prescribed in the Bye-laws especially where, as under the Law, the Regulations do not specify.

Under the Eastern Rules, it is required that a co-operative society may provide in its bye-laws that a person admitted to the society shall be deemed to have subscribed to a stated number of shares by virtue of his admission. The reference to a 'stated number of shares' is obviously a reference to a minimum number of shares which such an admitted member must subscribe to before he can be entitled to the rights of membership. In practice, this provision is usually reflected in most co-operative societies bye-laws in the following manner:

> Every member shall hold at least ....[13] fully paid[14] shares which shall not be transferrable[15] except to a nominee in accordance with the provisions of these bye-laws.

The position of the law therefore is that:

(a) every co-operative society should have a share capital,[16]

(b) every member of a co-operative society should hold or acquire an interest in the society by way of shareholding,

(c) every society shall be free to determine the quantum of shares which should be held or acquired by every member as a minimum requirement, and

(d) such minimum requirement shall be provided for in the society's bye-laws.

Maximum Shareholding – Section 28 of the Law makes express provision to the effect that

> no member, other than a registered society, shall hold more than one-fifth[17] of the share capital of any co-operative society.[18]

The provision is clear and self-explanatory. But observation must be made that there is no indication as to the size of the share capital of a co-operative society for purposes of computing the one-fifth. This leaves the share capital of most societies usually fluid.

---

13. The blank space contains a figure.
14. The monetary value of the shares are specified under 'Sources of Funds' in the Bye-laws.
15. See Rule 11 (2) of the Eastern Rules for a somewhat detailed provision on transfer of shares *inter vivos.*
16. In practice, some societies wrongfully do not.
17. Twenty percent.
18. All co-operative statutes including Cap. N98 have this provision.

Section 99 (2) of the Companies and Allied Matters Act expressly provides that

> no company ... shall be registered with an authorized share capital less than the authorized minimum share capital.

For purposes of companies, the Act then goes on to define 'authorised share capital' to mean

> N10,000.00 in the case of a private company and N500,000.00 in the case of a public company

while 'share capital' is defined as the share capital of a company at any given time.[19]

In practice and under the law, the amount of the share capital of a company is stated in the company's memorandum of association as the authorized share capital. So that when subsection 1 of Section 99 of the Act requires that not less than 25% of that capital be taken by the subscribers of the memorandum, the computation thereof shall constitute no difficulties and it will be easy to appreciate the size or quantum of the shares which must be taken as a requirement under the mandatory provision of the Act.

This is not the situation under the various co-operative societies statutes in relation to the determination of the share capital of co-operative societies which is not readily ascertainable at any given time by reference to the bye-laws. Some co-operative bye-laws contain a provision under 'sources of funds' that

> the funds of the society shall be composed of (among others) of an undetermined number of shares of the value of N ...... per share.

19. See Section 650 of the Act.

That the number of shares is stated to be 'undetermined' emphasizes the uncertain size of a co-operative society's share capital at any given time. This makes the provisions of Section 28 of the Law to the effect that no member of a co-operative society can hold more than twenty percent of the share capital of a society is itself vague.

It is therefore to be humbly recommended in this respect that the provisions of the various co-operative statutes need to be modified make them similar to those of Section 99 of the Companies and Allied matters Act but in such manner as to retain the peculiar characteristics of co-operatives.

Rationale for the Restriction – It is difficult to explain the reason for the restriction in Section 28 of the Law given that Section 25 thereof provides for an equality of votes in the conduct of the affairs of the society irrespective shareholding. The provisions of Section 25 is clear and unambiguous that irrespective of the number of shares held by any member of a co-operative society, every member shall have and exercise only one vote in the conduct of the affairs of a co-operative society. Under the law of companies, the opposite is the case as the number of votes exercisable by a member of the company is directly a function of the number of shares held.

Under the Universal Principles of Co-operatives, the payment of interests and dividends on the basis of the shareholding is forbidden. It should therefore be immaterial that any one member has a majority shareholding in excess of twenty percent as prescribed by the Law as dividends and interests as the end of the trading season will be computed only on the basis of the member's patronage of the society's business and not on the size of his shareholding.[20]

It is however plausible that the provision is designed to double check tyranny within the society or to avoid a situation where a single member arrogates to himself an overbearing importance in the conduct of the affairs of the society on the basis of his huge shareholding. Such a situation will defeat the other universal principle which requires that co-operative societies shall be run democratically. This is partly the reason why some co-operatives make provisions in their bye-laws for a mandatory equal number of shares to be held by all members.

However, where a society permits the freedom for members to acquire any number of shares of the society as they are financially capable of holding, Section 28 puts the maximum number of shares that can be held by any one member at not more than twenty percent of the total share capital of the society. Where a member becomes possessed of shares of a society the value of which is in excess of the maximum holding permissible under the Law, the member shall be required by the society to forfeit the excess to the

20. In practice, this universal principle is observed more in the breach especially by credit and thrift societies on the strength of an argument that the business of credit and thrift societies is financed in the main by funds realized from payments by members for the society's shares and which funds forms the capital base of the society from where loans are advanced to members who then pay interests thereon which create the surplus of the society. Payment for the shares therefore amounts to patronage of the society's business.

management committee who shall either sell same to other members, especially newly admitted members; or buy them and hold same in trust for the society which shall dispose of them as it shall see fit. This is usually provided for in the bye-laws.

Savings – Savings by members of a co-operative society is a veritable and regular source of funds for a society especially in credit and thrift societies where it is a mandatory requirement.

Savings is simply money set aside by a person for future. It is a reference to that part of a person's income which is not immediately required for use and is therefore put away or put aside for use at some future date. One of the advantages of co-operatives is that it encourages savings. Hence it is usual for credit and thrift societies to include in their bye-laws a provision to the effect that

> every member shall make regular thrift savings which shall be withdrawable only with the permission of the management committee for necessary or productive purpose.

Nature of Shares and Savings Distinguished - As veritable sources of funds, savings and shares constitute the most lucrative for co-operative societies. They are however different in their nature and character. Whereas shares are not acquired by members on a regular basis, savings are made piecemeal over time and on a regular basis.

While savings are more open to the member's control as he chooses, shares are not. A member enjoys greater freedom to withdraw from his savings but he is not usually so free with shares generally regarded as not withdrawable unconditionally. This is because shares form the capital base of the society. Shares constitute the foundation upon which the co-operative house is built hence they are not to be freely tampered with by uncontrolled and unrestricted withdrawals otherwise the society will collapse. The conditions for the withdrawal of shares are usually spelt out in the bye-laws and include that

> if at the end of the financial year the society's financial situation is favourable, the management committee may repay to any member whose membership was terminated[21] during the year a sum not exceeding the amount paid by him on account of shares provided that not more than five per cent of the total paid up share capital shall be thus paid out in any one year without the Registrar's permission.[22]

In effect, no withdrawal of a co-operative society shares by a member is to be allowed unless

(a) upon the termination of the membership of the member seeking to withdraw his shares,

(b) the financial situation of the society at the end of a trading season[23] is favourable as disclosed by the society's financial statements.

(c) the termination of the membership of the member took place during the year[24] and

(d) the payment on account of withdrawal of shares is made at the end of the financial year.

Accordingly, the management committee of a co-operative society is not under a duty to immediately make payment in

21. See 'Cessation of Membership' at Chapter Five *supra.*
22. See Bye-law 40 of the Delta State Model Bye-laws.
23. This means no payment can be made in respect of withdrawals midstream a financial year.
24. There may be unpaid withdrawals outstanding from previous years.

respect of an application by a member for withdrawal of shares. Also, the committee is precluded from paying more than five per cent[25] of the society's paid up capital in any one year on account of withdrawal of shares without the permission or approval of the Registrar.

With savings, on the other hand, withdrawals thereof carry less onerous conditions and regulations as the bye-laws will usually require only the approval of the management committee subject to other usual subsisting rules and guidelines made by the society. In this respect, the usual provision in the bye-laws runs to the effect that

> every member shall make regular savings which shall be withdrawable only with the approval of the management committee for necessary or productive purposes.

Societies without Share Capital – Co-operative societies without share capital usually make provisions only with respect to withdrawals of savings and deposits prohibiting same in words such as

> no member shall have a right to withdraw[26] part or all of his savings except on termination or final withdrawal of membership from the society.

Deposits are usually made withdrawable provided a notice in writing of at least a given duration, usually not less than seven days, shall have been served on the management committee by the member seeking to withdraw his deposit or part thereof.

---

25. This is a bye-law provision which means every society is free to fix the percentage as it suits its particular purposes.
26. The same reasons for prohibiting unconditional withdrawal of shares are applicable *mutatis mutandi* for savings since the savings in a society without a share capital form the financial base of the society.

Societies without share capital are a common occurrence with staff co-operative societies[27] whose bye-laws make provisions for deductions of savings from members' salaries at source by the employer and which deductions are credited to the account of the staff-member in the custody of the co-operative society. Such staff-members usually execute an authorization in favour of the employer for to give effect to the deductions.

The Society's Rights over Members' Shares – Notwithstanding that the shares or savings of a member may not be unconditionally withdrawable, they remain the property of the member. Whatever contributions to the business of the society that is made by a member of the society either by way of shares, savings or deposits remain the personal property of the member but which remain in the custody of the society for the purposes or objects of the society.

Therefore, a member of a co-operative society may at his discretion recover or call in such property at any time but subject to his compliance with subsisting rules and guidelines as contained in the society's bye-laws in relation thereto.

Society's Charge upon Shares – However, so long as the property in the member's shares, savings or deposits remain in the custody of the society, the Law provides that it shall be subject to a charge or set-off in favour of the society in respect of any debt due from the member to the society. This charging and set off rights are expressly conferred on the society by Section 16 of the Law thus:

---

27. See Chapter Four *supra* on Types and Formation of Societies.

> a registered society shall have a charge[28] upon the shares or interests in the capital and on the deposits of a member or past member or deceased member and upon any dividend,[29] bonus, or surplus payable to a member or past member or to the estate of a deceased member in respect of any debt due to the society from such member or past member or estate, and may set-off[30] any sum credited or payable to a member or past member or estate of a deceased member in or towards payment of any such debt.

The right to charge which this provision vests on the society covers not only shares but other interests of the member in the society's capital including bonuses, dividends or surpluses to which he has become entitled and deposits lodged with the society by the member including a member who may have withdrawn his membership or may have died.

The provision is Section 16 of the Law is especially useful to thrift and credit co-operative societies which are usually prone to being owed by their members to whom they have in the course of their usual and ordinary business advanced loans. Such societies can legally fall upon this

---

28. A right of interest over property usually of a company created or which exists in favour of a creditor as security for debt and which confers priority on the debt over unsecured debts. It comes either as a fixed charge i.e. where the right is attached to a specific property; or a floating charge where it is not attached to any specific property but to circulating assets to which the right will not crystallize until or upon the happening of a stated event.
29. The entitlement of a shareholder of an enterprise, usually a company, paid or payable to him from the profits of the enterprise. See *Kotoye v Saraki* (1994) 7 NWLR (Pt. 357) 414, 467.
30. A cross claim which operates also as a defence to the plaintiff's action.

provision in recovering the debts owed them by recalcitrant debtor-members.

This will be so notwithstanding the provisions of Regulation 24 to the effect that

> the shares of a society may not be pledged[31] to the society by any of its members as security for a loan.

The position of the law therefore is that whereas the Regulations forbid the pledging of a society's shares to the society by members of the society as security for the society's loans to such members, the Law on the other hand invests on the society powers to create charges in its favour over the shares of members in the society's capital to secure any debts, including debts arising from loans advanced to such members, owed to the society by such members.

A debt over which a charge is created is a secured debt and the creditor, in this case the society, is a secured creditor whose debt enjoys priority over all unsecured debts[32] such that in the event of the society going into liquidation or otherwise going under, the secured debts will first be met before consideration is given to the unsecured debts.

31. Same thing as a pawn which is a bailment of property as security for a debt. See *Labode v Otubu* (2001) 7 NWLR (Pt. 712) 256, 276 and *Halliday v Holgate* (1868) LR 3 Exch. 299. See also Chianu Emeka (2000) *Law of Securities for Bank Advances* (Ambik Press, Benin City) at page 9. A bailment involves the transfer of possession of a property from a bailor to the bailee. In the case of co-operatives loan, the shares (i.e. the property) which the Regulation forbids being pledged for a loan are usually at all material times in the possession of the society.
32. See Section 15 of the Law for how charges created in favour of co-operative societies operate.

Such a charge may extend to other interests which a member may have in the society's capital and to any deposits made by members with the society as well as to bonuses, dividends or surpluses to which such members may have become entitled or shall be entitled to.

Society's Right of Set-off – A co-operative society is also entitled to set up a set-off in respect of debts owed to it by a member against any sum of money which is due to such a member and credited or payable to him by the society.

A set-off generally operated as a cross claim to an action whereby the defendant against whom the plaintiff claims a sum of money asserts by his cross claim that the plaintiff also owes him a sum of money. In other words, a set-off is a monetary cross claim which also operates as a defence to the claim of the plaintiff.

Although a set-off is a cross claim, it depends on the existence of the plaintiff's action for its subsistence. Therefore, if the plaintiff discontinues his action, the set-off is automatically also discontinued.

A co-operative society's right of set-off is statutory[33] and may be enforced extra-judicially by the society against any sum credited or payable to a member or past member or the estate of a deceased member in or towards payment of any debt due to the society from such member. This is obvious from the wordings of Section 16 which is to the effect that

> a registered society … may set-off any sum credited or payable to ….

Co-operative Shares Privileged – Except by the provisions of Section 16 of the Law which permits the

33. See Section 16 of the Law.

charging of a member's shareholdings as discussed above, the shares or other interests of a member in the capital of a co-operative society are privileged by way of exemption from being liable to attachment and sale under any court order in respect of any debt or liability incurred by a member of a co-operative society.[34]

The Sheriffs and Civil Process Act[35] and the Judgement (Enforcement) Rules made pursuant to the Act make provisions for the enforcement of judgements of courts in Nigeria. Such enforcement involves the calling into play the coercive powers of the courts in respect of their judgements and orders.[36] By these enactments,

> any sum of money payable under a judgement of the court may be recovered ... by execution[37] against the goods and chattels and the immovable property of the judgement debtor.

The 'goods and chattels and the immovable property' as attached are usually sold for cash to raise the judgement debt. By Section 83 of the Act, properties such as money in bank accounts and shares can be directly attached by garnishee proceedings.

The provisions of Section 17 of the Co-operative Societies Law however makes the Sheriffs and Civil Process Act together with the Enforcement Rules and the

34. Section 17.
35. Laws of the Federation of Nigeria (Cap. 407) 1990. Some states such as Delta. Edo and Lagos have enacted their own Sheriffs and Civil Process laws which contain provisions impair material with the Act.
36. See Miakpo Emiaso (2010) *Law, Practice and Procedure: Area Customary Courts in Nigeria* (Peakmans Ltd., Lagos) at page 291.
37. Same as attachment

equivalent state laws inapplicable to the shares and interests of a co-operative society member in the capital of the society. This is a special privilege conferred by the Law on the co-operative shares and other interests in the capital of a co-operative society. The exemption from attachment privilege is also binding on the assignee in insolvency of a co-operative society member and a receiver duly appointed in respect of a member's bankruptcy proceedings.[38]

Other Sources of Co-operative Funds – The remaining sources of a co-operative society's funds are more miscellaneous in nature than substantial. They are not regular sources of income and they include, as listed supra,[39] deposits[40] and loans[41]made to the society by non-members, surpluses arising from the business of the society which are ploughed back and sundry other sources such as fines and other penalties approved by the society and provided for in the bye-laws.

38. Section 17 of the Law.
39. See p. 220
40. Very few societies receive deposits from non members or even members.
41. Some societies are recipients of government micro-credit facilities.

Chapter Nine
Co-operative Disputes

' ... the law impose(s) no responsibility on the (party) to have the dispute determined firstly by an arbitrator as a condition precedent to seeking remedies ... by action'. – Iguh JSC in Oseyomon v Ojo

Section 51 of the Law describes a referable dispute as one which touches the business of a registered society and which has arisen

(a) among members, past members, and persons claiming through members, past members and deceased members; or

(b) between a member, a past member or person claiming through a member, past member or deceased member and the society, its management committee, or any officer, agent or servant of the society; or

(c) between the society or its management committee and any officer, agent or servant of the society; or

(d) between the society and any other registered society.

By this description, only disputes which touch and concern the business of a co-operative society and which dispute is among or between persons who are current members or persons who are past members or persons claiming through members, past members, deceased members, the management committee, officers, agents, servants, and another co-operative society qualify as co-operative disputes and which may be referred to the registrar for determination.

A co-operative dispute may arise from a myriad of possible situations which may include:

(a) failure of members especially officers of the society to observe the society's bye-laws, the Regulations and even the provisions of the Law;
(b) non-repayment of overdue loans by members;
(c) ultra-*vires* acts or outright deviation from the registered objects of the society;
(d) misapplication or misappropriation of society funds;
(e) abuse or misuse of properties belonging to the society;
(f) arbitrariness or high-handedness on the part of the society's leadership involving sometimes the application of arbitrary rules and even unlawful rules;
(g) failure, neglect or refusal by the leadership to render accounts or submit reports of activities of the society as and at when due or at all;
(h) failure to call and hold periodic and regular meetings especially the annual general meeting;
(i) non-declaration of or inability to make and declare surplus and, by implication, dividends;
(j) personalization of the society whereby individuals arrogate to themselves ownership of the society;
(k) refusal of incumbent officers to conduct elections or to vacate office.

The list of what may give rise to a co-operative dispute is inexhaustible so long as membership and the running of co-operative societies remain activities of human beings and since disputes and differences are social imperatives. In every situation however, for a dispute to qualify as a referable co-operative dispute, it must touch and concern the business of the co-operative society.

Under Cap. C15 of the Lagos State, Section 44 thereof specifically excludes disputes which, though touching and concerning the business of the society, are in connection with 'disciplinary action taken by the society or its committee against a paid servant of the society'. Also under the same section in the Lagos State Law, where the dispute

> is one between a society registered in Lagos State and a society registered in another state of Nigeria of which the law contains provisions similar to those contained

in the Lagos State law particularly section 44 thereof, the dispute shall be referred simultaneously to both the Lagos State director of co-operatives and the equivalent officer of the other state both of whom shall be referred to as 'the joint directors' for the purpose of deciding the dispute.

A dispute touching and concerning the business of a co-operative society but which is between any of the above listed parties to a co-operative dispute and a third party e.g. a trader or supplier of goods (not being a member of the society) with whom the society had contracted in the ordinary course of the third party's business is not a dispute in the contemplation of Section 51 of the Law.

But if the third party is a co-operative society, the dispute is a co-operative dispute subject to reference to the registrar. If the co-operative society is registered in Lagos State and the third party co-operative society is registered in another state within Nigeria, the dispute shall be referred to a panel of 'joint directors'.

A claim by a co-operative society for a debt or a demand due to the society from a member or a past member, or a deceased member's nominee or personal representative is deemed a co-operative dispute touching and concerning the business of the society which is referable to the registrar; and it shall not be material that the claim is admitted or not.

Parties to a Co-operative Dispute – When any dispute which is subject to reference as discussed above arises, Regulation 21 (1) provides that any of the following parties may make a reference of it to the registrar:

(a) the management committee;
(b) the society itself by resolution in general meeting;
(c) any party to the dispute;
(d) any member of the society if the dispute is in relation to a sum due from a member of the society's management committee.

Compulsory Arbitration – Every dispute coming within the purview of Section 51 (1) of the Law must be referred to the registrar for decision. The provision, by implication, incorporates a mandatory arbitration agreement into the terms of operations of every co-operative society usually contained in the bye-laws and which bye-laws are binding on every member of the society including all persons who become qualified as party to a co-operative dispute.

Section 2 of the Arbitration and Conciliation Act[1] provides that an arbitration agreement can be revoked by agreement of the parties or by leave of court. Therefore the general position of the law is that a party to a dispute cannot be compelled to arbitrate[2] though no party to an

1. Cap. 19 Laws of the Federation 1990. This Act, by its section 35 is made not applicable to co-operative societies but is referred to herein only as a comparative guide.
2. See Ephraim Akpata: (1997)*The Nigerian Arbitration Law in Focus* (West African Book Publishers Ltd., Lagos) at p.21.

arbitration agreement may sustain a substantive action in court without first exhausting the terms of his agreement as to arbitration.

But Section 51 of the Law appears to leave a party to a co-operative dispute no choice. He must arbitrate and the outcome of such arbitration is binding on him and even so without any rights of appeal to the regular courts.

Powers of the Registrar under Arbitration – All the co-operative societies enactments in Nigeria are replete with provisions investing the Registrars of co-operative societies with sweeping powers including judicial powers especially in relation to the determination of disputes. This is because, as has been demonstrated above, every party to a co-operative dispute must arbitrate and all such co-operative disputes must be referred to the Registrar who, by virtue of subsection 2 of Section 51 of the Law, upon his receipt of the reference shall be at liberty to do any one of the following three things:

(a) decide the dispute himself i.e. play the role of a judge (a judicial function) in respect thereto; or
(b) refer it to a panel of three arbitrators for disposal; or
(c) appoint an arbitrator to decide the dispute.[3]

These powers of the Registrar with regards to the determination of every dispute touching the business of a registered co-operative society are very wide indeed. His decisions, in some cases, are final and are not to be called in question in any court.[4]

Even where the Registrar has referred a dispute to an arbitrator under his powers to do so as contained in

3. Regulation 21 (2).
4. Section 51 (5) (a) of the Law.

subsection 2 paragraph (b) of Section 51, he can nevertheless withdraw the dispute from the arbitrator, only subject to the provisions of any regulation; and decide the dispute himself.[5]

Also, the Registrar has powers to, either of his own motion or, on the application of a party to a dispute already decided by an arbitrator as a result of a reference, revise such a decision. This means that the registrar also functions as an appeal court even over matters where no party to a decided dispute has filed an appeal since he may revise a decision of an arbitrator acting on his own motion.

It needs stating that it is doubtful if these powers of the registrar meet with today's position of our constitutional law especially in view of the provisions of Section 4 (8) of the 1999 Constitution of the Federal Republic of Nigeria and in the face of quite a number of decisions of the Supreme Court of Nigeria including *Abu v Odugbo*[6] and *Oseyomon v Ojo.*[7] The constitution provides that

> the exercise of legislative powers ... shall be subject to the jurisdiction of courts of law and of judicial tribunals established by law, and accordingly, the National Assembly or a House of Assembly shall not enact any law, that ousts or purports to oust the jurisdiction of a court of law or of a judicial tribunal established by law.[8]

The provisions of Section 51 of the Law that 'such dispute *shall* be referred to the Registrar for decision' and that the

5. Section 51 (3).
6. (2001) FWLR (Pt. 69) 1260.
7. (1997) 7 S.C.N.J 365.
8. Section 4 (8) Constitution of the Federal Republic of Nigeria 1999.

Registrar's decision shall 'be final and ... not be called in question in any court' clearly amount to a provision of a law which 'ousts or purports to oust the jurisdiction of a court of law ...'. This is contrary to the provisions of the constitution and therefore doubtful if any court in Nigeria will give effect to it.

In the *Oseyomon v Ojo* case, the Supreme Court of Nigeria per Iguh J.S.C stated that the 1979 constitution conferred unlimited jurisdiction on the High Courts of a state and that

> all existing laws and or any provisions in a state law which are not in conformity with the provisions of the constitution or tend to derogate from the powers of such courts shall, to the extent of such inconsistency, be void

and that therefore

> the provisions of Sections 51 (1) (a), 51 (1) (b) and 51 (6) of the Co-operative Societies Law, Cap.45, Laws of Bendel State of Nigeria, 1976 which are state enactments must be regarded as void in so far as they purport to limit or oust the jurisdiction of the High Courts as therein provided contrary to the provisions of the 1979 constitution.[9]

The Supreme Court in this line of cases was construing Section 236 of the 1979 constitution which expressly defined the jurisdiction of the states High Courts to be 'unlimited'. In the 1999 constitution, this word has been dropped but it is submitted that notwithstanding this dropping of 'limited' from Section 272 of this constitution, the combined effect of the section with the provisions of

9. (1997) 7 S.C.N.J 365, 380. See the Supreme Court also in *Abu v Odugbo* (2001) FWLR (Pt. 69) 1260 and *Okulate v Awosanya* (2000) FWLR (Pt. 25) 1666.

Section 4 (8) thereof will still have the effect of making any law which derogates from, ousts or purports to oust the jurisdiction of courts of law in Nigeria are void. Therefore all the provisions in the Law and all other enactments on co-operative societies which oust or purport to oust the jurisdiction of courts are void.

It is to be pointed out that arbitration is a usual mode of resolving disputes, especially commercial disputes, and is ordinarily a matter of contract or the agreement of parties to a contract. And, as the courts do not and will not ordinarily interfere with the contracts of parties voluntarily entered into, all validly executed arbitration agreements are respected by the courts. [10] Therefore, if co-operative arbitration had not been made compulsory under the Law but left for co-operators to voluntarily provide for it in their bye-laws without ousting the jurisdiction of the courts, its constitutionality or validity would not be called into question.

Arbitration Procedure – The Regulations as made contain provisions as to procedure for arbitration and states that when a co-operative dispute arises, it may[11] be referred to

10. Indeed, with the Supreme Court's decision in *Oseyomon v Ojo (supra)* since 1997, Section 51 of the Law and all such provisions in other co-operative societies enactments are overdue for amendment to bring them in conformity with the constitution and general commercial practice of freedom of contract.
11. The usage of 'may' in the Regulations is a better choice and attitude unlike Section 51 of the Law which makes reference of a co-operative dispute to the registrar an imperative with the use of 'shall'. But the provisions of the Law are superior to those of the Regulations.

the Registrar who may either

(a) decide the dispute himself; or

(b) appoint[12] an arbitrator; or

(c) refer it to three arbitrators.

If the Registrar decides to refer the dispute to a panel of three arbitrators, he shall nominate (not appoint) the third arbitrator who_shall be the chairman. The person so nominated by the registrar must be acceptable to the two parties to the dispute who are to nominate one arbitrator each to make up the panel of three arbitrators.[13]

This is similar to the provisions of Sections 6 and 7 of the Arbitration and conciliation Act[14] which provides that where parties to an arbitration agreement have not provided for the number of arbitrators, it shall be deemed to be three and where no provision has been made specifying procedure to be followed in appointing the arbitrators, then in the case of an arbitration with three members, each party shall appoint (not nominate) one arbitrator and the two thus appointed shall appoint the third who (it is presumed) shall also be the chairman.

Where a party fails to appoint an arbitrator within the time limited for doing so or where the two arbitrators appointed by the parties fail to agree on the third arbitrator

12. There is not much difference between the registrar deciding the dispute himself and his appointing an arbitrator.
13. Regulation 21 (2).
14. Referred to here only as a comparative guide as the Act does not apply to co-operative societies.

within time, then the appointment shall be made by the court.[15]

In the case of co-operative disputes however, when a party fails to nominate a party within fifteen days, it is the Registrar (not the court) who may make a nomination instead. If the arbitrator nominated by the Registrar dies, or refuses or neglects to act or as a result of his absence or otherwise becomes incapable of acting, the Registrar shall nominate a fresh arbitrator to replace the one who has died or is refusing, neglecting, or incapable of acting.

Also, it is the Registrar who shall ultimately nominate a replacement if an arbitrator nominated by one of the parties dies, or refuses or neglects to act or by reason of absence or otherwise becomes incapable of acting. The party who nominated the arbitrator who is incapable of acting shall however first be called upon by the Registrar to nominate a replacement within fifteen days failing which the Registrar shall thereafter be entitled to nominate the replacement.[16]

Powers of Arbitrators – Every dispute referred to the registrar automatically becomes an arbitration proceedings whether the Registrar hears and determines same personally (in which case, for the purpose of determining the dispute, he is a sole arbitrator) or he refers it to arbitrators or appoints an arbitrator. In all arbitration proceedings, the Registrar, as sole arbitrator, and the

15. In this situation, by virtue of Section 57 of the Act, either the High Court of a state; or the High Court of the Federal Capital Territory, Abuja; or the Federal High Court.
16. Regulation 21 (3).

arbitrators shall have and exercise the following powers:[17]

(a) Oaths – This power enables the arbitrators to require the parties and their witnesses who are appearing before them to testify to subscribe to the usual oath which they declare to be binding on them and as is provided for in Section 180 of the Evidence Act.

The oath must be to the effect on the part of the subscriber thereto that the evidence that he is about to give is the truth. If he objects to the taking of an oath either on religious or other personal grounds, he shall be made to affirm to the like effect that he will tell the truth and only the truth before the arbitration. The fact of his subscribing to this oath or his affirmation to tell the truth must be recorded by the arbitrators as part of the proceedings.

The power of arbitrators to administer oaths includes also the power to administer or take affidavits in compliance with the provisions of PART V of the Evidence Act. Such affidavits must however be in connection only with the particular arbitration proceedings.

(b) Subpoena – This is a power usually exercisable by a court whereby the court makes an order compelling a person to attend the court as a witness either to testify only or to produce a document or to do both. Whenever such an order is made by a court requiring a person to testify only, the court is said to make an order of subpoena *ad testificandum.*

Where the order is one for the production of documents only, it is known as a subpoena *duces tecum* and this kind of subpoena may also be employed for the

17. Regulation 21 (5).

summoning of a witness both for the purpose of testifying and for the production of documents.

A subpoena is an order of the court which, as with all other orders of court, compels obedience. Accordingly, any person on whom a subpoena is served must obey as to disobey amounts to contempt of court the consequences of which could be very unpleasant.

By Regulation 21 (5), arbitrators have powers to make orders requiring the attendance of the parties and witnesses and to require the production of all necessary books and documents. This the arbitration does by way of a summons which it serves on the particular to whom the summons is addressed and whom the arbitrators require to attend before them for the purpose either to testify or produce documents or both. The service of the summons may be effected in any one of the following ways:

(i) orally i.e. by word of mouth; or
(ii) by hand; or
(iii) by registered post; or
(iv) through the nearest court having jurisdiction in the area in which the co-operative society operates.

This Regulation also provides that any person, having been duly served with an order of subpoena, who does not attend the arbitration proceedings in accordance with such summons, or making any other default or refusing to give evidence, or being guilty of any contempt to an arbitration during the investigation of the matter referred shall be liable to the same kind of punishment as if the contempt had been committed before a court.

The Regulation seems to suggest that while it is possible for a party or witness to be in contempt of an arbitration panel the panel cannot impose the punishment for the contempt since the 'disadvantages, penalties and punishments' prescribed in the regulation 'shall be subject on the presentation of the arbitrator or arbitrators'. If the regulation requires that the arbitrator or arbitrators must make representations of the contempt or default, this means that the actual power to punish for the contempt or default does not reside in the arbitrator or arbitrators but in the person or authority to whom the representation must be made.

The person to whom arbitrators are to make the representation is not stated in the Regulations nor in the Law. Under Nigerian constitutional laws, only a court of law can exercise the power to punish a citizen. Therefore, an arbitrator's representation with a view to subjecting a person to any 'disadvantages, penalties, and punishments' must made to a 'court having jurisdiction in the area in which the society operates'[18] or to 'any court which would have jurisdiction in civil suits between the parties to the dispute to give judgement for the payment of the amount awarded'[19]

Appropriate Court – It is obvious that from the inception of the concept of co-operatives in Nigeria, the intention has been to make the running of co-operative societies as simple as practicable and very accessible to the ordinary folks who were the primary targets for co-operative society

18. Regulation 21 (5).
19. Section 51 (5) (c).

membership. At the time C.F. Rickland wrote his report in 1934 containing his recommendations for a Co-operative Societies Ordinance and Regulations, the number of law courts and personnel with requisite knowledge in Nigeria were very few and were concentrated in the cities which were then very away from the remote rural settings of the larger number of members of the early co-operative societies.

The need for arbitration with respect to co-operative disputes was therefore a natural choice as, even if parties had access to the law courts, the technicalities of legal procedures in these courts would defeat the expectation of a speedy and cheap resolution of disputes. Therefore, requiring the registrar, in those early days of the introduction of co-operative societies, to resolve all disputes arising from and touching the business of registered co-operative societies was more in line with the expectation.

But times have radically changed. The reasons and arguments which informed the enactment of those provisions conferring such wide powers on the registrar and ousting the jurisdiction of the courts of law are no longer present and tenable. The number of trained personnel in requisite knowledge has increased tremendously over the years. So also has the number of law courts grown.

Standing Co-operative Arbitration Panel

In Lagos State, there is now a 'court' specifically set up to exercise the special jurisdiction of adjudicating over co-operative disputes. It is a standing Co-operative Arbitration Panel established by the state's ministry of agriculture and co-operatives which is invested with such judicial powers as may be exercisable by a magistrate court but only with regards to matters and causes arising from and relating to co-operative businesses.

The powers and jurisdiction of this standing Co-operative Arbitration Panel include, among other powers, to:

(a) "examine the causes of problems and disputes within and among co-operative societies in Lagos State;
(b) determine and judge cases according to the judicial authority conferred upon it;
(c) make appropriate recommendations and awards that will enhance justice over disputes before it; and
(d) hear all cases brought before it on application, reference, or appeal.

The Standing Co-operative Arbitration Panel in Lagos State is headed by a senior state counsel (i.e. a legal practitioner in the employment of the government) as chairman sitting with members drawn from other departments of the state government, the co-operative movement in the state, and the police. It sits as 'court' every Tuesday where parties present their cases personally since by Regulation 21 (4) and pursuant to the provisions of Section 44 of Cap. C.15, it is said that legal practitioners are 'barred' from representing parties.[20]

---

20. See Bello, S. Muhammed (2005) *Conflicts and Crisis Management in Co-operative Societies under the Law,* Reading 6 from *Selected Readings in Co-operative Development.*

Constitutionality of the Standing Panel

The desire of the Lagos State ministry in charge of co-operatives to ensure speedy and proper resolution of co-operative disputes by setting up the standing arbitration panel is to be appreciated but it is doubtful if its setting up is supportable under the law. Judicial powers in Nigeria are constitutionally vested in the courts either as courts established for the federation or as established for a state[21] and which powers

> extend to all matters between persons ... and to any person in Nigeria, and to all actions and proceedings relating thereto, for the determination of any question as to the civil rights and obligations of that person.[22]

Section 8 of the constitution also makes express provisions prohibiting the legislatures both at the federal and state levels from making any laws which oust or purport to oust the jurisdiction of courts. A standing arbitration panel sitting like a court is not a court. It is at best usurping the judicial functions of a court – a situation analogous to the ousting of the jurisdiction of the court which ought to exercise the jurisdiction.

Under the doctrine of separation of powers as entrenched in the 1999 constitution of Nigeria, a ministry of government including the Lagos State Ministry of Agriculture and Co-operatives comes under the executive arm of government with no powers to legislate. No court properly so-called with requisite judicial powers as spelt out in the constitution can come into being in Nigeria except by legislation.

21. Section 6 (1) and (2) of the 1999 Constitution.
22. Ibid at subsection 6 (b).

A state House of Assembly is seised of legislative powers including the powers to legislate a court into being.[23] There is no evidence that the Lagos State House of Assembly has created any court known as the Co-operative Arbitration Panel with judicial powers to adjudicate specially or exclusively on co-operative disputes.

Accordingly, it is humbly submitted with respect that any such 'court' being in existence can hardly be constitutional.

Effect on Parties' Right to Nominate Arbitrators

Also where, by the Law and the Regulations, a dispute has been referred to the director of co-operatives in Lagos State and the director makes up his mind not to 'decide the dispute himself' but to 'refer the dispute to three arbitrators', each of the parties to the dispute is invested with the right to nominate one of the three arbitrators.[24] A standing arbitration panel with permanent members robs the parties of this right.

In effect, the operations of such a standing panel which is established by an organ of the executive arm of government, operates to amend the law, in this instance Section 44 (2) (b) of the Lagos State Co-operative Societies Law (Cap. C.15) – a power which the executive arm of government does not constitutionally possess. Although it is conceded that the commissioner in charge of co-operatives may, by Section 64 of Cap.C.15, exercise powers to make regulations for the purposes of the Law and which powers may be said to extend to the amendment of

23. ibid at Section 6 (5) (k).
24. Regulation 21 (2) and Section 44 (2) (b) of Cap. C.15.

such regulations, the powers certainly do not extend to the making of and or amendment of the substantive law.

There is no evidence that the Lagos State House of Assembly which possesses exclusive legislative powers with regards to co-operative matters in Lagos State has amended Section 44 (2) (b) of Cap. C.15. This puts serious doubts on the legality of the operations of the standing co-operative arbitration panel in the state

Legal Representation

Bello, in his *Readings*[25] declares that 'Regulation 21 (4) under Section 44 of the Law has barred representation by legal practitioners'. The said Regulation which the erudite author refers to provides that

> no legal practitioner may be nominated as arbitrator by a party to a dispute.[26]

The operative words in the provision are *may*, *nominate* and *arbitrator*. What the provision intends and means therefore is that a person, being a legal practitioner by profession, *may* not be *nominated* as an *arbitrator* in a co-operative dispute. Even this is not an imperative provision in view of the use of "may" by the law maker so that when the opposite is considered, the provision can be taken to also mean that a legal practitioner may be nominated as an arbitrator to a co-operative dispute.

There is a difference between when a legal practitioner is an arbitrator and when he represents a party to a co-operative dispute in his professional capacity and in

25. *Supra.*
26. The provision is peculiar to co-operative societies and does not represent the general position of the law on arbitration. It is not contained in the Arbitration and Conciliation Act (Cap.19).

his ordinary course of business as a legal practitioner. With due respect, Regulation 21 (4) relates to the former situation and does not extend to the latter. In effect, a party to a co-operative dispute may not, in the exercise of his rights under this Regulation to nominate one of the arbitrators where a dispute has been referred to arbitrators,[27] nominate a legal practitioner as an arbitrator.

There is nothing in the Law or In the Regulations in Nigeria which bars or precludes legal practitioners from professionally representing their clients who are parties to a co-operative dispute with a view to presenting their clients' cases. The general position of the law in this regard is that every person whose civil rights and obligations come up for determination shall be entitled to fair hearing by a court or other tribunal established by law and constituted in such a manner as to secure its independence and impartiality.

A party to a co-operative dispute who desires that he be represented by counsel for the purpose of fairly and effectually presenting his case before a co-operative arbitration panel but is denied such representation has been denied his constitutional right to fair hearing and would, on appeal, succeed in having the arbitral award set aside.

Suitability of Existing Courts

The reference in Regulation 21 (5) to a 'court having jurisdiction in the area in which the society operates' and in Section 51 (5) (c) to 'any court which would have jurisdiction in civil suits between the parties to the dispute to give a judgement for the payment of the amount awarded' is an indication that, were the lawmaker to give a

27. Other co-operative societies enactments specifically provide for '... three arbitrators'.

definition of the court to which co-operative disputes are to be referred, he would have defined a neighbourhood court with a requisite jurisdiction in terms of monetary value.

Such courts now abound all over the country. In Delta and Edo states, the Area Customary Courts squarely fits this bill. In all other states in the federation, the Magistrates courts should do. The Area Customary Courts are particularly well suited for the purposes of co-operative disputes. They are truly neighbourhood courts and are found in every local government area in both Delta and Edo states. Their civil jurisdiction is wide enough to cover almost any suit arising from a co-operative dispute.

By Section 21 (1) of the Customary Courts Law 1984 (as amended) these courts have jurisdiction for any cause or matter

> under any law (not being customary law) ... where the amount of debt, demand, or damages does not exceed

N600.000.00 (six hundred thousand Naira) in Edo State and N500,000.00 (five hundred thousand Naira) in Delta State. The civil jurisdiction in terms of monetary limits of most magistrate courts in Nigeria currently hovers around N1,0000,000.00 (one million Naira).

These courts are courts of summary jurisdiction whose procedures are free of the tedious technicalities of the High Courts and are therefore very well suited to the purposes of co-operative disputes. It is humbly recommended that the various co-operative societies enactments be amended to expressly confer jurisdiction for co-operative disputes on these courts irrespective of the monetary value of the co-operative claim.

(c) Costs – An arbitration panel over a co-operative dispute also has powers to order the payment of the costs of the arbitration. The Regulations provide that the registrar or arbitrators shall further have powers to order the expenses incurred in determining the co-operative dispute to be paid either

(i) out of the funds of the co-operative society in respect of which the dispute had arisen; or

(ii) such party or parties to the dispute as he (i.e. the registrar as sole arbitrator) or they (i.e. three arbitrators) may think fit.

The Arbitration Hearing – The Regulations are silent as to when an arbitration over a co-operative dispute can be said to have commenced or deemed to have commenced or indeed the manner or procedure for commencing same.

Article 3 of the Arbitration Rules as contained in the First Schedule to the Arbitration and Conciliation Act[28] provides clearly that:

> the party initiating recourse to arbitration … shall give to the other party a notice of arbitration (and that) arbitral proceedings shall be deemed to commence on the date on which the notice of arbitration is received by the (other party).[29]

But Section 51 (1) of the Law as in all the other co-operative societies enactments provides only that a co-operative dispute shall be referred (without providing for how) to the registrar and 'the registrar shall on receipt of such reference … decide the dispute …'.[30] Regulation 21 (1) and (6) contain similar provisions without any

28. This Act and its Rules are not applicable to co-operative societies but are referred to here only for comparative purpose.
29. See also Section 17 of the Act.
30. Section 51 (2).

procedural provisions as to how the reference is to be made and by what means or mode the person making the reference is to bring the existence of the reference to the notice or knowledge of the other party.

However, Regulation 48 (2) of the Ogun State Co-operative Societies Regulations provides that

> every reference ... shall be made by a statement in writing in Form B[31] in the Schedule to (the) Regulations and shall be addressed to the Registrar.

The said Form B is headed *'Application for Settlement of a Dispute under the Co-operative Societies Law'*. The 'statement in writing' is required to be signed by the party making the reference and it must contain such other details as the

(a) date of making the statement;
(b) dispute (that is, a concise statement indicating what the disputant claims and the reason therefor); and
(c) full particulars of the dispute.

By Regulation 21 (6), once a reference of a co-operative dispute has been made, 'the registrar or arbitrators shall

(a) hear the evidence of the parties and of
(b) the witnesses who attend, and

upon the evidence and after consideration of any documentary evidence produced by either side, a decision or award shall be given in accordance with justice, equity and good conscience'.

The decision or award shall be reduced into writing,

31. See Appendix D for this form which is obviously an adaptation from the Co-operative Societies Act (Laws of the Federation and Lagos) 1958.

announced to the parties and the written decision or award shall be handed over to the successful party. When, however, neither party is entirely successful, the award shall be deposited with the appropriate registrar who will issue a copy of it to any party who applies for it.

In arriving at its decision when the arbitration is by a panel of three arbitrators, the opinion of the majority (i.e. two arbitrators) shall prevail[32] and any party who is not satisfied with an award of an arbitrator or of arbitrators may appeal within one month from the date of the award to the registrar.[33] He may appeal in person or by agent.

Where no appeal is filed against an arbitrator's award within one month, it shall become final and binding on the parties in all respects and shall not thereafter be liable, as between the parties, to be called in question in any court. The same is applicable to a registrar's decision on a co-operative dispute whether entered on appeal from an arbitrator's award or an original decision of his.[34]

The above brief procedure for determining a co-operative dispute makes a co-operative arbitration one determinable summarily. Under it, the parties are entitled to be heard in evidence, call witnesses in support of their respective cases, and to tender documentary evidence. This is different from the arrangement under the Arbitration and Conciliation Act[35] which provides that the arbitral tribunal shall upon the commencement of the proceedings first

32. Regulation 21 (8).
33. Regulation 21 (9).
34. Regulation 21 (10).
35. Section 20.

decide whether the proceedings shall be conducted

(a) by holding oral hearings for the presentation of evidence or oral arguments; or
(b) on the basis of documents or other materials; or
(c) by both holding oral hearings and on the basis of documents or other materials.

Also, the arbitral tribunal is, by the Act, under duty to give to all the parties to the proceedings sufficient advance notice of any hearing and of any meeting of the arbitral tribunal which is held for the purpose of inspection of any documents, goods, or other property in relation to the proceedings. Every statement, document or other information supplied to the arbitral tribunal shall be communicated to the other party by the party supplying the statement, document or other information; and every statement, document or other information supplied by the tribunal to one party shall be supplied to the other party.[36]

There is therefore a clear intention under the Act that the arbitral tribunal does substantial justice as between the parties through the observance of basic canons of natural justice whereby every party to the proceedings is treated equally and given full opportunity to be heard by presenting his case.[37]

36. See generally Section 20 of the Act.
37. Article 15 of Arbitration Rules.

Chapter Ten

Dissolution, Division and Amalgamation of Societies

The end of anything is better than its beginning

– Ecclesiastes 7:8

Introduction – In Chapter Four, the perpetual succession of a co-operative society was discussed as one of the effects of its registration whereby the society is said to exist in perpetuity, permanently, *ad infinitum* and beyond the lives of its members. By this doctrine of perpetual succession, a co-operative society as a juristic personality never dies in the eyes of the law.[1]

Perpetual Succession not Absolute – The above position is not absolute. There are circumstances provided by the Law itself under which the existence of a co-operative society may be brought to an end. As an entity which came into existence under the instrumentality of the law, its continued existence can also be brought to an end by and only through the provisions of the law. This much the court agreed with in *Kwara Investment Co. Ltd v Garba*[2] when it declared that

> where a legal entity was brought into being by statutory proclamation, only the instrumentality of a statute can bring its existence to a legal end.

Parts 7 and 10 of the Co-operative Societies Law makes provisions for three modes by which the existence of a co-operative society may be brought to a legal end. These are:

1. See Section 9 of the Co-operative Societies Law (Cap. 45) Laws of Bendel State 1976 as applicable to Delta and Edo states. See also *Okon v Ubi* (2006) All FWLR (Pt. 328) 717.
2. (2002) FWLR (Pt. 2) 198,201.

(a) Dissolution[3] (b) Division and (c) Amalgamtion.[4]

DISSOLUTION – This word is not defined in the Law but what it means in the context of the existence of co-operative societies can be understood from the last leg of Section 39 of the Law which provides that

> if the Registrar … is of opinion that (a) society ought to be dissolved,[5] he may make an order for the cancellation of the registration of the society.

Therefore, just as by Section 7 (1) of the Law the Registrar is empowered to register a society into being and thereby render it a body corporate with perpetual succession, so also may the Registrar, by powers conferred on him under Section 39, dissolve a co-operative society out of existence and thereby render it lifeless notwithstanding that the society had been invested with perpetual succession i.e. having life *ad infinitum* from inception.

The power to so wind up[6] a co-operative society and thereby bring its life to an end is exclusively[7] that of the Registrar.[8] This power he can exercise if,

(a) after holding an inquiry, or

(b) making an inspection,

---

3. See Part 7 of the Law.
4. See Part 10.
5. This word means to end a legal relationship or to bring something such as a marriage or a business partnership to a formal end.
6. The term 'wind up' is interchangeably usable to also mean 'dissolved' or 'cancellation of certificate' or liquidate.
7. Except by Section 38 (6) of Cap. N98 which provides that the power can be exercised 'by an order of the Director or of a court'.
8. See Section 39 (5) of the Law. This is one of the excessive powers and functions of the Registrar under the co-operative societies statutes.

as provided for under Section 38 (1) of the Law, or
(c) when he receives an application made by 75% of the members of the society

he becomes of opinion that the society ought to be dissolved.

Inquiry – By the provisions of Section 38 of the Law, the Registrar may *suo motun* hold an inquiry into the constitution, working and financial condition of any co-operative society. He may also do so where an application requesting him to do so has been served on him made by no less that one third of the members of the society or a majority of the members of the management committee.

The Registrar may hold the inquiry personally or direct some other person authorised by him by order in writing to do so.

Inspection – The power of the Registrar to wind up a co-operative society is also exercisable by him if he is of opinion that the society ought to be dissolved following his conduct of an inspection of the society's books upon an application made to him by a creditor of the society. By Section 38 (2) of the Law, the Registrar is required to

> inspect or direct some person authorised by him in writing ... to inspect the books of (a) society

any time a creditor of the society applies to him and 'proves that an ascertained sum[9] of money' is, as at the date of the application, owed to the applicant which remains unpaid 'within a reasonable time'[10] despite the creditor's demand therefor.

9. Vague and imprecise. Compare Section 4 (1) (a) of the Bankcruptcy Act (Cap. 30) Laws of the Federation of Nigeria 1990.
10. Vague and imprecise provision.

Upon making his application to the Registrar, the creditor-applicant shall deposit a sum of money to be assessed by the Registrar with the Registrar as security for the costs of the inspection before the Registrar carries out the inspection. At the conclusion of the inspection, the creditor-applicant and the society shall be informed of the results of the inspection.

Exercise of Power to Dissolve Society – By the provisions of Section 39 (1) of the Law, if the Registrar,

> after holding an inquiry or making an inspection under Section 38 or on receipt of an application made by three-fourths of the members of a registered society, is of opinion that the society ought to be dissolved, he may make an order for the cancellation of the registration of the society.

Similarly, where it is proved to the satisfaction of the Registrar at any time that the number of the members of any primary co-operative society has been reduced to less than ten persons, the Registrar may by order in writing cancel the registration of the society.

By cancelling the registration of a society, the Registrar extinguishes the life of the society as the society will then stand dissolved from the date of the order and it shall 'it shall cease to exist as a corporate body[11] ...'.

Dissolution Order *Nisi* – The Registrar's order cancelling the registration of a society and made pursuant to Section 40 of the Law on the basis of a shortfall in the number of members of the society takes effect from the date the order is made. In other words, this order takes immediate effect.

But where the order cancelling a society's

11. See Section 41.

registration is one made pursuant to Section 39 (1) of the Law and following an inquiry or an inspection, the order shall be one in the nature of an order *nisi* pending appeal.

This is because any member of the society who is aggrieved by such an order may within one[12] month from the date of the order appeal[13] against the order to the appropriate authority.[14]

In other words, the order shall not take effect until the period during which an appeal may be lodged against it shall have expired so that until then, the order is but an order *nisi* and shall not be effective until it has been confirmed.

Dissolution Order Absolute - Where no appeal is presented by any member of the society against the order *nisi* within the time within which an appeal may be lodged, the order shall become absolute and it shall take effect.[15]

Upon making an order *nisi* for the cancellation of the registration of a society, the Registrar may also make such further order as he may think fit for the custody of the

12. Two months under other co-operative societies statutes including Cap. N98 except those from the old Western Region.
13. The appeal, under the Eastern and Northern co-operative societies statutes, is to the Minister to whom is assigned responsibility for co-operative societies. In Lagos State, it is to the State Commissioner while under Cap. N98, it is to the Minister or Commissioner.
14. Section 2 of the Law defines 'appropriate authority' to mean the member of the government of the state for the time being charged with responsibility for co-operative societies.
15. There is no provision in the Law for what the appropriate authority should do with the appeal or how he should treat it where an appeal is lodged against the Registrar's order *nisi*.

books and documents of the society including making an order for the protection of the society's assets until the order becomes absolute and takes effect.

Liquidation following Dissolution – When a co-operative society is dissolved, there may be outstanding issues and matters as consequences thereof requiring resolution. Such issues and matters may be in connection with how the society's creditor's claims, if any, can be satisfied and how may the assets and funds of the society may be deployed.

In general terms and in particular with regards to company law, a liquidated company is the same as a dissolved company. Both a liquidated company as well as a dissolved company means a dead company. The process of liquidating or winding up a company is a process which leads to the bringing to an end of the life of the company.

Therefore, whether it is called a winding up or a liquidation or even a dissolution, it means a process or a procedure by which the life of the company is extinguished. The process usually involves the appointment of a liquidator who assumes the control of the company while the company is still alive and runs same with the sole objective of prudently bringing it to a close.

The liquidator replaces the directors of the company but with legally well defined duties and functions geared towards bringing to an end the life of the company in an orderly manner. A liquidator's duties usually involve the realization or collection of the company's assets, payment of its debts, and the distribution of whatever surpluses remaining among the company's members.

Under the co-operative societies statutes however, it would appear that the process of liquidating a co-operative society follows only after its dissolution. This means that under the co-operative societies statutes, unlike as under companies, a dissolution is not necessarily the same thing as a liquidation. Section 42 of the Law in this regard provides that

> where the registration of (a) society is cancelled[16] by an order under Section 39 or under Section 40, the Registrar may appoint a suitable person to be, subject to his discretion and control, the liquidator of the society.

This means that the Registrar has to first dissolve[17] a co-operative society under either of Section 39 or Section 40 of the Law and thereby make the society 'cease to exist as a corporate body'[18] before proceeding under Section 42 to 'appoint … the liquidator of the society'. In effect, the powers conferred on the liquidator under Section 43 are to be exercised by him in respect of a corporate body which is no longer alive.

The reverse is the case with companies where the company to be wound up by the liquidator remains a living corporate entity which becomes dead only at the completion of the liquidator's liquidation.[19]

The Liquidator – Generally, a liquidator is a person who conducts the winding up of a company. He is usually

16. The cancellation of the registration of a society is the same thing as the dissolution of the society. See Sections 39 and 40 of the Law.
17. By cancelling its registration.
18. See Section 41 of the Law.
19. See Paul L. Davies (1997) *Gower's Principles of Modern Company Law* (Sweet & Maxwell) at p. 833.

appointed either by the court[20] or by the company in general meeting.[21]

However, by Section 42 of the Co-operative Societies Law, it is only the Registrar who 'may appoint' the liquidator in the liquidation of a co-operative society.

Overbearing Powers of Registrar - This is one other example of over concentration of powers on the Registrar in the Law which is replete with such conferment of powers on the Registrar. These excessive powers include even judicial powers which may not have been out of place in the circumstance of Nigeria in 1934 when C.F. Rickland made his recommendation for a legislation on co-operative societies but hardly tenable in today's Nigeria.

Stretching the Registrar's extensive powers with regard to the appointment of the liquidator, Sections 42 and 43 provide that the liquidator's appointment shall be subject to the Registrar's 'discretion and control'[22] and to his 'guidance and control ... and to any limitations imposed'[23] by him and who may further by order control and revise the liquidator's exercise of his powers pursuant to Section 44 (1) of the Law which provides thus:

> A liquidator shall exercise his powers subject to the control and revision of the Registrar, who may –
> (a) rescind or vary any order made by a liquidator and make whatever new order is required;
> (b) remove a liquidator from office;
> (c) call for all books, documents and assets of the society;

20. See Sections 422 and 489 Companies and Allied Matters Act.
21. Section 464 Companies and Allied Matters Act.
22. Section 42.
23. Section 43 (1).

(d) by order in writing limit the powers of a liquidator under Section 43;
(e) require accounts to be rendered to him by the liquidator;
(f) procure the auditing of the liquidator's accounts and authorise the distribution of the assets of the society;
(g) make an order for the remuneration of the liquidator; or
(h) refer any subject of dispute between a liquidator and any third party to arbitration if that party shall have consented in writing to be bound by the decision of the arbitrator.

There is therefore no gainsaying that the powers of the Registrar over the liquidator's exercise of his powers are so over-bearing that the liquidator is but a mere puppet of the Registrar and such that the office of the liquidator becomes so very unattractive. The situation is compounded further by the provisions of Section 46 of the Law which ousts the jurisdiction of the courts in the following words:

> save in so far as is hereinbefore expressly provided, no civil court shall have jurisdiction in respect of any matter concerned with the dissolution of a registered society under this Law.[24]

Even more worrisome are provisions such as is in Section 44 (2) which seem to confer on the Registrar powers to convict and sentence persons to terms of imprisonment.

---

24. This provision and all such like provisions which are replete in the Law can have no effect in law for being void as it breaches Section 4 (8) of the 1999 Constitution of Nigeria and in the face of the Supreme Court's decision in *Oseyomon v Ojo* (1997) 7 SCNJ 365.

The subsection provides that

> any person willfully neglecting or refusing ... shall be guilty of an offence and shall be liable on conviction to imprisonment for six months.

The provision is bare as to which court has the jurisdiction for the conviction and sentencing so that it will be apt to presume that, since the section is all about the powers of the Registrar to control the liquidation of a co-operative society, it must be the Registrar who has the power to convict and sentence under the section.

This is without arguments unsupportable under our laws. The power to subject a person to any form of punishment under Nigerian laws is exclusively vested in the judiciary[25] of which the Registrar of Co-operatives and his office are not part They are part of the executive arm of government.

The lawmaker must be taken to know and to understand this position of our laws as by Section 45 (2) of the Law he had proceeded to declare that

> an order[26] made by the liquidator[27] or by the Registrar under Section 43 or Section 44 shall be enforced by *any civil court* having jurisdiction over the place where the registered office of the society is situated in like manner as a decree of that court.

In effect, the position of the Co-operative Societies Law is that the Registrar can conduct a criminal trial of a citizen over an offence committed under the Co-operative Societies Law, find the citizen guilty and convict him and

25. See section 35 of the 1999 Constitution of the Federal Republic of Nigeria.
26. A sentence of court is an order.
27. Section 44 (1) (h) of the Law.

thereon proceed to sentence him by imposing a six months term of imprisonment on him. He then gets stuck because his office is without the necessary legal machinery for enforcing his order of imprisonment. But by Section 45 (2) of the Law, the Registrar can however, having convicted and sentenced, turn the citizen over to 'any court' – the same courts whose jurisdiction had been ousted – to enforce his order 'in like manner as a decree of (the) court'.

The co-operative societies statutes in Nigeria are replete with similar provisions as above such as Sections 34(4), 36(4), 37(3), 38(6), 43(3), 48(2), 49(1) and (2). Indeed, Section 49(1) is an unwarranted usurpation of judicial functions as it directly provides that

> the Registrar … may direct the interim attachment of … property … as he thinks necessary; and such attachment shall have the same effect as if it had been made by a competent court.

All the provisions in the co-operative statutes conferring judicial powers on the Registrar of Co-operatives are clearly not only unconstitutional but also offend the principle of separation of powers inherent in our constitutional system of government.

They are also in direct breach of the important canon of natural justice of *nemo judex in causa sua* which forbids that a person shall be a judge in his own cause. By Section 44 of the Law for instance, it is the Registrar who has to complain of a willful neglect or of a willful refusal against a person; it is him who will have to prosecute the charge; and it will be him yet who will pronounce a judgement. It is very like the case of the cockroach charged before a court manned and presided over by cocks. There can be only one premeditated result!

A Dictatorial Registrar? – All the co-operative statutes unwittingly present the Registrar as a medieval dictator whose word was the law. The decisions of the Registrar of Co-operatives are in most cases final, conclusive and beyond question even by the courts. Section 51 subsection (5) (a) and (b) and subsection (6) of the Law, for instance, declare that

> (5)(a) any decision given by the Registrar under subsection (2) or under subsection (4) shall, save as otherwise provided in subsection (6), be final and shall not be called in question in any court.
>
> (b) Any decision given by an arbitrator under paragraph (b) of subsection (2) shall, save as otherwise provided in subsection (4), be final and shall not be called in question in any court.
>
> (6) Any party aggrieved by any order of the Registrar made under subsections (4) and (5) may appeal to the appropriate authority within twenty-one days from the date of such order and the decision of the appropriate authority shall be final and conclusive.[28]

The only possible explanation why the co-operative statutes are replete with these kind of provisions must be in connection with the rudimentary state of the Nigerian judiciary at the time in 1934 when C.F. Strickland made his recommendations for legislation on co-operative societies.

---

28. See also Section 44 (6) and (7) of the Lagos State Co-operative Societies Law (Cap. C.15); Section 53 (9) of the Eastern Region Co-operative Societies Law (Cap. 28); Section 54 (6) and (7) of the Northern Region Co-operative Societies Law (Cap. 26). But compare Section 49 (6) of the unconstitutional Cap. N98 Federal Act which removes the usurpation of judicial functions from the Director and donates same to the 'Minister or Commissioner'.

In the 1930s, it was not uncommon to have laymen,[29] usually white British citizens, preside over regular courts for reasons of a dearth of professionally qualified personnel. But as Emiaso states in the preface[30] to his book, the reasons and circumstances why the early courts were manned by laymen no longer exists anywhere in today's Nigeria. So also is there any more the need for any person, not being professionally qualified in law, to perform judicial functions outside the court system in Nigeria.

Indeed, the offending provisions in the co-operative societies statutes do not any longer have any force of law since the decision of the Supreme Court in *Oseyomon v Ojo*[31] where the apex court declared that

> ... the provisions of Section 51 (5) (a), 51 (5) (b) and 51 (6) of the Co-operative Societies Law, Cap. 45 Laws of Bendel State of Nigeria, 1976 which are state enactments must be regarded as void in so far as they purport to limit or oust the jurisdiction of the High Courts as therein provided contrary to the express provisions of the 1999 constitution.

More fundamentally, the 1999 Constitution of Nigeria has, by its Section 4 (8), expressly prohibited Nigerian legislatures from enacting any law

> that ousts or purports to oust the jurisdiction of a court (not just the High Court) of law or of a judicial tribunal established by law.

---

29. See for instance Miakpo Emiaso (2010) *Law, Practice and Procedure: Area Customary Courts in Nigeria* (Peakmans Ltd., Lagos) at p.7.
30. ibid at p. ix.
31. (1997) 7 SCNJ 365, 380.

Therefore, any law which contains provisions such as are replete in the co-operative societies statutes shall be void for being unconstitutional in so far and to the extent that it ousts or purports to oust the jurisdiction of any court established by law in respect of any subject matter.

Powers and Duties of the Liquidator – The powers and duties of the liquidator who is appointed to liquidate the operations of a dissolved co-operative society are spelt out in Section 43 (1) of the Law. These powers must be exercised by the liquidator subject to the guidance and control of the Registrar and also subject to any limitations which the Registrar may by order impose thereon pursuant to Section 44. These powers are that:

> 43. (1) a liquidator appointed under Section 42 shall, subject to the guidance and control of the Registrar and to any limitations imposed by the Registrar by order under Section 44 have power to –
>
> (a) decide, subject to any bye-laws defining the liability of members, the contributions to be made by members and past members or by the estates of deceased members of the society to its assets;
>
> (b) appoint a day by proclamation or notice before which creditors whose claims are not already recorded in the books of the society shall state their claims for admission or be excluded from any distribution made before they have proved them;
>
> (c) decide any question of priority which arises between creditors;
>
> (d) refer disputes to arbitration and institute[32] and defend

32. Is this not contrary to the provisions of Section 51 which ousts the jurisdiction of courts?

suits and other legal proceedings on behalf of the society by his name or office;

(e) decide by what persons and in what proportions the costs of liquidation are to be borne;

(f) give such directions in regard to the collection and distribution of assets as may be necessary in the course of winding up the society;

(g) compromise any claim by or against the society provided the sanction of the Registrar has first been obtained;

(h) call such general meetings[33] of members as may be necessary for the proper conduct of the liquidation, giving not less than fourteen days' notice of every such meeting;

(i) take possession of the books, documents and assets of the society;

(j) sell the property of the society;

(k) carry on the business[34] of the society so far as may be necessary for winding up[35] it up beneficially, provided that he shall not for this purpose be entitled to issue any loan;

(l) arrange for the distribution of the assets of the society in a convenient manner when a scheme of distribution has been approved by the Registrar.

In carrying out these powers, the liquidator shall be invested with magisterial powers with respect to the summoning of parties, the enforcement of attendance of

---

33. How does one call a meeting of a society that has been dissolved and which consequentially is no longer in existence let alone talk about it having members?
34. Carry on the business of a society that is already dead to the law?
35. Winding up an already wound up society?

witnesses and compelling of persons to produce documents and, of course, where in the course of exercising his powers under subsections 2 and 3 of Section 43 any person willfully neglects or refuses to do any act or to furnish the liquidator with any information or furnishes information he knows to be false or he, without reasonable excuse disobeys any of the liquidator's summons, requisition, or order

> shall be guilty of an offence and shall be liable on conviction to imprisonment for six months or to a fine of two hundred Naira or to both such imprisonment and fine.

Subsections 2 and 3 of Section 43 in effect invests on the liquidator judicial powers such as the Registrar himself can exercise particularly the power to convict and sentence persons to jail terms even though all the powers conferred on the liquidator are to be exercised by only subject to the guidance and control of the Registrar and further subject under Section 44 (1) to the further 'control and revision' of the Registrar who may exercise all those powers thereat including and especially power to rescind or vary the liquidator's order and substitute his own therefor.

Deployment of Society Funds upon Liquidation – In the liquidation of a co-operative society whose registration has been cancelled, the funds of the society including those in the reserve fund shall be deployed subject to the following order of priority:

(a) the cost of the liquidation followed by

(b) the discharge and settlement of the society's liabilities, then

(c) the payment for or refund of share capital to members followed by

(d) the payment of a dividend to members at a rate not exceeding five per cent per annum but only for such period in the past for which no disposal of surplus i.e. payment of dividend, was made.[36]

(e) After meeting the demands of (a) to (d) above and any outstanding claims by creditors not met under the scheme of distribution and there remains still any surplus, such remaining surplus shall be deployed by the Registrar towards any co-operative purpose at his discretion.[37]

DIVISION – One other mode by which the life of a co-operative society can be brought to an end is for the society to split into two or more societies. This is provided for in Section 52 of the Law.

Special Notice of First Meeting – Whenever it is desired, for any reason, that a co-operative society should split into more than one society, a first meeting of the society's general body specially called for the purpose shall be convened 'of which at least seven clear days notice shall (have been) given to its members.'[38]

Preliminary Resolution – At the First Meeting, the society shall 'resolve to divide itself into two or more societies' and the resolution to this effect shall be known as a preliminary resolution which shall contain proposals for the division of the assets and liabilities of the society among the new societies into which it is proposed to divide.

The preliminary resolution may also prescribe the area of operations of each of the new societies and specify

36. Section 47 (1) of the Law.
37. Section 47 (3).
38. Section 52 (1).

the members who will constitute each of the new societies.[39]

Member's Freedom to Opt Out – Every member and every creditor of the splitting society must be served a copy of the preliminary resolution and he shall, within two months from the date of the service on him thereof, be entitled to exercise an option not to become a member and, in the case of a creditor, that he intends to demand a payment to him of the amount due to him from the old society.

Final Meeting – After the expiration of the two months period from the date of receipt[40] of the preliminary resolution by all the members and creditors of the society, a second and final meeting of the general body of the society of which at least seven clear days notice shall (have been) given to its members shall be convened for considering the preliminary resolution which, if confirmed by a fresh resolution passed by a majority of not less than two-thirds of the members of the society present[41] at the meeting, shall form the ground upon which the Registrar may register the new societies and the bye-laws thereof.

The preliminary resolution shall be confirmed with or without changes. If there are changes, such changes must not be material and the Registrar has exclusive powers to determine whether a change is material or not. His decision

39. ibid.
40. It will be less vague to compute the period from the date the resolution is passed.
41. It is safer to be of the total number of members on the society's register of members.

in this respect 'shall be final and no appeal shall lie therefrom.'[42]

Upon confirmation as aforesaid by the second resolution, the Registrar may then register the new societies and their bye-laws whereupon such registration, the registration of the old society shall be deemed to have been cancelled and thereby extinguishing its life.
The registration of the new societies as discussed above shall operate as sufficient conveyance to vest the assets and liabilities of the original society in the new societies in the manner specified in the preliminary resolution and as confirmed by the fresh resolution at the second and final meeting.[43]

At the second and final meeting leading to the division of the society, provision shall be made by a third resolution for the repayment of share capital to all members who have by notice to the society within the specified period of two months indicated their intention not to be members of the new societies. Provision shall also be made at this meeting by a resolution for the satisfaction of the claims of all those creditors who gave notice to the society within the specified period indicating their desire that the amount owed to them by the society be paid to them.[44] These members and creditors shall not be entitled to the repayment of their share capital and satisfaction of their claims if the preliminary resolution is not confirmed.[45]

Also by subsection 5 of section 52 of the Law, the

42. Section 52 (3) of the Law.
43. Section 52 (6).
44. Section 52 (4).
45. Proviso to subsection 4 of Section 52.

Registrar shall fix 'such time'[46] as he 'considers reasonable'[46] within which the repayment for shares to members and the satisfaction of claims to creditors shall be made failing which 'the Registrar may refuse[47] to register the new societies.

AMALGAMATION – The third mode by which a co-operative society's life may be brought to an end is to combine two or more existing societies into one. This is the same as what is referred to as merger under companies law. It is the fusion of two or more companies usually of similar size into one.

Section 52 (7) of the Co-operative Societies Law makes provision for the merger of co-operative societies which in effect brings to an end the lives of the merging societies while bringing into being a new society. The provision repeats with appropriate modification but almost verbatim the provisions in relation to the division of societies discussed above. The provision provides similar[48] arrangements as for the division of a society including the calling of a first meeting, a second and final meeting, the preliminary resolution, the second and third resolutions etc.

46. Vague, arbitrary, and excessively subjective.
47. This is absurd as the new societies would have already been registered by the Registrar pursuant to Section 52 (3) long before the default would be known. It is humbly recommend that this should read ' … may rescind' or 'may revoke' the registration of the new societies.
48. See subsections 7 to 12 of Section 52.

APPENDIX A

CO-OPERATIVE SOCIETIES LAW (DELTA STATE)

ARRANGEMENT OF SECTIONS

PART 1

Introductory

PART 2

Registration

PART 3

Duties and Privileges of Registered Societies

PART 4

Rights and Liabilities of Members

22. Qualifications for membership.
23. Members not to exercise rights till due payment is made.
24. Restrictions of members.
25. Vote of members
26. Representation by proxy
27. Contracts of members who are minors with society.
28. Restriction on interest of members of society
29. Restriction on transfer of share or interest
30. Liability of past member and estate of deceased member for debt of society.

PART 5

Property Funds of Registered Societies

31. Restriction on loans
32. Deposits and loans receivable by a registered society.
33. Restrictions on other transactions with non- members.
34. Investment of funds.
35. Disposal of surplus.

PART 6

Audit, Inspection and Inquiry

36. Audit
37. Power of registrar to inspect books and to require returns.

PART 7

Dissolution

39. Dissolution
40. Cancellation of registration of society due to lack of membership.
41. Effect of cancellation of registration.
42. Liquidation after cancellation of registration of society.
43. Liquidator's power.
44. Power of registrar to control liquidation.
45. Enforcement of order.
46. Limitation of the jurisdiction of civil court.
47. Disposal of funds on liquidation.

CHAPTER 42

CO-OPERATIVE SOCIETIES

Law to make provision with respect to Co-operative Societies

PART 1

Introduction

1. This Law may be cited as the Co-operative Societies Law.

2. In this Law –

'**the appropriate authority**' means the member of the Government of the State for the time being charged with responsibility for co-operative societies;

"**bonus**" means a share of the surplus of a registered society divided among its members in proportion to the volume of business done by them with the society from which the surplus of the society was derived;

"**by-laws**" means the registered by-laws made by a society in the exercise of any power conferred by this Law and includes any registered amendment thereof;

"**central financing society**" means a registered society of which the principal object is to make loans to other registered societies;

"**central society**" means a registered society established to facilitate the operations of registered societies in accordance with co-operative principles and includes a central financing society;

"**committee**" means the governing body of a registered society to whom the management of its affairs is entrusted;

"**co-operative society**" means co-operative society registered under the provisions of the Co-operative Societies Act or under the provisions of this law.

"**dividend**" means a share of the surplus of a registered society divided among its members in proportion to the share capital held by them;

"**member**" include a person or registered society joining in the application for the registration of a society and a person or registered society admitted to membership after registration in accordance with the by-laws and regulations;

"**officer**" includes a president, chairman, secretary, treasurer, member of committee or other person empowered under the regulations or by-laws to give directions in regard to the business of a registered society;

"**primary society**" means a registered society consisting of individuals as members;

"**registered society**" means a co-operative society registered under this Law;
"**registrar**" means the registrar of co-operative societies appointed under section 3 of this Law and includes any person when exercising such powers of the registrar as may have been conferred upon him under that section;
"**regulation**" means regulations made under this law.

PART 2
Registration

3. (1) The Public Service Commission may appoint a person to be registrar of co-operative societies, and may appoint persons assist such registrar, and may, by notice publish in the state Gazette, confer on any such persons all or any of the powers of a registrar under this Law.
(2) Any person appointed as registrar under this section shall have a seal of such device as may be approved by the Military Governor and impressions of such seal shall be judicially noticed.

4. Subject to the provisions hereinafter contained, a society which has as its object the promotion of the economic interests of its members in accordance with co-operative principles, or a society established with the object of facilitating the operations of such a society, may be registered under this Law with or without limited liability as the registrar may decide.

5. (1) No primary society shall be registered under this Law which does not consist of at least ten individuals each of whom is qualified under section 22 of this Law for membership.
(2) No central society shall be registered unless at least two registered societies are members thereof.
(3) (a) The word "co-operative" or its vernacular equivalent shall form part of the name of every society registered under this Law.
(b) The word "limited" or its vernacular equivalent shall be the last word in the name of every society with limited liability registered under this Law.
(c) Save in the case of a central financing society the word "bank" or "banking" shall not form part of the name of any society registered under this Law.

(4) When for the purposes of this section, any question arises as to age, residence or occupation of land constituting the qualification of any person, that question shall be decided by the registrar whose decision shall be final.

6. (1) For the purposes of registration, an application shall be made to the registrar.

(2). The application shall be signed –

(a) in the case of a primary society by at least ten individuals qualified for membership under section 22 of this Law; and

(b) in the case of a society of which a member is a registered society, by a duly authorized person on behalf of every such registered society, and where all ten other members or when there are less than ten other members by all of them.

(3) The application shall be accompanied by three copies of the proposed by-laws of the society and the persons by whom or on whose behalf such application is made shall furnish such information in regard to the society as the registrar may require.

(4) The registrar may make sure alterations in the proposed by-laws as he may deem advisable subject to the ratification of the applicants being obtained when such alterations are material.

7. (1) If the registrar is satisfied that a society has complied with the provisions of this Law and the regulations and that its proposed by-laws are not contrary to this Law or to the regulations, he may register the society and its by-laws. Where the registrar refuses to register a society an appeal shall lie to the appropriate authority within one month from the date of such refusal.

(2) On registration the society shall pay such fee as may be required by the regulations.

8. The registration of a society shall render it a body corporate by the name under which it is registered, with perpetual succession and a common seal and with power to hold movable and immovable property of every description, to enter into contracts, to institute and defend suits and other legal proceedings and to do all things necessary for the purpose of its constitution.

9. A certificate of registration signed and sealed by the registrar shall be conclusive evidence that the society therein mentioned is duly registered, unless it proved that the registration of the society has be cancelled.

10. Notwithstanding anything contained in this Law the Military Governor may by writing under his hand and subject to such conditions, if any, as he may impose, exempt any particular society from any of the requirements of this Law as to registration.

PART 3

Duties and Privileges of Registered Societies

11. (1) Any registered society may, subject to this Law and the regulations, amend its by-laws, including the by-law which declares the name of the society.

(2) No amendment of the by-laws of a registered society shall be valid until the same has been registered under this law, for which purpose three copies of the amendment shall be forwarded to the registrar.

(3) If the registrar is satisfied that any amendment of the by-laws is not contrary to this Law or to the regulations, he may register the amendment. Where the registrar refuses to register an amendment of any by-law an appeal shall lie to the appropriate authority within one month from the date of such refusal.

(4) An amendment which changes the name of the society shall not affect any right or obligation of the society or any of its members or past members, and any legal proceedings pending may be continued by or against the society under its new name.

(5) When the registrar registers an amendment of the by-laws of a registered society, he shall issue to the society a copy so certified and sealed shall be conclusive evidence that the amendment is duly registered.

(6) In this section, "amendment" includes the making of a new by-law and the variation or revocation of a by-law.

12. Every registered society shall have an address registered in accordance with then regulations, to which all notices and communications may be sent, and shall send to the registrar notice of every change thereof.

13. Every registered society shall keep a copy of this Law and of the regulations and of its by-laws and a list of its members open to inspection free of charge at all reasonable times at the registered address of the society.

14. (1) A registered society which has as one of its objects the disposal of any article produced or obtained by the work or industry of its members whether the produce of agriculture, animal husbandry, forestry, fisheries, handicrafts or otherwise may provide in its by-laws or may otherwise contract with its members –

(a) that every such member who produces any such article shall dispose of the whole or any specified amount, proportion or description thereof to or through the society; and

(b) that any member who is proved or adjudged in such manner as may be prescribed by the regulations to have committed a breach of the by-laws or contracts shall pay to the society as liquidated damages a sum ascertained or assessed in such manner as may be prescribed by the aforesaid regulations.

(2) No contract entered into under the provision of this section shall be contested in any court on the ground only that it constitutes a contract in restraint of trade.

(3) Any person who, having knowledge of the existence of a marketing contract between a registered society and a member, willfully induces, or attempts to induce, a violation of the contract, shall be liable to pay damages to the registered society.

(4) It shall be lawful for a registered society to apply for an injunction in restraint of an attempt to induce violation of any such contract.

15. Subject to any prior claim of the Government on the property of the debtor and to the lien or claim of a landlord in respect of rent or any money recoverable as rent and in the case of immovable property to any prior registered charge thereon –

(a) any debt or outstanding demand payable to a registered society by any member or past members shall be a first charge on all crops or other agricultural produce, felled timber or other forest produce, marine produce, fish (fresh water and salt water), livestock, fodder, agricultural, industrial and fishing implements, plant, machinery, boats, tackle and nets, raw materials, stock in trade and generally all produce of labour and things used in connection with production raised, purchased or produced in whole or in part from any loan whether in money or in goods given him by the society: provided that nothing herein contained shall affect the claim of any bona fide purchaser or transferee without notice;

(b) any outstanding demands or dues payable to a registered housing society by any member or past member in respect of rent, shares, loans or purchase money or any other rights or amount payable to such society shall be a first charge upon his interest in the immovable property of the society.

16. A registered society shall have a charge upon the shares or interest in the capital and on the deposits of a member or past member or deceased member and upon any dividend, bonus, or surplus payable to a member or past member or to the estate of a deceased member in respect of any debt due to the society from such member or past member or estate and may set off any sum credited or payable to a member or past member or estate of a deceased member in or towards payment of any such debt.

17. Subject to the provisions of section 16, the share or interest of a member in the capital of a registered society shall not be liable to attachment or sale under any decree or order of a court in respect of any debt or liability uncured by such member, and neither his assignee in insolvency nor a receiver duly appointed shall be entitled to or have any claim on such share or interest.

18. (1) On the death of a member, a registered society may transfer the share or interest of the deceased member to the person nominated in accordance with the regulations made in this behalf, or, if there is no person so nominated, to such persons as may appear to the committee to be the heir or legal representative of the deceased member, or may pay to such nominee, heir or legal representative, as the case may be, a sum representing the value of such member's share or interest, as ascertained in accordance with the regulations or bye-laws:

Provided that –

(a) in the case of a society with unlimited liability, such nominee, heir or legal representative, as the case may be, may require payment by the society of the value of the share or interest of the deceased member ascertained as aforesaid;

(b) in the case of a society with limited liability, the society may transfer the share or interest of the deceased member to such nominee, heir or legal representative, as the case may be, being qualified in accordance with the regulations and bye-laws for membership of the society, or, on his application within six months of the death of the deceased member, to any person specified in the application who is so qualified.
(2) A registered society shall pay all other moneys due to the deceased member from the society to such nominee, heir or legal representative, as the case may be.
(3) All transfers and payments made by a registered in accordance with the provisions of this section shall be valid and effectual against any demand made upon the society by any other person.

19. (1) A registered society may receive deposits from or for the benefit of minors and it shall be lawful for a registered society to pay such minors the interest which may become due on such deposits. Any deposit made by a minor may, together with the interest accrued thereon, be paid to that minor; and any deposit made on behalf of a minor may, together with the interest accrued thereon, be paid to the guardian of the minor for the use of the minor.
(2) The receipt of any minor or guardian for money paid to him under this section shall be a sufficient discharge of the liability of the society in respect of that money.

20. Any register or list of members kept by any registered society shall be *prima facie* evidence of any of the following particulars entered therein –

(a) the date at which the name of any person was entered in such register or list as a member;
(b) the date at which any such person ceased to be a member.

21. (1) A copy of any entry in a book of a registered society regularly kept in the course of business shall, if certified in such manner as may be prescribed by the regulations, be received in any legal proceeding, civil or criminal, as *prima facie* evidence of the existence of such entry and shall be admitted as evidence of the matters, transactions and accounts therein recorded in every case where, and to the same extent as, the original entry itself is admissible.

(2) No officer of any such society shall, in any legal proceedings to which the society is not a party, be compelled to produce any of the society's books, the contents of which can be proved under subsection (1) or to appear as a witness to prove any matter, transactions or accounts therein recorded, unless the court for special reasons so directs.

PART 4

Rights and Liabilities of Members

22. (1) To be qualified for membership of –

(a) a society, a person must –

(i) have attained the age of eighteen years;

(ii) be resident within, or in occupation of land within, the registered society's area of operations as described by the bye-laws; or

(b) a central society, if the applicant is a registered society, it must -

(i) have its registered address within the central society's area of operations as defined by the bye-laws; and

(ii) be a holder of property within the central society's area of operations as defined by the bye-laws:

Provided that the registrar shall have power in the case of a society of limited liability to grant exemption from this qualification.

(2) When, for the purposes of this section, any question arises concerning the age, residence, property qualification or status of any person, then the same shall be decided by the committee subject to an appeal to the registrar whose decision shall be final.

23. No member of a registered society shall exercise the rights of a member unless or until he has made such payment to the society in respect of membership or acquired such interest in the society as may be prescribed by the regulations or bye-laws.

24. Except with the sanction of the registrar, no person shall be a member of more than one registered society whose primary object is to grant loans to its members.

25. No member of any registered society shall have more than one vote in the conduct of the affairs of the society:
Provided that in the case of an equality of votes the chairman shall have a casting vote:
And provided further that in the case of societies of which a registered society is a member that society may have such voting powers as are provided in the regulations.

26. A registered society which is a member of any other registered society may appoint a proxy for the purpose of voting in the conduct of the affairs of such other registered society:
Provided that the person so appointed shall be a member of a registered society.

27. The minority or underage of any person duly admitted as a member of any registered society shall not debar that person from executing any instrument or giving any acquitance necessary to be executed or given under this Law or the regulations made thereunder, and shall not be a ground for invalidating or avoiding any contract entered into by any such person with the society, and any such contract entered into by any such person with the society, whether as principal or as surety, shall be enforceable by or against such person notwithstanding his minority or underage.

28. No member, other than a registered society, shall hold more than one-fifth of the share capital of any co-operative society.

29. (1) The transfer or charge of the share or interest of a member or past member or deceased member in the capital of a registered society shall be subject to such conditions as to maximum holding as may be prescribed by this Law or by the regulations.
(2) In the case of a society registered with unlimited liability, a member shall not transfer any share held by him or his interest in the capital of the society or any part thereof unless –

(a) he has held such share or interest for not less than one year; and

(b) the transfer or charge is made to the society or to a member of the society, or to a person whose application for membership has been accepted by the committee.

30. (1) The liability of a past member for the debts of a registered society as they existed on the date on which he ceased to be a member shall continue for a period of two years reckoned from that date.
(2) The estate of a deceased member shall be liable for the debts of the society as they existed on the date of his decease for a period of two years reckoned from the date of his decease.

PART 5

Property and Funds of Registered Societies

31. (1) A registered society shall not, except as provided in section 34, make any loan to any person other than a member:
Provided that, with the consent of the registrar, a registered society may make loans to another registered society.
(2) Except with the permission of the registrar, a registered society shall not lend money on the security of any movable property other than produce or goods in which the society is authorized to deal.
(3) The Military Governor may, by order, prohibit or restrict the lending of money on mortgage of any description of immovable property by any registered society.

32. A registered society shall receive deposits and loans from persons who are not members only to such extent and under such conditions as may be prescribed by the regulations or bye-laws.

33. Save as provided for in sections 31 and 32, the transactions of a registered society with persons other than members shall be subject to such prohibitions and restrictions as may be prescribed by the regulations.
34. A registered society may invest or deposit its funds –

(a) in the Post \office Savings Bank or with any Bank or person carrying on the business of banking approved for this purpose by the registrar; or
(b) in any securities issued or guaranteed by the Government of a Commonwealth country; or
(c) with any other registered society approved for this purpose by the registrar; or
(d) in any other mode approved by the registrar.

35. (1) No society shall pay a dividend or bonus or otherwise distribute any part of its net surplus except as provided in its bye-laws and until the proposed payment or distribution has been approved by the registrar.

(2) At least one-fourth of the net surplus of every registered society, as ascertained by the audit prescribed by section 36, shall be carried to a fund to be called the reserve fund which shall be employed as prescribed by the regulations:

Provided that the registrar shall have power in the case of any registered society of limited liability to grant from time to time exemptions from further contribution to the reserve fund, or to reduce the rate thereof, and may at any time revoke such exemption or reduction:

And provided further that in the case of a society of unlimited liability, no distribution of surplus shall be made without the order of the Military Governor.

(3) Any registered society may, with the sanction of the registrar, after one-fourth of the net surplus in any year has been carried to a reserve fund, contribute an amount not exceeding ten *per centum* of the remaining net surplus to any charitable purpose or to a common-good fund.

(4) Any registered society or an officer or a member thereof willfully neglecting or refusing to comply with any of the provisions of subsections (1) and (2) hereof shall be guilty of an offence and shall be liable on conviction to imprisonment for six months or to a fine of two hundred *naira* or to both such imprisonment and fine.

PART 6

Audit, Inspection and Inquiry

36. (1) The registrar shall audit or cause to be audited by some persons authorized by him by general or special order in writing the accounts of every registered society at least once in every year.

(2) The audit under subsection (1) shall include an examination of overdue debts, if any, and a valuation of the assets and liabilities of the registered society.

(3) The registrar and every other person appointed to audit the accounts of a society shall have power when necessary –

(a) to summon at the time of his audit any officer, agent, servant or member of the society who he has reason to believe can give material information in regard to any transactions of the society or the management of its affairs; or

(b) to require the production of nay book or document relating to the affairs of, or any cash or securities belonging to, the society by the officer, agent, servant or member in possession of such book, document, cash or securities.

(4) Any officer, agent, servant or member of a registered society willfully or neglecting or refusing to do any act or to furnish any information or furnishing information known to be false or without any reasonable excuse disobeying any summons, requisition or order under subsection (3) hereof, shall be guilty of an offence and shall be liable on conviction to imprisonment for six months or to a fine of two hundred *naira* or to both such imprisonment and fine.

37. (1) The registrar, or any person authorized by order in writing by the registrar, shall at all times have access to all the books, accounts, papers and securities of a registered society, and shall be entitled to inspect the cash in hand; and every officer of the society shall furnish such information in regard to the transactions and working of the society as the person making such inspection may require.

(2) The registrar may give directions prescribing the returns to be submitted by a registered society to the registrar and the persons by whom and the form in which such returns shall be submitted.

Directions given by the registrar under this subsection shall apply to all or any registered society.

(3) Any registered society or an officer or member thereof willfully neglecting or refusing to do any act or to furnish any information, or willfully submitting information or a return known to be false under subsections (1) and (2) hereof, shall be guilty of an offence, and shall be liable on conviction to imprisonment for six months or to a fine of two hundred *naira* or to both such imprisonment and fine.

38. (1) The registrar may of his own motion, and shall on the application of a majority of the committee, or of not less than one-third of the members of a registered society, hold an inquiry or direct some person authorized by him by order in writing in this behalf to hold an inquiry into the constitution, working and financial condition of a registered society; and all officers and members of the society shall furnish such information in regard to the affairs of the society and produce the cash in hand and such books, accounts, papers and securities of the society as the registrar or the person authorized by him may require.

(2) The registrar shall, on the application of a creditor of the registered society, inspect or direct some person authorized by him in writing in this behalf to inspect the books of gthe society, if the applicant –

(a) that an ascertained sum of money is then due to him and that he has demanded payment thereof and has not received satisfaction within a reasonable time; and

(b) deposits with the registrar such sum as security for the costs of the proposed inspection as the registrar may require.

(3) The registrar shall communicate the results of any such inspection to the creditor and to the society into whose affairs inquiry has been made.

(4) Where an inquiry is held under subsection (1) or an inspection is made under subsection (2), the registrar may by a certificate under his hand and seal make an award apportioning the costs or such part of the costs, as he may think right, between the registered society, the members demanding an inquiry, the officers or former officers of the society, and the creditor, if any, on whose application the inquiry is made.

(5) Any sum awarded by way of costs under subsection (4) shall be recoverable in the same manner as a fine imposed by any court having jurisdiction over the person against whom the award is made, on the production before the court of the certificate referred to in the subsection.

(6) Any officer or member of a registered society willfully neglecting or refusing to do any act or to furnish any information or furnishing information known to be false under the provisions of subsection (1) hereof, shall be guilty of an offence, and shall be liable on conviction to imprisonment for six months or to a fine of one hundred *naira* or to both such imprisonment and fine.

PART 7

Dissolution

39. (1) If the registrar, after holding an inquiry or making an inspection under section 38 or on receipt of an application made by three-fourths of the members of a registered society, is of opinion that the society ought to be dissolved, he may make an order for the cancellation of the registration of the society.

(2) Any member of a registered society may, within one month from the date of an order under subsection (1), appeal from such order to the appropriate authority.

(3) Where no appeal is presented within one month from the making of an order cancelling the registration of a society, the order shall take effect on the expiry of that period. Where an appeal is presented within one month, the order shall not take effect until it is confirmed.

(4) Where the registrar makes an order for the cancellation of the registration of a society under subsection (1), he may make such further order as he may think fit for the custody of the books and documents and the protection of the assets of the society until the order cancelling registration takes effect.

(5) No society shall be wound up save by an order of the registrar.

40. The registrar may, by order in writing, cancel the registration of any primary society if at any time it is proved to his satisfaction that the number of the members has been reduced to less than ten. Every such order shall take effect from the date thereof.

41. Where the registration of a society is cancelled by an order under section 39 or under section 40, the society shall cease to exist as a corporate body from the date on which the order takes effect, hereinafter referred to as the date of dissolution:

Provided that any privileges conferred on the society under sections 15, 16, 17, and 18 shall be deemed to be vested in any liquidator appointed for that society by the registrar.

42. Where the registration of the society is cancelled by an order under section 39 or under section 40, the registrar may appoint a suitable person to be, subject to his discretion and control, the liquidator of the society.

43. (1) A liquidator appointed under section 42 shall, subject to the guidance and control of the registrar and to any limitations imposed by the registrar by order under section 44 have power to –

(a) decide, subject to any bye-laws defining the liabilities of members, the contributions to be made by members and past members or by the estates of deceased members of the society to its assets;

(b) appoint a day by proclamation or notice before which creditors whose claims are not already recorded in the books of the society shall state their claims for admission or be excluded from any distribution made before they have proved them;

(c) decide any question of priority which arises between creditors;

(d) refer disputes to arbitration and institute and defend suits and other legal proceedings on behalf of the society by his name or office;

(e) decide by what persons and in what proportions the costs of liquidation are to be borne;

(f) give such directions in regard to the collection and distribution of assets as may be necessary in the course of winding up the society;

(g) compromise any claim by or against the society provided the sanction of the registrar has first been obtained;

(h) call such general meetings of members as may be necessary for the proper conduct of the liquidation, giving not less than fourteen days' notice of every such meeting;

(i) take possession of the books, documents and assets of the society;

(j) sell the property of the society;

(k) carry on the business of the society so far as may be necessary for winding it up beneficially, provided he shall not for this purpose be entitled to issue out any loan;

(l) arrange for the distribution of the assets of the society in a convenient manner when a scheme of distribution has been approved by the registrar.

(2) Subject to such regulations as may be made in this behalf, any liquidator appointed under this Law shall, in so far as such powers are necessary for carrying out the purposes of this section, have all such powers as are vested in a magistrate on the occasion of any action in respect of summoning parties, enforcing the attendance of witnesses and compelling the production of documents.

(3) Any person willfully neglecting or refusing to do any act or to furnish any information or furnishing information known to be false, required for the purpose of this section, or without reasonable excuse disobeying any summons, requisition or order issued thereunder, shall be guilty of an offence and shall be liable on conviction to imprisonment for six months or to a fine of two hundred *naira* or to both such imprisonment and fine.

44. (1) A liquidator shall exercise his powers subject to the control and revision of the registrar, who may –

(a) rescind or vary any order made by a liquidator and make whatever new order is required;

(b) remove a liquidator from office;

(c) call for all books, documents and assets of the society;

(d) by order in writing limit the powers of a liquidator under section 43;

(e) require accounts to be rendered to him by the liquidator;

(f) procure the auditing of the liquidator's accounts and authorize the distribution of the assets of the society;

(g) make an order for the remuneration of the liquidator; or

(h) refer any subject of dispute between a liquidator and any third party to arbitration if that party shall have consented in writing to be bound by the decision of the arbitrator.

(2) Any person willfully neglecting or refusing to do any act or to furnish any information or furnishing information known to be false, required for the purposes of subsection (1) or without reasonable excuse disobeying any order issued thereunder, shall be guilty of an offence and shall be liable on conviction to imprisonment for six months or to a fine of one hundred *naira* or to both such imprisonment and fine.

45. (1) The decision of an arbitrator on any matter referred to him under section 44 shall be binding upon the parties, and shall be enforceable in like manner as an order made by the registrar under that section.

(2) An order made by the liquidator or by the registrar under section 43 or section 44 shall be enforced by any civil court having jurisdiction over the place where the registered office of the society is situated in like manner as a decree of that court.

46. Save in so far as hereinbefore expressly provided, no civil court shall have any jurisdiction in respect of any matter concerned with the dissolution of a registered society under the Law.

47. (1) In the liquidation of a society whose registration has been cancelled, the funds, including the reserve fund, shall be applied first to the costs of liquidation, then to the discharge of the liabilities of the society, then to the payment of the share capital and then, provided that the bye-laws of the society permit, to the payment of a dividend at a rate not exceeding five *per centum* per annum for any period for which no disposal of surplus was made.
(2) When the liquidation of a society has been closed and any creditor of that society has not claimed or received what is due to him under the scheme of distribution, notice of the closing of the liquidation shall be published in the State Gazette; and no claim against the funds of the society liquidated shall lie after two years have elapsed from the date of the publication of the State Gazette notice.
(3) Any surplus remaining after the application of the funds to the purposes specified in subsection (1) and the payment of any claims for which an action is instituted under subsection (2) shall be available for use by the registrar for any co-operative purpose at his discretion.

PART 8

Surcharge and Attachment

48. (1) Where in the course of the winding up of a registered society it appears that any person who has taken part in the organization or management of such society or any past or present officer of the society has misapplied or retained or become liable or accountable for any money or property of such society or has been guilty of misfeasance or breach of trust in relation to such society, the registrar may, on the application of the liquidator or of any creditor or contributor, examine into the conduct of such person and make an order requiring him to repay or restore the money or property or any part thereof with interest at such rate as the registrar thinks just or to contribute such sum to the assets of such society by way of compensation in regard to the misapplication, retainer, dishonesty or breach of trust as the registrar thinks fit.

(2) Any person who without reasonable excuse fails to comply with the provisions of an order issued under subsection (1) shall be guilty of an offence and shall be liable on conviction to imprisonment for six months or to a fine of two hundred *naira* or to both such fine and imprisonment.

49. (1) When the registrar is satisfied that any person with intent to defraud or delay the execution of any order which may be made against him under section 48 (1) or section 51 (1) or of any decision given in a dispute referred to the registrar or to any arbitrators under any regulations –

(a) is about to dispose of the whole or any part of his property; or

(b) is about to remove the whole or any part of his property from the local limits of the jurisdiction of the registrar, the registrar may, unless adequate security is furnished, direct the interim attachment of said property or such part thereof as he thinks necessary; and such attachment shall have the same effect as if it had been made by a competent court.

(2) Any person who without reasonable excuse fails to comply with the provisions of an order issued under subsection (1), shall be guilty of an offence and shall be liable on conviction to imprisonment for six months or to a fine of two hundred *naira* or to both such fine and imprisonment.

50. Any person aggrieved by any order of the registrar made under sections 48 and 49 may appeal to the appropriate authority within twenty-one days from the date of such order and the decision of the appropriate authority shall be final and conclusive.

PART 9

Disputes

51. (1) If any dispute touching the business of a registered society arises –

(a) among members, past members and persons claiming through members, past members and deceased members; or

(b) between a member, past member or person claiming through a member, past member, or deceased member and the society, its committee, or any officer, agent or servant of the society; or

(c) between the society or its committee and any officer, agent or servant of the society; or

(d) between the society and other registered society,

such dispute shall be referred to the registrar for decision.

Without prejudice to the generality of the provisions of this subsection, a claim by a registered society for any debt or demand due to it from a member, past member, or the nominee, or legal representative of a deceased member, whether such debt or demand be admitted or not, shall be deemed to be a dispute touching the business of the society within the meaning of this subsection.

(2) The registrar shall on receipt of such reference –

(a) decide the dispute; or

(b) subject to the provisions of any regulations, refer it for disposal to an arbitrator.

(3) Subject to the provision of any regulations the registrar may withdraw any reference transferred under paragraph (b) of subsection (2) and decide the dispute under paragraph (a) of the said subsection.

(4) The registrar may of his own motion or on the application of a party to a reference revise any decision thereon by an arbitrator to whom it was referred.

(5) (a) Any decision given by the registrar under subsection (2) or under subsection (4) shall, save as otherwise provided in subsection (6), be final and shall not be called in question in any court.

(b) Any decision given by an arbitrator under paragraph (b) of subsection (2) shall, save as otherwise provided in subsection (4), be final and shall not be called in question in any court.

(c) The decision shall, on the application of the party in whose favour it is given, be enforced by any court which would have jurisdiction in civil suits between the parties to the dispute to give a judgement for the payment of the amount awarded or, where the decision does not relate to the payment of money, to give a similar decision, in the same manner as if the decision had been a judgement or decision of such court.

(6) Any party aggrieved by any order of the registrar made under subsections (4) and (5) may appeal to the appropriate authority within twenty-one days from the date of such order and the decision of the appropriate authority shall be final and conclusive.

PART 10

Division and Amalgamation

52. (1) Any registered society may, at a meeting of its general body specially called for the purpose, of which at least seven clear days' notice shall be given to its members, resolve to divide itself into two or more societies.

The resolution (hereinafter in subsections (2) to (6) referred to as the preliminary resolution) shall contain proposals for the division of the assets and liabilities of the society among the new societies into which it is proposed to divide it and may prescribe the area of operations of, and specify the members who will constitute, each of the new societies.

(2) (i) A copy of the preliminary resolution shall be sent to all the members and creditors of the society.

(ii) Any member of the society may, notwithstanding any bye-law to the contrary, by notice given to the society within a period of two months from his receipt of the preliminary resolution, intimate his intention not to become a member of any of the new societies.

(iii) Any creditor of the society may, notwithstanding any agreement to the contrary, by notice given to the society within the said period, intimate his intention to demand a return of the amount due to him.

(3) After the expiry of two months from the receipt of the preliminary resolution by all the members and creditors of the society, a meeting of the general body of the society, of which at least seven clear days' notice shall be given to its members, shall be convened for considering the preliminary resolution.

If, at such meeting, the preliminary resolution is confirmed by a resolution passed by a majority of not less than two-thirds of the members present, either without changes or with such changes as, in the opinion of the registrar, are not material, he may register the new societies and the bye-laws thereof.

On such registration, the registration of the old society shall be deemed to have been cancelled.

The opinion of the registrar as to whether the changes made in the preliminary resolution are or are not material shall be final and no appeal shall lie therefrom.

(4) At the meeting referred to in subsection (3), provision shall be made by another resolution for –

(i) the repayment of the share capital of all the members who have given notice under paragraph (ii) of subsection (2); and

(ii) the satisfaction of the claims of all the creditors who have given notice under paragraph (iii) of subsection (2):

Provided that no member or creditor shall be entitled to such repayment or satisfaction until the preliminary resolution is confirmed as provided in subsection (3).

(5) If, within such time as the registrar considers reasonable, the share capital of the members referred to in subsection (4) is not repaid or the claims of the creditors referred to in that clause are not satisfied, the registrar may refuse to register the new societies.

(6) The registration of the new societies shall be a sufficient conveyance to vest the assets and liabilities of the original society in the new societies in the manner specified in the preliminary resolution as confirmed under subsection (3) above.

(7) Two or more registered societies may, at meetings of their respective general bodies specially called for the purpose, of which at least seven clear days' notice shall be given to their respective members, resolve to amalgamate into one society. This resolution is hereinafter in this section referred to as the preliminary resolution.

(8) (i) A copy of the preliminary resolution of each society shall be sent to all the members and creditors thereof.

(ii) Any member of any such society, notwithstanding any bye-law to the contrary, by notice given to the society of which he is a member within a period of two months from his receipt of the preliminary resolution, intimate his intention not to become a member of the new society.

(iii) Any creditor of any such society may, notwithstanding any agreement to the contrary, by notice given to the society of which he is a creditor within the said period, intimate his intention to demand a return of the amount due to him.

(9) After the expiry of two months from the receipt of the preliminary resolution by all the members and creditors of all the societies, a joint meeting of the members of such societies, of which at least seven clear days' notice shall be given to them, shall be convened for considering the preliminary resolution.

If, at such meeting, the preliminary resolution is confirmed by a resolution passed by a majority of not less than two-thirds of the members present, either without changes or with such changes as in the opinion of the registrar are not material, the new society and the bye-laws thereof may be registered.

On such registration, the registration of the old societies shall be deemed to have been cancelled.

The opinion of the registrar as to whether the changes made in the preliminary resolution are or are not material shall be final and no appeal shall lie therefrom.

(10) At the joint meeting referred to in subsection (9), provision shall be made by another resolution for –

(i) the repayment of the share capital of all the members who have given notice under paragraph (ii) of subsection (8); and

(ii) the satisfaction of the claims of all the creditors who have given notice under paragraph (iii) of subsection (8):

Provided that no member or creditor shall be entitled to such repayment or satisfaction until the preliminary resolution is confirmed as provided in subsection (9).

(11) If, within such time as the registrar considers reasonable, the share capital of the members referred to in subsection (10) is not repaid or the claims of the creditors referred to in that subsection are not satisfied, the registrar may refuse to register the new society.

(12) The registration of the new society shall be a sufficient conveyance to vest in it all the assets and liabilities of the original society.

PART 11

Regulations

53. (1) The Military Governor may make all such regulations as may be necessary for the purpose of carrying out or giving effect to the principles and provisions of the Law.

(2) In particular and without prejudice to the generality of the foregoing power, such regulations may –

(a) prescribe the forms to be used and the conditions to be complied with in the making of applications for the registration of societies, and the procedure to be followed with regard to such applications;

(b) prescribe the conditions to be complied with by persons applying for admission or admitted as members and provide for the election and admission of members, and the payment to be made and the interest to be acquired before the exercise of the right of membership;

(c) subject to the provisions of section 28, prescribe the maximum number of shares or portion of the capital of a society which may be held by a member;

(d) prescribe the extent to which a society may limit the number of its members;

(e) provide for the appointment, withdrawal or expulsion of members and for the payments, if any, to be made to members who withdraw or are expelled, and for the liabilities of past members;

(f) provide for general meetings of the members, empower the registrar or any person authorized by him to summon such meetings, provide for the procedure at such meetings, and the powers to be exercised at such meetings, and the appointment and voting powers of representatives of affiliated societies to the meetings of central societies;

(g) provide for the appointment, suspension and removal of the members of the committee and other officers, and for the procedure at meetings of the committee, and for the powers to be exercised and the duties to be performed by the committee and other officers;

(h) prescribe the matters in respect of which a society may or shall make bye-laws and for the procedure to be followed in making, altering and rescinding bye-laws, and the conditions to be satisfied prior to such making, alteration or rescission;

(i) prescribe the payments to be made, the conditions to be complied with, and the forms of the bonds, instruments or other documents to be executed, by members applying for loans or cash credits, the period for which loans may be made or credits granted, and the maximum amount which may be lent and maximum credit which may be allowed to individual members with or without the consent of the registrar;

(j) provide for the mode in which the value of a deceased member's interest shall be ascertained and for the nomination of a person to whom such interest may be paid or transferred;
(k) provide for the mode in which the value of the interest of a member who has become of unsound mind and incapable of managing himself or his affairs shall be ascertained, and for the nomination of any person to whom such interest may be paid or transferred;
(l) provide for the formation and maintenance of reserve funds, and the objects to which such funds may be applied, and for the investment of any funds under the control of the society;
(m) prescribe the conditions under which accumulated funds may be distributed to the members of a society and the maximum rate of dividend which may be paid by a society;
(n) prescribe the accounts and books to be kept by a registered society, and for the periodical publication of a balance sheet showing the assets and liabilities of a registered society;
(o) provide for the audit of the accounts of registered societies and for the charges, if any, to be made for such audit and provide for the levy of contributions from all or any registered societies to a fund to be used for the audit and the supervision of existing societies and co-operative propaganda and prescribe for the administration of such a fund;
(p) provide for the persons by whom, and the form in which, copies of entries in books of societies may be certified;
(q) provide for the formation and maintenance of a register of members, and, where the liability of members is limited by shares, of the register of shares;
(r) provide for the inspection of documents and registers at the registrar's office and the fees to be paid therefor and for the issue of copies of such documents or registers;
(s) prescribe the manner in which any question as to the breach of any bye-law or contract relating to the disposal of produce to or through a society may be determined and the manner in which the liquidated damages for any such breach may be ascertained or assessed;

(t) prescribe the mode of appointing an arbitrator or arbitrators and the procedure to be followed in proceedings before the registrar or such arbitrator or arbitrators;

(u) prescribe the procedure to be followed by a liquidator appointed under section 42 and the cases in which appeals shall lie from the orders of such liquidator;

(v) prescribe the forms to be used,. The fees to be paid, the procedure to be observed and all other matters connected with or incidental to the presentation, hearing and disposal of appeals under this Law or the regulations.

(3) In any case where the registrar is satisfied that a substantial number of members of any society are unacquainted with the English language, he shall cause such regulations to be translated into a language with which such members are acquainted and additionally to be made known in such manner as is customary for the community concerned.

PART 12

Miscellaneous

54 (1) Notwithstanding anything contained in section 51, the registrar at any time when proceeding to a decision under this Law, or the appropriate authority at any time when an appeal has been referred to him against any decision of the registrar under this Law, may refer any question of law arising out of such decision for the opinion of the High Court.

(2) Any judge, or judges, of the high Court as the Chief Justice may direct, may consider and determine any question of law so referred and the opinion given on such question shall be final and conclusive.

(3) The Chief Justice may make rules of court regulating the procedure of the High Court on determining questions of law under this section.

55. (1). Such sums as may be due from a registered society or from an officer or member or past member of a registered society as such to the Government under section 38 may be recovered in the manner provided for the recovery of debts due to the Government under the law for the time being in force.

(2) Sums due from a registered society to the Government and recoverable under subsection (1) may be recovered first, from the property of the society; secondly, in the case of a society of which the liability of members is limited, from the members

subject to the limit of their liability; and thirdly, in the case of other societies, from the members.

56. The Military Governor, by writing under his hand, may exempt any particular registered society from any of the provisions of the Law or direct that such provisions shall apply to such society with such modification as the Military Governor may specify.

57. (1) No person other than a registered society shall trade or carry on business under any name or title of which the word "co-operative" is part without the sanction of the registrar.
(2) Any person who contravenes the provision of this section shall be guilty of an offence and shall be liable on conviction to a fine not exceeding twenty *naira* and in the case of a continuing offence to a further fine not exceeding two *naira* for each day during which the offence continues.

58. All information contained in the books and accounts of a registered relating to the property or the financial situation of the society's members shall be wholly exempt from disclosure for any purpose relating to any income tax or to rating.

59. Nothing in the law relating to the registration of instruments for the time being in force shall apply to –

(a) any instrument relating to shares in a registered society, notwithstanding that the assets of such society consist in whole or in part of immovable property; or

(b) any debenture issued by any such society and not creating, declaring, assigning, limiting or extinguishing any right, title or interest to or in immovable property except in so far as it entitles the holder to a security afforded by a registered instrument whereby the society has mortgaged, conveyed or otherwise transferred the whole or part of its immovable property or any interest therein to trustees upon trust for the benefit of the holders of such debentures; or

(c) any endorsement upon or transfer of any debentures issued by any such society; or

(d) any charge created in favour of a registered society by a member of that society in respect of any produce of his agriculture or his land.

60. All co-operative societies possessing a registered address within the state and registered under the Co-operative Societies Act shall be deemed to be registered under this Law and subject to its provisions.

61. (1) Nothing in this Law shall affect any Order in Council, order, rule, regulation, appointment, conveyance, mortgage, deed or agreement made, resolution passed, direction given, proceedings taken, instrument issued or thing done under the Co-operative Societies Act but any such Order in Council, order, rule, regulation, appointment, conveyance, mortgage, deed, agreement, resolution, direction, proceeding, instrument or thing shall, if in force at the commencement of this Law, continue in force, and so far as it could have been made, passed, given, taken issued or done under this Law, shall have effect as if made, passed, given, taken, issued or done under this Law.

(2) Any document referring to the Co-operative Societies Act shall be construed as referring to the corresponding provisions of this Law.

(3) Any register kept under the Co-operative Societies Act shall be deemed part of the register to be kept under the corresponding provisions of this Law.

(4) All funds and accounts constituted under this Law shall be deemed to be in continuation of the corresponding funds and accounts constituted under the co-operative Societies Act.

(5) Nothing in the Law shall affect the incorporation of co-operative societies referred to in section 60.

(6) Where any offence, being an offence for the continuance of which a penalty was provided, has been committed under the Co-operatives Act, proceedings may be taken under this Law in respect of the continuance of the offence after the commencement of this Law, in the same manner as if the offence had been committed under the corresponding provisions of this Law.

APPENDIX B

CO-OPERATIVE SOCIETIES REGULATIONS

1. These regulations may be cited as the Co-operative Societies Regulations.

2. (1) Every application for the registration of a society shall be submitted to the registrar in the form approved by him.
(2) If the registrar refuses to register a society or its bye-laws, he shall inform the applicants in writing of the reasons for his refusal.

3. Every society shall include in its name a word or words clearly indicating the nature and situation of the society but shall not include the name of a person.

4. (1) A society shall make bye-laws in respect of the following matters-

(a) name and registered address;
(b) the area of its operations;
(c) objects for which the society is established;
(d) purposes to which the funds may be applied, the mode of custody and investment of funds;
(e) qualifications for membership, the terms of admission of members, the entrance fees, if any, and the mode of election;
(f) nature and extent of the liability of members;
(g) withdrawal and expulsion of members, and the payments, if any, to be made to such members;
(h) transfer of shares or interest of members;
(i) manner of raising the share capital, if any, and other funds;
(j) general meetings, and the procedure and powers of such meetings;
(k) appointment, suspension and removal of members of the committee and officers; the powers and duties of the committees and officers;
(l) the authorization of an office to sign documents and to use the seal on behalf of the society;
(m) in the case of a building society, the duration of the society.

(2) If the objects of the society include the creation of funds to be lent to the members, additional bye-laws shall be made on the following matters –

(a) the conditions on which loans may be made to members including –

(i) the rate of interest;

(ii) the maximum amount which may be lent to a member;

(iii) the maximum period which can be granted for the repayment of a loan;

(iv) extension of the term and renewal of loans;

(v) the purpose of loans;

(vi) security for repayment;

(b) the consequences of default in payment of any sum due on account of shares or loan and the consequences of failure to use a loan for the purpose for which it was granted;

(c) disposal of the annual surplus.

5. (1) Subject to the provisions of section 10 of the Co-operative Societies Law (hereinafter referred to as the Law) and of regulation 4 a society may from time to time make new bye-laws for the conduct of its business, or may amend or cancel bye-laws already made, provided that –

(a) due notice of nay proposal to make, amend or cancel bye-laws is given in accordance with the bye-laws; and

(b) the resolution is passed –

(i) by not less than three-fourths of the members present at a general meeting at which at which not less than one half of the members of the registered society are present; or

(ii) by the written vote of a clear majority (without a casting vote) of the total number of members of the society, provided that voting papers have been sent to all members of the society and that the written votes are examined and counted at a general meeting at which a quorum is present in terms of the bye-laws of the society; and

(c) provided that no new bye-law or amendment or cancellation of an existing bye-law shall have any legal force till it has been registered by the registrar.

(2) Two copies of every such amendment, signed by two officers of the society, shall be submitted to the registrar accompanied by –

(a) a statement that the provisions of regulations 5 (1) (a) and 5 (1) (b) have been fully complied with; and

(b) an application that the change in the bye-laws have been registered.

If the registrar approves of the amendment he shall register the same, retain a copy in his office and return the other to the society with a certificate that the amendment has been registered.

(3) In regulation 5 (2) the term "amendment" includes a new bye-law and a resolution rescinding a bye-law.

6. (1) No person shall be admitted as a member of an urban credit society if he resides outside the sphere of operations of the society as prescribed by the bye-laws, and all persons who have for one year resided outside the sphere of operations shall cease to be members, and the managing committee shall remove their names from the register.

(2) A thrift society or a building society may accept as a member any person not residing in Nigeria but possessing or holding immovable property within the sphere of operations of the society.

No other society shall admit or retain as a member a person not residing in Nigeria.

7. The Military Governor may general or special order direct that any society or class of societies shall not incur a liability towards non-members in excess of a sum fixed from time to time by the registrar.

No society shall receive or renew any loan or deposit which will make its liability to non-members exceed the limit thus laid down.

8. (1) No society shall issue a series of bonds or debentures without the sanction of the Military Governor.

(2) No benefit, including interest, premium, prize or loan any terms, to the purchaser or holder of any debenture, bond, certificate, deposit, receipt or other acknowledgement shall be dependent in whole or in part on any method containing an element of chance.

9. (1) Every society shall from time to time hold general meetings as provided in the bye-laws for the disposal of necessary business including –

(a) the fixing of a maximum liability towards non-members;

(b) the fixing of a maximum credit which shall not be exceeded by any member;

(c) the election of officers (other than the secretary) and the members of committee;

(d) the consideration of audited balance sheet and the disposal of the surplus;

(e) the consideration of the audit note and any inspection note by the registrar or inspector.

(2) Subject to the Law, the regulations and the bye-laws, the general meeting shall have the sole right to decide the disposal of the surplus.

(3) Questions before the general meeting shall be decided, unless otherwise specifically provided, by a majority of members present, voting as required by section 25 of the Law.

(4) The registrar or any person authorized by him at any time shall summon a special general meeting of the society in such manner and at such time and place as he may direct.

He may also direct what matters shall be discussed by the meeting.

Such meeting shall have all the powers and be subject to the same rules as a meeting called according to the bye-laws of the society.

10. An officer of a society shall not be appointed to his office for an indefinite period or for a period exceeding one year.

A retiring officer shall, unless the bye-laws otherwise provide, be eligible for re-election:

Provided that in a society formed among the members of a military or police force, the president and vice-president may be appointed *ex-officio*.

11. Every representative of a society in a meeting of a central society to which it is affiliated shall be selected from among the members of the committee of his society.

12. A member is not eligible for the committee if –

(a) he is under twenty-one years of age; or

(b) he is entrusted in his individual capacity with secretarial or managerial duties (other than the joint business of the

committee), and receives pay or an honorarium on that account; or
(c) in a credit society, he lends money on his own account; or
(d) in a marketing society, he deals in the commodities which the society markets otherwise than through or with the society.

13. A member of the society shall cease to hold office if –
(a) he ceases to be a shareholder, or
(b) he is declared insolvent, or
(c) he becomes of unsound mind, or
(d) he is convicted of any offence involving dishonesty or is imprisoned for three months or longer, or
(e) he is entrusted in his individual capacity with secretarial or managerial duties (other than the joint business of the committee), and receives pay or an honorarium on that account, or
(f) in a credit society, he lends money on his own account, or
(g) in a marketing society, he deals in the commodities which the society markets otherwise than through or with the society.

14. The committee shall exercise all the powers of the society except those reserved for the general meeting, and subject to any instructions or restrictions duly laid down by the society in a general meeting or in the bye-laws.

15. The duties of the committee shall include the following –
(a) to comply with the Law and regulations made thereunder, and the bye-laws of the society, and properly to conduct the business of the society;
(b) to maintain true and accurate accounts;
(c) to keep a true account of the assets and liabilities;
(d) to keep a correct register of members;
(e) to lay before the annual general meeting o profit and loss account and a balance sheet;
(f) to assist the inspection of the books by any person authorized to see them;
(g) to take adequate security from officers and employees;
(h) in a credit society, to watch that loans are applied to the approved purpose for which they are made; and

(i) in a marketing society, to watch that produce marketed is of good quality and duly graded.

16. Every society shall maintain a register of members showing –

(a) the name, address and occupation of each member, and a statement of the shares held by him;

(b) the date on which each member's name was entered in the register;

(c) the date on which any person ceased to be a member;

(d) the nominee, if any, appointed under regulation 23.

17. Registered societies shall keep such accounts and books as may be required or prescribed by the registrar.

18. (1) Every registered society shall prepare yearly in such form as may be prescribed by the registrar –

(a) an account showing the income and expenditure for the year,

(b) a profit and loss account, and

(c) a balance sheet.

(2) The account shall be made up to the 31st day of March or such other date as the registrar may direct, and a copy of each account shall be sent to the registrar within such time as he may direct.

19. Every society shall pay annually such fee, if any, to an audit and supervision fund as the registrar may assess.

The fund shall be held and administered by the registrar under the general orders of the Military Governor, until such time as a registered co-operative union may be formed to hold and administer it.

20. For the purpose of section 21 of the Law a copy of an entry in the books of a society may be certified by a certificate written at the foot of such copy, declaring that it is a true copy of such entry, and that the book containing the entry is still in the custody of the society, such certificate being dated and signed by the secretary of the society and another member of the committee.

21. (1) When any dispute described in section 51 of the Law arises reference may be made to the registrar, either by the committee or by the society by resolution in general meeting or by any party to the dispute, or if the dispute concerns a sum due from a member of the committee to the society, by any member of the society.

(2) The registrar may either decide the dispute himself, or appoint an arbitrator, or refer the dispute to three arbitrators, of whom one shall be nominated by each of the parties and the third shall be nominated by the registrar and shall act as chairman.

(3) When a dispute is referred to three arbitrators, if any party to the dispute fails to nominate an arbitrator within fifteen days, the registrar may make the nomination instead.

If an arbitrator nominated by one of the parties dies, or refuses or neglects to act, or, by absence or otherwise, becomes incapable of acting, the registrar shall call upon the party concerned to nominate a fresh arbitrator within fifteen days, and if no arbitrator is nominated accordingly, he may nominate one himself; and if such arbitrator was nominated by himself he shall nominate a fresh one in his place.

(4) No legal practitioner may be nominated as arbitrator by any party to a dispute.

(5) In all arbitration proceedings under this rule the registrar or arbitrators shall have power to administer oaths, to require the attendance of the parties and witnesses and to require the production of all necessary books and documents by a summons delivered orally or sent by hand or by registered post, or through the nearest court having jurisdiction in the area in which the society operates, and shall further have power to order the expenses incurred in determining the dispute to be paid either out of the funds of the society or by such party or parties to the dispute as he or they may think fit.

Persons not attending in accordance with such summons, or making any other default or refusing to give evidence or guilty of any contempt to an arbitrator during the investigation of the matter referred, shall be subject on the representation of the arbitrator or arbitrators, as the case may be, to such disadvantages, penalties and punishments as they would incur for the same offences if committed in suits tried before a court.

(6) The registrar or arbitrator shall hear the evidence of the parties and witnesses who attend, and upon that evidence and after consideration of any documentary evidence produced by either side a decision or award shall be given in accordance with justice, equity and good conscience and shall be reduced to writing, announced to the parties and handed over to the successful parties.

When neither party is entirely successful, the award shall be deposited with the appropriate registrar who will issue a copy of it to any party that applies for it.

(7) In absence of any party duly summoned to attend, the dispute may be decided *ex parte*.

(8) When three arbitrators are appointed, the opnion of the majority shall prevail.

(9) Any party aggrieved by an award of an arbitrator may appeal to the registrar in person or by agent within one month of the date of the award.

(10) An arbitrator's award, if no appeal has been made within a month, or a decision of the registrar originally or on appeal, shall not, as between the parties to the dispute, be liable to be called in question in any court, and shall be in all respects final and binding on the parties to the dispute.

22. A member of a registered society –

(a) may withdraw from the society after such notice and on such conditions as are prescribed in the bye-laws;

(b) if he ceases to be qualified under the bye-laws, shall be removed by the committee;

(c) may be removed or expelled from the society for such cause only as may be prescribed in the bye-laws;

(d) shall, on withdrawing or being removed or expelled from the society, be entitled to repayment without interest of any money (not exceeding the face value of his shares) paid by him or his predecessor in interest towards the purchase of shares, after the period prescribed in the bye-laws:

Provided that no repayment on account of shares shall be made to any member or past member if after subtraction of the reserve fund and any other undistributed surplus of the society a net loss appears in the audited balance sheet.

23. (1) Every member of a society may nominate a person or persons to whom his share or interest referred to in section 18 of the Law shall on his death be transferred or the sum specified shall be paid, and may from time to time revoke or modify such nomination.

But no member may nominate more than one person in societies with share capital, unless he holds more than one share, and in any case,

unless the amount to be paid to such nominee, whether by way of whole shares or by fixed proportion of the amount available for transfer, as the case may be, is duly specified when the nominee is appointed.
The nomination and any change thereof shall be recorded in the register of members and attested by the thumb mark or signature of the member.
The value of the share or interest shall be represented by the sum actually paid by him to acquire such share or interest unless the bye-laws provide for calculation otherwise, provided that no repayment shall be made if the balance sheet of the society shows a net loss.
(2) A receipt signed by a minor or guardian of a minor for money paid to him under this regulation shall be a sufficient discharge therefor.

24. The shares of a society may not be pledged to the society by any of its members as security for a loan.

25. Interest payable on deposits made by members or non-members shall in no case exceed nine *per cent per annum* and shall not exceed three-fourths of the rate of interest charged by the society on loans to members.

26. The reserve fund of a society shall be invested or deposited as provided in section 34 of the Law, and shall not be utilized in the business of the society except with the written permission of the registrar.

27. The reserve fund shall be indivisible and no member shall be entitled to claim a specified share in it.

28. (1) On the dissolution of a society, the reserve fund shall be applied to discharging the liabilities of the society and to the repayment of the share capital.
(2) Any sum that thereafter remains may be applied to such object of local or public utility or tending to promote the co-operative movement as may be selected by a general meeting and approved by the appropriate registrar.
If within three months of the closing of the accounts of the liquidator the society fails to select an object that is approved by the registrar the reserve fund shall be treated as unclaimed money subject to the provisions of section 47 of the Law.

29. (1) No dividend or payment on account of profits shall be made by a society registered with unlimited liability until the reserve fund has reached a proportion of not less than one-tenth of the society's total liabilities.
(2) No society shall pay a dividend if the rate of interest on loans granted by it to its members exceeds twelve and one half *per cent per annum,* if payable annually, or, one kobo in the *naira per mensem* if payable at intervals of less than one year.
(3) No society shall pay a dividend at a rate in excess of ten *per cent per annum*.
(4) No part of the funds of the society shall be divided as bonus or dividend or otherwise among members until the entire expenditure incurred by the society during the year has been debited in the annual profit and loss account and the net surplus calculated.
(5) No dividend shall be paid by any society while any claim due from the society to a depositor or lender remains unsatisfied.
30. (1) Any member of the public shall be permitted, on payment of twenty-five kobo for each occasion of inspecting, to inspect in the office of the registrar for any lawful purpose the following documents –

(a) the registration register;
(b) the registration certificate of the society;
(c) the registered bye-laws of a society and amendments effected in such bye-laws;
(d) an order cancelling the registration of a society;
(e) the annual statements of a society.

2. The fees prescribed for certified copies of any public documents, which any person has under this regulation a right to inspect, are as follows –

(a) for a registration certificate fifty kobo, and
(b) in case of other documents, a sum calculated at the rate of forty kobo for each hundred words of the copy or extract.

Appendix C

FORM A

Application for Registration as a Co-operative Society

Regulations 2 (1) Ogun State

1. Name of proposed society..
2. Address of society for purpose of ....
3. Area of operations..
4. Exact objects of society..

....

5. Number and amount of shares which it is proposed to issue......................
6. Is it proposed to raise capital otherwise than by issuing shares..................
   If so, what amount and by what means? ....
7. Is liability to be limited or unlimited? ....
8. Qualification proposed for membership..
9. Brief description of the proposed working of the society........................
10. Names of president, vice-president ....

President

....

Vice President

........................*Treasurer*

........................*Secretary*

11. Actual membership at date of application................................

We, the undersigned, certify that the details given above are correct and apply that the society described may be registered as a co-operative society under Section 4 of the Co-operative Societies Law

Signature*

Name+	Occupation	Residence	
		Village or town	Local Government

1..
2. ....
3. ....
4. ....
5. ....
6. ....
8. ....
9. ....
10. ....

Appendix D

FORM B

Application for Settlement of a Co-operative Dispute

Regulation 48 (2) Ogun State

Whereas a dispute has arisen between ....
....
concerning ....

I/We (Name or Names and Title) ....
hereby apply to the Registrar of Co-operative Societies, Ogun State, for the said dispute to be settled in accordance with Section 51 of the Co-operative Societies Law.

I/We request that the dispute be decided by the Registrar himself.

Date .... *Signature(s)* ....
....
....
....
....
....
....
....

Appendix E

Name……….
Address…….
Regn. No……
Phone No……
Date………..

The President……………..

Dear Sir,

APPLICATION FOR N………………… LOAN

I/We do hereby apply for a loan of N………….. (……..) at prevailing interest rate of ……… to enable me/us to………………… My **business**/occupation is…… and my monthly **income** is N………..

I undertake to repay the loan within …………….. months at a monthly instalment of N………………. and further undertake to pay a penal interest of ………….. per month in default of any instalment due.

I hereby **charge** my total assets with the ……….. Co-operative Society Ltd as security in part for the loan and by this present authorize the said …………. Co-operative Society Ltd to make a direct debit deduction from my account in satisfaction of any unpaid instalment due on the loan.

The loan is **guaranteed** by the persons whose membership details appear hereinbelow who, by their signatures hereunder, have accepted liability for any unpaid balance of the loan and have also authorized the ………….. Co-operative Society Ltd to make a direct debit deduction from their respective accounts in satisfaction of such unpaid balance without notice to them:

Name	**Reg. No.**	**Address**	**Signature**
1. …………	………	…………	……………….
2…………..	………	…………	……………….

Yours faithfully

……………….
Signature

FOR OFFICE USE ONLY – …………………..CO-OPERATIVE SOCIETY LTD

Applicant's total shares/thrift savings N……………....... / N...………………………….
Guarantors' total shares/thrift savings 1. N …………….. / N ……………………………
2. N …………..... / N ……………………………
Loan of N ……………………………………………… is Approved / Not Approved

……………………………….. ………………………….
PRESIDENT SECRETARY

INDEX

Made in the USA
Monee, IL
08 November 2026

68174119R00204